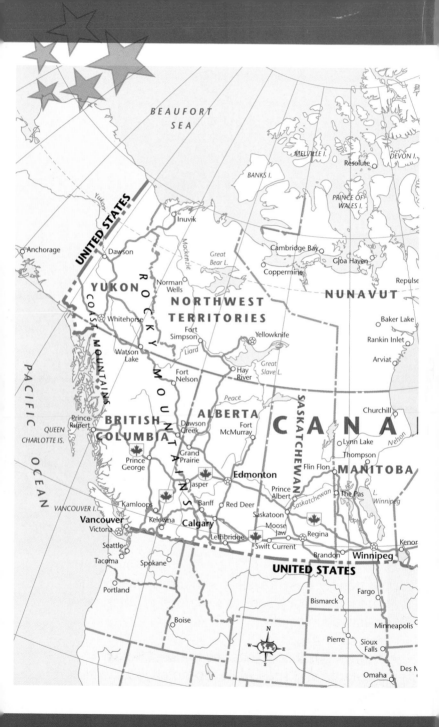

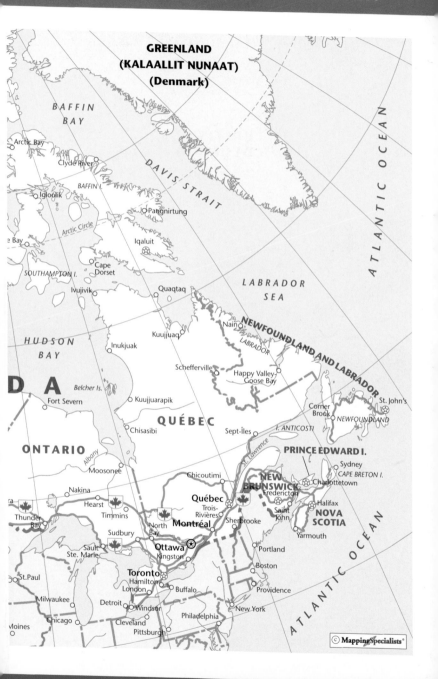

GREENLAND
(KALAALLIT NUNAAT)
(Denmark)

BAFFIN
BAY

Arctic Bay

Clyde River

DAVIS STRAIT

Igloolik

BAFFIN I.

Pangnirtung

Arctic Circle

e Bay

Iqaluit

LABRADOR
SEA

SOUTHAMPTON I.

Cape
Dorset

Quaqtaq

Ivujivik

ATLANTIC OCEAN

HUDSON
BAY

Inukjuak

Kuujjuaq

Nain

NEWFOUNDLAND AND LABRADOR

LABRADOR

Scefferville

Happy Valley-
Goose Bay

D A

Belcher Is.

Fort Severn

Kuujjuarapik

Corner
Brook

NEWFOUNDLAND

St. John's

QUÉBEC

Chisasibi

Sept-Îles

I. ANTICOSTI

ONTARIO

Albany

Moosonee

Chicoutimi

St. Lawrence

PRINCE EDWARD I.

Sydney
CAPE BRETON I.

Charlottetown

NEW
BRUNSWICK

Nakina

Hearst

Timmins

Québec

Trois-
Rivières

Fredericton

Halifax

Thunder
Bay

North
Bay

Montréal

Sherbrooke

Saint
John

NOVA
SCOTIA

Sudbury

Sault
Ste. Marie

Ottawa

Kingston

Portland

Yarmouth

St. Paul

Toronto

Hamilton

Buffalo

Boston

London

Providence

Milwaukee

Detroit

Windsor

Chicago

Cleveland

Philadelphia

New York

Moines

Pittsburgh

ATLANTIC OCEAN

© MappingSpecialists

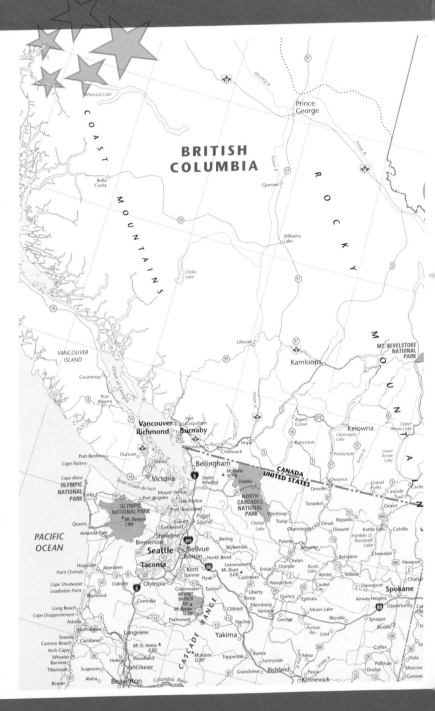

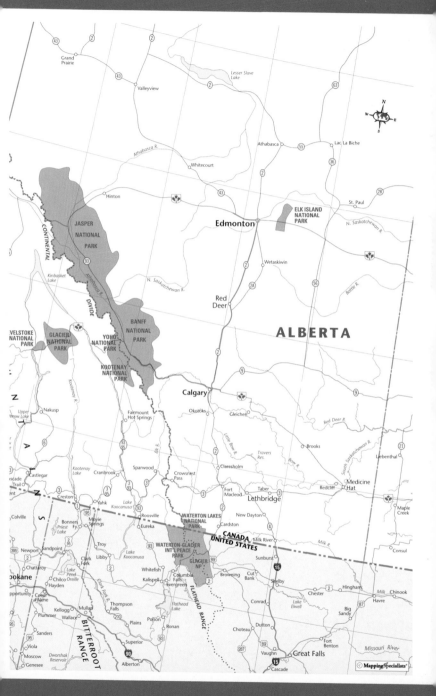

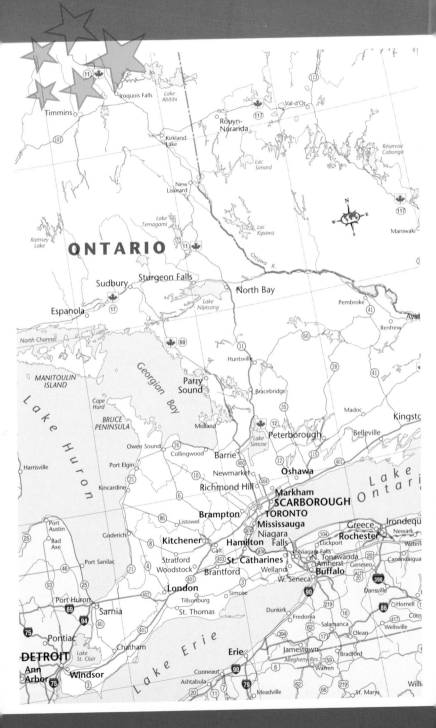

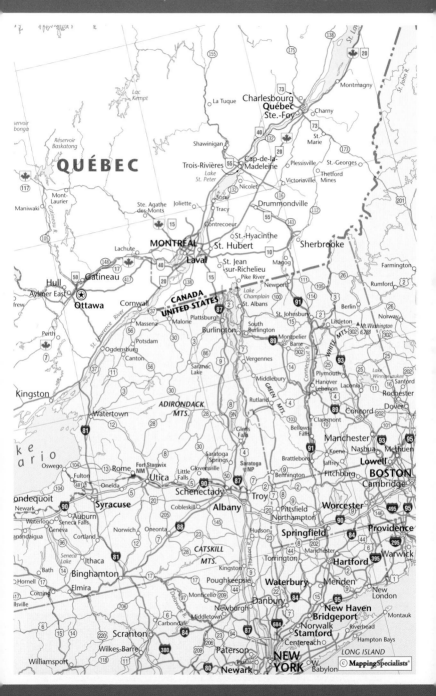

CANADA

ACKNOWLEDGMENTS

We gratefully acknowledge the help of our representatives for their efficient and perceptive inspections of the lodging and dining establishments listed, the establishments' proprietors for their cooperation in showing their facilities and providing information about them, and the many users of previous editions who have taken the time to share their experiences. Mobil Travel Guide is also grateful to all the talented writers who contributed entries to this book.

Front and back cover images: ©iStockPhoto.com

All maps: created by Mapping Specialists

The information contained herein is derived from a variety of third-party sources. Although every effort has been made to verify the information obtained from such sources, the publisher assumes no responsibility for inconsistencies or inaccuracies in the data or liability for any damages of any type arising from errors or omissions.

Neither the editors nor the publisher assume responsibility for the services provided by any business listed in this guide or for any loss, damage or disruption in your travel for any reason.

ISBN: 9-780841-60856-6   Manufactured in Canada

10 9 8 7 6 5 4 3 2 1

TABLE OF CONTENTS

3

CANADA

★
★
★
★
★

WRITTEN IN THE STARS

Because time is precious and the travel industry is ever-changing, having accurate, reliable travel information at your fingertips has never been more important. With this in mind, Mobil Travel Guide has provided invaluable insight to travelers through its Star Rating system for more than 50 years.

The Mobil Corporation (known as Exxon Mobil Corporation since a 1999 merger) began producing the Mobil Travel Guide books in 1958 following the introduction of the U.S.-interstate highway system in 1956. The first edition covered only five Southwestern states. Since then, our books have become the premier travel guides in North America, covering all 50 states and Canada, and beginning in 2008, international destinations such as Hong Kong and Beijing.

Today, the concept of a "five-star" experience is one that permeates the collective conciousness, but few people realize it's one that originated with Mobil. We created our star rating system to give travelers an easy-to-recognize quality scale for choosing where to stay, dine and spa. Based on an objective process, we make recommendations to our readers that we believe will enhance the quality and value of their travel experiences. Our trusted Mobil One- to Five-Star rating system is the oldest and most respected lodging and restaurant inspection and rating program in North America. Most hoteliers, restaurateurs and industry observers favorably regard the rigor of our inspection program and understand the prestige and benefits that come with receiving a Mobil Star rating.

The Mobil Travel Guide process of rating each establishment includes unannounced inspections, incognito evaluations and a review of unsolicted comments from the general public. We inspect more than 500 attributes at each property we visit, from cleanliness to the condition of the rooms and public spaces, to employee attitude and courtesy. It's a system that rewards those properties that strive for and achieve excellence each year. And the very best properties raise the bar for those that wish to compete with them.

Only facilities that meet Mobil Travel Guide's standards earn the privilege of being listed in the guide. Properties are continuously updated, and deteriorating, poorly managed establishments are removed. We wouldn't recommend that you visit a hotel, restaurant or spa that we wouldn't want to visit ourselves.

★★★★★The Mobil Five-Star Award indicates that a property is one of the very best in the country and consistently provides gracious and courteous service, superlative quality in its facility and a unique ambience. The lodgings and restaurants at the Mobil Five-Star level consistently continue their commitment to excellence, doing so with grace and perseverance.

★★★★The Mobil Four-Star Award honors properties for outstanding achievement in overall facility and for providing very strong service levels in all areas. These award winners provide a distinctive experience for the ever-demanding and sophisticated consumer.

★★★The Mobil Three-Star Award recognizes an excellent property that provides full services and amenities. This category ranges from exceptional hotels with limited services to elegant restaurants with a less formal atmosphere.

★★The Mobil Two-Star property is a clean and comfortable establishment that has expanded amenities or a distinctive environment. These properties are an excellent place to stay or dine.

★The Mobil One-Star property is limited in its amenities and services but provides a value experience while meeting travelers' expectations. The properties should be clean, comfortable and convenient.

We do not charge establishments for inclusion in our guides. We have no relationship with any of the businesses and attractions we list and act only as a consumer advocate. We do the investigative legwork so that you won't have to.

Restaurants and hotels—particularly small chains and stand-alone establishments—change management or even go out of business with surprising quickness. Although we make every effort to continuously update information, we recommend that you call ahead to make sure the place you've selected is still open.

STAR RATINGS

MOBIL RATED HOTELS

Whether you're looking for the ultimate in luxury or the best bang for your travel buck, we have a hotel recommendation for you. To help you pinpoint properties that meet your needs, Mobil Travel Guide classifies each lodging by type according to the following characteristics.

★★★★★The Mobil Five-Star hotel provides consistently superlative service in an exceptionally distinctive luxury environment. Attention to detail is evident throughout the hotel, resort or inn, from bed linens to staff uniforms.

★★★★The Mobil Four-Star hotel provides a luxury experience with expanded amenities in a distinctive environment. Services may include automatic turndown service, 24-hour room service and valet parking.

★★★The Mobil Three-Star hotel is well appointed, with a full-service restaurant and expanded amenities, such as a fitness center, golf course, tennis courts, 24-hour room service and optional turndown service.

★★The Mobil Two-Star hotel is considered a clean, comfortable and reliable establishment that has expanded amenities, such as a full-service restaurant.

★The Mobil One-Star lodging is a limited-service hotel, motel or inn that is considered a clean, comfortable and reliable establishment.

For every property, we also provide pricing information. The pricing categories break down as follows:

$$\mathbf{\$} = \text{Up to } \$150$$

$$\mathbf{\$\$} = \$151\text{-}\$250$$

$$\mathbf{\$\$\$} = \$251\text{-}\$350$$

$$\mathbf{\$\$\$\$} = \$351 \text{ and up}$$

All prices quoted are accurate at the time of publication; however, prices cannot be guaranteed.

MOBIL RATED RESTAURANTS

Every restaurant in this book has been visited by Mobil Travel Guide's team of experts and comes highly recommended as an outstanding dining experience.

★★★★★The Mobil Five-Star restaurant offers one of few flawless dining experiences in the country. These establishments consistently provide their guests with exceptional food, superlative service, elegant décor and exquisite presentations of each detail surrounding a meal.

★★★★The Mobil Four-Star restaurant provides professional service, distinctive presentations and wonderful food.

★★★The Mobil Three-Star restaurant has good food, warm and skillful service and enjoyable décor.

★★The Mobil Two-Star restaurant serves fresh food in a clean setting with efficient service. Value is considered in this category, as is family friendliness.

★The Mobil One-Star restaurant provides a distinctive experience through culinary specialty, local flair or individual atmosphere.

Because menu prices can fluctuate, we list a pricing category rather than specific prices. The pricing categories are defined as follows, per diner, and assume that you order an appetizer or dessert, an entrée and one drink:

$ = $15 and under

$$ = $16-$35

$$$ = $36-$85

$$$$ = $86 and up

CANADA

★
★
★
★
★

MOBIL RATED SPAS

Mobil Travel Guide's spa ratings are based on objective evaluations of hundreds of attributes. About half of these criteria assess basic expectations, such as staff courtesy, the technical proficiency and skill of the employees and whether the facility is clean and maintained properly. Several standards address issues that impact a guest's physical comfort and convenience, as well as the staff's ability to impart a sense of personalized service. Additional criteria measure the spa's ability to create a completely calming ambience.

★★★★★The Mobil Five-Star spa provides consistently superlative service in an exceptionally distinctive luxury environment with extensive amenities. The staff at a Mobil Five-Star spa provides extraordinary service beyond the traditional spa experience, allowing guests to achieve the highest level of relaxation and pampering. These spas offer an extensive array of treatments, often incorporating international themes and products. Attention to detail is evident throughout the spa, from arrival to departure.

★★★★The Mobil Four-Star spa provides a luxurious experience with expanded amenities in an elegant and serene environment. Throughout the spa facility, guests experience personalized service. Amenities might include, but are not limited to, single-sex relaxation rooms where guests wait for their treatments, plunge pools and whirlpools in both men's and women's locker rooms, and an array of treatments, including a selection of massages, body therapies, facials and a variety of salon services.

★★★The Mobil Three-Star spa is physically well appointed and has a full complement of staff.

INTRODUCTION

If you've been a reader of Mobil Travel Guides, you may have noticed a new look and style in our guidebooks. Since 1958, Mobil Travel Guide has assisted travelers in making smart decisions about where to stay and dine. Fifty-one years later, our mission has not changed: We are committed to our rigorous inspections of hotels, restaurants and, now, spas, to help you cut through all the clutter, and make easy and informed decisions on where you should spend your time and budget. Our team of anonymous inspectors are constantly on the road, sleeping in hotels, eating in restaurants and making spa appointments, evaluating hundreds of standards to determine a property's star rating.

As you read these pages, we hope you get a flavor of the places included in the guides and that you will feel even more inspired to visit and take it all in. We hope you'll experience what it's like to stay in a guest room in the hotels we've rated, taste the food in a restaurant or feel the excitement at an outdoor music venue. We understand the importance of finding the best value when you travel, and making the most of your time. That's why for more than 50 years, Mobil Travel Guide has been the most trusted name in travel.

If any aspect of your accommodation, dining, spa or sightseeing experience motivates you to comment, please contact us at Mobil Travel Guide, 200 W. Madison St., Suite 3950, Chicago, IL 60606, or send an email to info@mobiltravelguide.com Happy travels.

ALBERTA

ALBERTA IS A RICH FRONTIER—CANADA'S ECONOMIC BOOMTOWN, THANKS TO PROFITABLE oil sands—and home to some of the continent's most awe-inspiring scenery and outdoor adventure. Here you'll find sweeping plains, towering Rocky Mountains, sparkling emerald lakes, cowboys and cattle ranches, champagne powder snow, a colorful gold rush heritage and some of the most delectable steak in the world.

Alberta boasts the widest variety of geographical features of any province in Canada, including badlands rich in dinosaur fossils, rolling prairies and vast forests. All along its western border are the magnificent Canadian Rockies, which encompass six national and provincial parks, including the legendary Jasper and Banff.

Enter Alberta, which is easily accessible from Montana, from Waterton Lakes National Park and drive north to Calgary, where you'll intersect with the Trans-Canada Highway. The view of the Rockies from the Calgary Tower and the excitement of the Calgary Stampede, a 10-day event held each July, are not to be missed. From Calgary, drive northwest to Banff, Lake Louise and Jasper National Park for some of the finest mountain scenery, outdoor activities and resorts and restaurants on the continent. Heading due north from Calgary, visit Red Deer, a town famous for agriculture, oil and its beautiful parkland setting. Farther north is the provincial capital, Edmonton. A multicultural city noted for its oil, Gold Rush past, parks, cultural celebrations, magnificent sports facilities and rodeos. Northwest of Edmonton, Alberta provides paved access to Mile 0 of the Alaska Highway at Dawson Creek, B.C. There is also paved access to the Northwest Territories—Canada's northern frontier land.

Drive southeast from Calgary and enter an entirely different scene: cowboy-and-Indian territory. Fort Macleod brings you back to the early pioneer days. Lethbridge is famous for its replica of the most notorious 19th-century whiskey fort, Fort Whoop-Up and the Nikka Yuko Japanese Gardens. Farther east, visit Medicine Hat, known for its parks, pottery and rodeos. Don't go to Alberta without plenty of space on your camera's memory stick.

Information: www.travelalberta.com

FUN FACTS

The world's largest herd of free-roaming bison is located in Wood Buffalo National Park.

BANFF

As early as 1885, Albertans knew what treasure lay in their backyards. The Banff Hot Springs Reservation was incorporated to protect the steaming, healing grottos abundant to the area, and by 1887 that vision was expanded to become Rocky Mountains Park. Today the vast recreation area is known as Banff National Park—Canada's first national park, the second in North America and only the third in the world. A UNESCO World Heritage site, the park covers 2,564 square miles (6,641 square kilometers).

Banff comes alive each summer with its music and drama festival at Banff Centre. In winter, the Rockies provide some of the best skiing on the North American continent. A fantastic blend of both culture and natural beauty, Banff offers exciting nightlife, sleigh rides, Western barbecues, gondola rides, boat and raft tours, concerts, art galleries, museums, hot springs, ice-field tours, hiking and trail rides.

Snowy peaks tower over glassy alpine lakes. Massive canyons carved out of plain landscapes and more than 1,000 prehistoric glaciers await eco-warriors and everyday shutterbugs alike. Animals are so plentiful that traveling throughout the province (and camping and outdoor eating) requires special care. Watch for bighorn sheep, mountain goats, moose, elk, deer and grizzly and black bears.

Information: www.bannflakelouise.com

WHAT TO SEE AND DO

BANFF GONDOLA

403-762-2523; www.banffgondola.com

Travel up to 7,500 feet in elevation for spectacular vistas. Gift shops and restaurants are at the top. Open year-round; hours vary by season.

BANFF NATIONAL PARK

403-762-1550; www.pc.gc.ca/pn-np/ab/banff

Canada's first national park, Banff was initially famous for its hot springs, and visitors still flock here to check out the bubbling thermal waters at the Cave and Basin National Historic Site. The town is home to many of the park's resorts and lodges, perhaps the most notable being the opulent Fairmont Banff Springs, fashioned after a Scottish baronial castle. Upscale accommodations also can be found near the wondrous Lake Louise, its placid blue-green waters reflecting the sharply angled mountain peaks surrounding the shoreline. Budget-minded visitors to Banff National Park typically opt to sleep under the stars, with the park offering 2,468 campsites on a first-come, first-served basis. Banff National Park stands tall among the spectacular peaks of the Canadian Rockies as one of the premier year-round vacation destinations in all of North America. Downhill skiers and snowboarders come from around the world to Banff's legendary slopes, with three major ski resorts serving the area. The summer months bring boot-clad hikers eager to take advantage of more than 1,000 miles (1,600 kilometers) of trails that cut across diverse but consistently striking terrain, winding through open meadows and dense forests, passing alongside ancient glaciers and glistening lakes. Other popular activities include mountaineering, fishing, canoeing, kayaking, golf, horseback riding and wildlife viewing.

BANFF PARK MUSEUM

403-762-1558; www.pc.gc.ca/lhn-nhs/ab/banff

One of the oldest museums in Canada. Displays animals, insects and other collections found in Banff National Park. Reading room, hands-on discovery room.

BANFF UPPER HOT SPRINGS

403-762-1515, 800-767-1611; www.hotsprings.ca

Originally built in 1932, the therapeutic waters of Canada's most revered hot spring produces average temperatures of 100 degrees, with an expansive outdoor pool and rich selection of spa indulgences.

11

ALBERTA

BREWSTER CANADA MOTORCOACH TOURS

403-762-6767, 877-791-5500; www.brewster.ca

Tours take passengers onto the Columbia Icefield for a glacier-bound SnoCoach tour.

CAVE AND BASIN CENTENNIAL CENTRE

403-762-1557; www.pc.gc.ca/lhn-nhs/ab/caveandbasin/index_E.asp

The birthplace of Canada's national park system and a national historic site. Hot springs, cave, exhibits, trails, theater.

FAIRMONT BANFF SPRINGS GOLF COURSE

403-762-6801; www.fairmont.com/banffsprings/Recreation/Golf/

This spectacular 27-hole golf course is situated along the Bow River and framed by the majestic peaks of the Canadian Rockies. Driving range, practice greens, pro shop. May-October.

JOHNSTON CANYON

16 miles west of Banff; www.banff.com

Self-guided, 3.5-mile (5.6-kilometer) walk through the scenic canyon. View Ink Spots and six cool water springs.

NATURAL HISTORY MUSEUM

403-762-4652; www.pc.gc.ca/lhn-nhs/ab/banff/natcul/index_e.asp

More than 60 displays; slide shows and films depict prehistoric life, precious stones, and trees and flowers, as well as the origins of the earth and the formation of mountains and caves.

ROCKY MOUNTAIN RAFT TOURS

403-762-3632; www.banffrafttours.com

One- or two-hour float trips travel on the Bow River through Banff National Park.

SUNSHINE VILLAGE

403-762-6500, 877-542-2633; www.skibanff.com

This legendary ski area offers 3,168 acres of terrain with an elevation of 8,954 feet (2,729 meters) and a vertical drop of 3,514 feet (1,071 meters). One high-speed six-passenger gondola, four high-speed detachable quads, one fixed quad, one triple chair, two double chairs, one T-bar and two magic carpets. Restaurants, lounges, ski and snowboard school, rental shop, day care, snowboard park and more.

SPECIAL EVENTS

ANNUAL BANFF/LAKE LOUISE WINTER FESTIVAL

403-762-8421; www.bannflakelouise.com

This two-week festival, including cultural events, winter athletic contests, a Town Party and bar socials, has been a Banff tradition since 1916. Late January-early February.

BANFF SUMMER ARTS FESTIVAL

403-762-6301, 800-413-8368; www.banffcentre.ca/bsaf

Main stage productions and workshops in opera, ballet, music theater, drama, concerts, poetry reading and visual arts. May-September.

BANFF TELEVISION FESTIVAL
403-678-9260; www.banff2009.com

While this event is primarily for industry networkers, the public can view some of the best international television free of charge. June.

HOTELS
★BANFF AVENUE INN
433 Banff Ave., Banff, 403-762-4499, 888-762-4499; www.banffavenueinn.com

18 rooms. Complimentary continental breakfast. Wireless Internet access. **$$**

★★BANFF CARIBOU LODGE
521 Banff Ave., Banff, 403-762-5887, 800-563-8764; www.banffcaribouproperties.com

195 rooms. Restaurant. Bar. High-speed Internet access. Exercise room. **$$**

★★BUFFALO MOUNTAIN LODGE
700 Tunnel Mountain Road, Banff, 403-762-2400, 800-661-1367;
www.buffalomountainlodge.com

108 rooms. Restaurant, bar. Exercise room. Business center. **$$**

★★★BANFF PARK LODGE
222 Lynx St., Banff, 403-762-4433, 800-661-9266; www.banffparklodge.com

Stunning mountain views can be seen from any room of this full-service hotel located just two blocks from Banff's shopping district and near the Bow River. After a long day at play, enjoy a quiet dinner in the hotel's fine-dining restaurant, The Terrace. A casual dinner can be found at The Chinook where there are theme-night dinners that range from Italian to Western fare. 211 rooms. Two restaurants, bar. Pool. Business center. High-speed Internet access. **$$**

★★BANFF PTARMIGAN INN
337 Banff Ave., Banff, 403-762-2207, 800-661-8310; www.bestofbanff.com

134 rooms. Restaurant, bar. Exercise room. **$**

★★BREWSTER'S MOUNTAIN LODGE
208 Caribou St., Banff, 403-762-2900, 888-762-2900;
www.brewstermountainlodge.com

77 rooms. Restaurant, bar. Exercise room. Business center. **$$**

★DOUGLAS FIR RESORT AND CHALETS
Tunnel Mt. Road, Banff, 403-762-5591, 800-661-9267; www.douglasfir.com

133 rooms, all suites. Exercise room. Pool. Tennis. Business center. **$**

★★★THE FAIRMONT BANFF SPRINGS
405 Spray Ave., Banff, 403-762-2211, 800-441-1414; www.fairmont.com

A striking backdrop of snow-capped peaks and towering trees makes for a magical experience, with regal accommodations, luxurious amenities and plentiful activities—including world-class skiing and championship golf. The Willow Stream spa offers a well-rounded treatment menu to help guests further relax in this majestic setting. 770 rooms. Restaurant, bar. Pets accepted. Fitness center. Spa. Pool. Golf. Tennis. Business center. **$$$**

★★★RIMROCK RESORT HOTEL

300 Mountain Ave., Banff, 403-762-3356, 888-746-7625; www.rimrockresort.com

Terraced into the side of a mountain in Banff National Park, this sophisticated hotel offers alpine vistas with world-class skiing nearby. A comprehensive health center and saltwater pools appeal to fitness-minded visitors, while the spa indulges all. Three dining establishments echo the elegance of the hotel while catering to a variety of tastes. 346 rooms. Three restaurants, bar. Fitness center. Pool. Spa. Business center. $$$

★★★ROYAL CANADIAN LODGE

459 Banff Ave., Banff, 403-762-3307, 800-661-1379; www.charltonresorts.com

In the serene setting of Banff, this small, rustic hotel charms with spacious guest rooms featuring high ceilings, Canadian maple furnishings, granite vanities and either gas fireplaces or views of the Alpine Garden. Evergreen, the restaurant, serves three meals daily and features Canadian cuisine, while the Grotto Spa includes a mineral pool and whirlpool and offers several types of treatments. 99 rooms. Restaurant, bar. Spa. Fitness center. Pool. $$

RESTAURANTS

★★BALKAN

120 Banff Ave., Banff, 403-762-3454; www.banffbalkan.ca

Greek menu. Lunch, dinner. $$

★★★★BANFFSHIRE CLUB

405 Spray Ave., Banff, 403-762-6860; www.fairmont.com

The jewel of the lavish Fairmont Banff Springs, the Banffshire Club prides itself on having one of the most extensive wine cellars in Canada. Warm up with one of many single malt scotches in view of Sulphur Mountain and enjoy game dishes and a uniquely fresh, Alberta-inspired menu with hints of French cuisine. Reservations recommended. Contemporary menu. Dinner. Closed Sunday and Monday. Reservations recommended. $$$$

★★★BOW VALLEY GRILL

405 Spray Ave., Banff, 403-762-6896; www.fairmont.com

Housed in the historic, castle-like Fairmont Banff Springs Hotel, this French restaurant was recently remodeled to restore its romantic brilliance. The formal, special-occasion space is the property's signature dining room and offers the excitement of tableside preparations and nightly dancing. Steak menu, Breakfast, lunch, dinner, Sunday brunch. Casual attire. Reservations recommended. $$$

★★BUFFALO MOUNTAIN LODGE DINING ROOM

Tunnel Mountain Road, Banff, 403-762-2400, 800-661-1367; www.crmr.com/dining-buffalo.php

American menu. Breakfast, lunch, dinner. $$$

★★GIORGIO'S TRATTORIA

219 Banff Ave., Banff, 403-762-5114; www.giorgiosbanff.com

Italian cuisine. Dinner. $$

★★★LE BEAUJOLAIS

212 Buffalo St., Banff, 403-762-2712; www.lebeaujolaisbanff.com

A prestigious destination in a beautiful town, this restaurant is awash in fresh flowers, candlelight and mountain views. Comfortably formal service and occasional table-side preparations are a treat. French menu. Lunch, dinner. Closed November-mid-December. $$$

★★★THE PRIMROSE

300 Mountain Ave., Banff, 403-762-3356, 800-661-1587; www.rimrockresort.com

High on Sulphur Mountain, this restaurant is the more casual dining option at the Canadian Rockies Rimrock Resort Hotel. Enjoy great views and a straightforward American menu. American menu. Lunch, dinner. $$$

★★★SEASONS

1029 Banff Ave., Kananaskis Village, 403-591-7711; www.rockymountainresort.com

This fireside café is housed at the Banff Rocky Mountain Resort and Conference Center in the heart of the Canadian Rockies. The atmosphere is casual, and the regionally influenced menu is broad. Views of the Rockies add drama to the experience. American menu. Breakfast, lunch, dinner. $$

★★★TICINO

415 Banff Ave., Banff, 403-762-3848; www.ticinorestaurant.com

Named after the region in Switzerland that borders on Italy, this restaurant serves cuisine with influences of both countries. The bistro emphasizes hearty pasta, meat and fish dishes with a variety local vegetables and herbs. The rustic, Italian alpine room has attracted diners for more than 30 years. Italian and Swiss menu. Dinner. $$$

SPA

★★★★WILLOW STREAM SPA

405 Spray Ave., Banff, 403-762-6860; www.fairmont.com

Willow Stream Spa is a shining star in the world-class mountain paradise of Banff Springs. This top-rated facility has it all, along with an outdoor whirlpool, an indoor Hungarian mineral pool and three waterfall-style whirlpools. A diverse treatment menu is available, offering therapies customized for reawakening, balancing, rejuvenating, and revitalizing. Sport-specific treatments include massages designed for golfers and skiers, while those who want to enjoy their spa treatments together can do so in the specially designed couple's suite. A full-service fitness center offers guided hikes and fitness consultations in addition to its two pools, cardiovascular equipment and free weights. $$$$

CALGARY

The gateway to the Canadian Rockies, Calgary was founded in 1875 by the North West Mounted Police at the confluence of the Bow and Elbow rivers. Surrounding the city are fertile farmlands, and to the west, the rolling foothills of the Rockies. A city couldn't be more ideally situated for both economic luster and gawk value—lush ranchlands and profitable grain farming have made the Calgary Canada's principle agribusiness center, while majestic peaks overlook the urban landscape.

Site of the 1988 Olympic Winter Games, Calgary offers endless pursuits for outdoor enthusiasts, with world-class golf, skiing, snowboarding, hiking, mountaineering and whitewater rafting in its foothills and alpine environs.

Powering Calgary's recent phenomenal growth is oil. Since 1914, the petroleum industry has centered its activities here. Today, more than 85 percent of Canada's oil and gas producers are headquartered in Calgary. Despite this influx of cash and ambition, Calgary retains a small town feel with a Wild West atmosphere well demonstrated by the enthusiasm and pride that brims over during Stampede Week—arguably one of the most voracious parties in the entire country.

Information: www.tourismcalgary.com

WHAT TO SEE AND DO

CALGARY FLAMES (NHL)

Pengrowth Saddledome, 14th Avenue and Fifth Street S.E., Calgary, 403-777-4646; www.calgaryflames.com

Professional hockey team.

CALGARY SCIENCE CENTRE

701 11th St. S.W., Calgary, 403-268-8300; www.calgaryscience.ca

Discovery Dome, astronomy displays, exhibitions, observatory and self-guided tours; science and technology demonstrations. Open daily.

CALGARY TOWER

101 Ninth Ave. S.W., Calgary, 403-266-7171; www.calgarytower.com

A 626-foot (191-meter) tower with a spectacular view of Calgary and the Rocky Mountains. Also a revolving restaurant, observation terrace, lounge and shopping.

THE CALGARY ZOO, BOTANICAL GARDEN AND PREHISTORIC PARK

1300 Zoo Road N.E., Calgary, 403-232-9300, 800-588-9993; www.calgaryzoo.ab.ca

One of Canada's largest zoos, with more than 900 animals; botanical garden; Canadian Wilds (25 acres) features Canadian ecosystems populated by their native species. Prehistoric Park.

CANADA OLYMPIC PARK

88 Canada Olympic Road S.W., Calgary, 403-247-5452; www.coda.ab.ca

The premier site of the 1988 Olympic Winter Games. Olympic Hall of Fame and Museum, plus winter sports facilities with one double and two triple chairlifts, a T-bar, ski school and rentals. Summer facilities include mini-golf, beach volleyball, a summer bobsled ride, mountain biking and softball.

DEVONIAN GARDENS

317 Seventh Ave. S.W., Calgary, 403-268-3830; www.calgary.ca/parks/devonian

A lush, welcoming oasis of green in the heart of the city with waterfalls, fountains and fish ponds as well as concerts, art displays, a playground and a reflecting pool. Below the gardens are stores and restaurants.

ALBERTA

★
★
★
★
★

EAU CLAIRE FESTIVAL MARKET

200 Barclay Parade S.W., Calgary, 403-264-6450; www.eauclairemarket.com

A two-story warehouse with boutique shops, specialty food stands, restaurants, bars and a five-screen cinema, including an IMAX theater.

EPCOR CENTRE FOR THE PERFORMING ARTS

205 Eighth Ave. S.E., Calgary, 403-294-7455; www.epcorcentre.org

Four theaters noted for excellent acoustics house the Calgary Philharmonic, Orchestra Theatre Calgary and other performing arts.

FORT CALGARY HISTORIC PARK

750 Ninth Ave. S.E., Calgary, 403-290-1875; www.fortcalgary.com

This vast riverside park is the site of the original North West Mounted Police (NWMP) fort at the meeting place of the Bow and Elbow Rivers. Abandoned in 1914, the site of the fort is now being rebuilt. An interpretive center highlights NWMP and Calgary history. Adjacent is Deane House, restored and opened as a restaurant.

GLENBOW MUSEUM

130 Ninth Ave. S.E., Calgary, 403-268-4100; www.glenbow.org

Combining a museum, art gallery, library and archives all under one roof, Glenbow boasts more than a million artifacts and some 28,000 works of art in its vast collections. Regional, national and international fine arts; displays of native cultures of North America and the development of the West; mineralogy, warriors, African and personal adornment. Museum shop. Open Monday-Sunday, 9 a.m.-5 p.m., Thursday until-9 p.m.

HERITAGE PARK HISTORICAL VILLAGE

1900 Heritage Drive S.W., Calgary, 403-268-8500; www.heritagepark.ab.ca

Recreates life in Western Canada before 1914. More than 150 exhibits; steam train, paddle wheeler, horse-drawn wagon and electric streetcars, wagon rides, antique midway.

MUSEUM OF THE REGIMENTS

4520 Crowchild Trail S.W., Calgary, 403-974-2850; www.themilitarymuseums.ca

One of North America's largest military museums, the Museum of the Regiments honors four Calgary regiments. Films, traveling art exhibits. Monday-Friday 9 a.m.-5 p.m.; Saturday-Sunday 9:30 a.m.-4 p.m.

ROYAL TYRRELL MUSEUM OF PALEONTOLOGY

Highway 838, Midland Provincial Park, 403-823-7707, 888-440-4240;
www.tyrrellmuseum.com

The world's largest display of dinosaurs in a state-of-the-art museum setting. More than 35 complete dinosaur skeletons; paleoconservatory with more than 100 species of tropical and subtropical plants that once thrived in this region; hands-on exhibits include interactive terminals and games throughout. Summer bus service from Calgary.

SPRUCE MEADOWS

18011 Spruce Meadows Way S.W., Calgary, 403-974-4200; www.sprucemeadows.com

Only internationally sanctioned outdoor horse jumping show held in North America; offers the world's richest show jumping purse. June-September.

17

ALBERTA

★
★
★
★
★

SPECIAL EVENTS

CALGARY STAMPEDE

Stampede Park, 1410 Olympic Way S.E., Calgary, 403-261-0101, 800-661-1260; www.calgarystampede.com

Billed as "The World's Greatest Outdoor Show," the Stampede has been held every year since 1912. Revelers gather with vivid enthusiasm for parades, rodeos, chuck wagon races, stage shows, exhibitions, square dances, marching bands and vaudeville shows. Ten days in early July.

CALGARY WINTER FESTIVAL

100-634 Sixth Ave. S.W., Calgary, 403-543-5480; www.calgarywinterfest.com

Music, entertainment, sports competitions, children's activities, carnival, dance. Eleven days in mid-February.

HOTELS

★★BLACKFOOT INN

5940 Blackfoot Trail S.E., Calgary, 403-252-2253, 800-661-1151; www.blackfootinn.com

200 rooms. Restaurant, bar. Business center. Exercise room. Pets accepted. $

★★★DELTA BOW VALLEY

209 Fourth Ave. S.E., Calgary, 403-266-1980, 800-268-1133; www.deltahotels.com

Guests have the choice of a room with a city, mountain or river view at this downtown full-service hotel, which is located east of the grand Canadian Rockies. Elements Bistro emphasizes regional cuisine and Canadian wines are featured. 394 rooms. Restaurant, bar. Children's activity center. Pets accepted, fee. Exercise room. Pool. Business center. $$

★★★THE FAIRMONT PALLISER

133 Ninth Ave. S.W., Calgary, 403-262-1234, 800-540-4477; www.fairmont.com/palliser

This palace-style building is a city favorite and its downtown location makes it a convenient base for business or leisure travelers. The hotel features traditional European styling, and a skywalk connects it to the Telus Convention Centre, Calgary Tower and Glenbow Museum. The Oak Room and Rimrock restaurants feature a variety of savory treats, while guests with a sweet tooth can visit the twice-weekly all-chocolate buffets. 405 rooms. Restaurant, bar. Pets accepted, fee. Exercise room. Pool. Business center. $$

★★GREENWOOD INN CALGARY

3515 26th St. N.E., Calgary, 403-250-8855, 888-233-6730; www.greenwoodcalgary.com

210 rooms. Restaurant, bar. High-speed Internet access. Pets accepted, fee. Exercise room. Pool. $

★★★HYATT REGENCY CALGARY

700 Centre St. South, Calgary, 403-717-1234, 800-233-1234; www.calgary.hyatt.com

This Hyatt's downtown location is ideal for both leisure and business travelers. Spacious rooms, vast amenities and 24-hour room service as well as a fitness center and indoor pool keep guests pampered. Relaxing dinners and small get-togethers can be had at Thomsons Restaurant and the Sandstone Lounge. 355 rooms. Restaurant, bar. High-speed Internet access. Pets accepted, fee. Exercise room. Fitness center. Pool. Business center. $$$

★★★INTERNATIONAL HOTEL SUITES CALGARY

220 Fourth Ave. S.W., Calgary, 403-265-9600, 800-661-8271;
www.internationalhotel.ca

This high-rise hotel is conveniently located in the heart of the city center, within walking distance of area attractions. The hotel's onsite restaurant, 4th Avenue Cafe, features international cuisine and offers a children's menu. For lighter fare, head over to the 4th Avenue Lounge and order from the tapas menu. 248 rooms, all suites. Restaurant, bar. Business center. Spa. Pool. $$

★★★MARRIOTT CALGARY

110 Ninth Ave. S.E., Calgary, 403-266-7331, 800-228-9290; www.marriott.com

Situated in the heart of downtown Calgary, the Marriott is connected by skywalk to the Calgary Tower and Telus Convention Center and located near the Glenbow Museum and the Calgary Zoo. An array of amenities and services provides guests with the comforts of home. 384 rooms. Restaurant, bar. High-speed Internet access. Pets accepted. Pool. Fitness center. Business center. $$

★★★SHERATON CAVALIER HOTEL

2620 32nd Ave. N.E., Calgary, 403-291-0107, 800-325-3535; www.sheratoncalgary.ca

Many families choose the Sheraton Cavalier Hotel when staying in Calgary not only for its spacious guest rooms but for its indoor water park. With a well-equipped business center and a cyber café onsite, the hotel attracts a number of business travelers as well. It is located 10 minutes from the airport, and a complimentary shuttle is available. 306 rooms. Restaurant, bar. High-speed Internet access. Fitness center. Airport transportation available. Pets accepted, fee. Spa. Pool. Business center. Complimentary parking. $$

★★★SHERATON SUITES CALGARY EAU CLAIRE

255 Barclay Parade S.W., Calgary, 403-266-7200, 888-784-8370;
www.sheratonsuites.com

This downtown hotel facing Eau Claire Market is a great choice for both business and leisure travelers, and the indoor pool with waterslides is a hit with kids. Guest suites are spacious and dining options diverse, including the Irish pub Fionn McCool's and Barclay's, an upscale-casual restaurant. 323 rooms, all suites. Restaurant, bar. Pets accepted, fee. Exercise room. Pool. Business center. $$$

19

ALBERTA

★
★
★
★
★

SPECIALITY LODGING
RAFTER SIX RANCH RESORT
Highway 1 and South Ranch Road, Seebe, 403-673-3622, 888-267-2624;
www.raftersix.com
Wilderness camping facilities plus 18 rooms. Restaurant, bar. Pool. **$$**

RESTAURANTS
★★★THE BELVEDERE
107 Eighth Ave. S.W., Calgary, 403-265-9595; www.thebelvedere.ca
Housed in the restored Union Bank building, this contemporary dining room has a plush, clubby feel. The restaurant offers a seasonal, unhurried experience featuring globally inspired, creative cuisine. American, seafood, steak, vegetarian menu. Lunch, dinner. **$$$**

★★★CENTINI RESTAURANT AND LOUNGE
160 Eighth Ave. S.E., Calgary, 403-269-1600; www.centini.com
Fresh, seasonal food is prepared and served with a passion at this Italian restaurant located in downtown Calgary's Telus Convention Center, near many businesses and shops. On offer are house-made specialty pastas and an extensive wine list featuring 650 wines and 8,500 bottles. Italian menu. Lunch, dinner. Reservations recommended. **$$$**

★★HY'S STEAK HOUSE
316 Fourth Ave. S.W., Calgary, 403-263-2222; www.hyssteakhouse.com
Steak menu. Dinner. **$$$**

★★THE KEG STEAKHOUSE AND BAR
7104 MacLeod Trail S., Calgary, 403-253-2534; www.kegsteakhouse.com
Steak menu. Lunch, dinner. Outdoor seating. Reservations recommended. **$$**

★★QUINCY'S ON SEVENTH
609 Seventh Ave. S.W., Calgary, 403-264-1000; www.quincysonseventh.com
Steak menu. Dinner. Reservations recommended. **$$$**

★★★RIMROCK ROOM
133 Ninth Ave. S.W., Calgary, 403-260-1219, 800-441-1414; www.fairmont.com
Located in the landmark Palliser Hotel, this regionally influenced restaurant has been serving guests for more than 80 years. The elegant dining room is a popular choice for special-occasion dinners and for seating during the lobby's Sunday buffet brunch. Canadian regional menu. Breakfast, lunch, dinner brunch. **$$$**

★★RIVER CAFÉ
200 Barclay Parade S.W., Calgary, 403-261-7670; www.river-cafe.com
Canadian regional menu. Lunch, dinner, Saturday-Sunday brunch. Outdoor seating. Reservations recommended. **$$**

CANMORE
Canmore burst onto the tourist scene after hosting Nordic events during the 1988 Calgary Winter Olympics. Today, it is an authentic Alpine village that's a destination for thrills and vistas, with a significant selection of exquisite galleries and unique

gift shops. Most of Canmore can be traversed within an hour by foot; the town center surrounds Eighth Street, (or "Main Street" as it is known colloquially), originally a residential road boasting some of the oldest architecture in the town.

Much of the area to the northeast of Canmore is located in a critical wildlife corridor which hosts bears, cougars, wolves and elk as they move between habitats. A series of hiking and walking paths traverse this area, known as The Benchlands, and are watched over by various stakeholders (Bow Valley Mountain Bike Alliance, the B.V. Riding Association and local hiking groups) in order to protect wildlife and its habitat while providing high-quality recreational trails. Climbing is popular, with trad, sport and multipitch climbs throughout the Bow Valley, and the area is a world destination for ice climbing. Kayakers and canoeists can take guided trips with one of the many local outfitters or independently navigate the surrounding rivers and lakes. Caving enthusiasts will enjoy the extensive Rat's Nest Caves.

Information: www.tourismcanmore.com

SPECIAL EVENTS

THE CANMORE ARTSPEAK FESTIVAL

Canmore, 403-996-0293; www.artspeakcanmore.com

Celebrates Canmore's artistic spirit by featuring various artists, an art walk, a literary festival, film screenings and street performers. June.

CANMORE CHILDREN'S FESTIVAL

Canmore, 403-678-1878; www.canmorechildrensfestival.com

A two-day event providing an array of children's entertainment, including acrobats, magicians, jugglers, music, theatre, storytelling, crafts, stilt-walking, dancing, face painting and clowns. Late May.

THE CANMORE FOLK MUSIC FESTIVAL

Canmore, 403-678-2524; www.canmorefolkfestival.com

Held annually on the Heritage Day long weekend in August at Centennial Park on the Stan Rogers Stage. The festival is the longest running music festival in Alberta. Late August.

THE CANMORE HIGHLAND GAMES

Canmore, 403-678-9454; www.canmorehighlandgames.ca

Presented annually by the Three Sisters Scottish Society on the September long weekend. The games host heavy lifting competitions, piping, drumming and highland dance events. September.

THE CANMORE ICE CLIMBING FESTIVAL

200-50 Lincoln Park, Canmore, 403-678-4164; www.canmoreiceclimbingfestival.com

An international event featuring an 18-meter (60-foot) man-made ice wall constructed on Canmore's downtown fringe from chicken wire, scaffolding and long hoses. Events include an exhibitor tent, climbing clinics and renowned guest speakers. December.

FESTIVAL OF EAGLES

Canmore; www.eaglewatch.ca

A celebration of the Golden Eagle autumn migration over Canmore and the Bow Valley. The weekend celebration includes guided hikes, bird walks, interpretive displays, theatrical performances and guest speakers. Spotting scopes are set up at Canmore Collegiate High School. Mid-October.

MOZART ON THE MOUNTAIN

Canmore, 403-571-0270; www.cpo-live.com/main/content.php?content_id=80

An outdoor concert presented annually by the Calgary Philharmonic Orchestra. Late August.

HOTELS

★★CHATEAU CANMORE

1718 Bow Valley Trail, Canmore, 403-678-6699, 800-261-8551;
www.chateaucanmore.com

93 rooms, all suites. Restaurant, bar. Exercise room. Pool. Tennis. Business center. $

★★RADISSON HOTEL AND CONFERENCE CENTER CANMORE

511 Bow Valley Trail, Canmore, 403-678-3625, 800-333-3333;
www.radisson.com/canmoreca

224 rooms. Restaurant, bar. Complimentary high-speed Internet access. Business center. Pets accepted, fee. Spa. Pool. $

SPECIALITY LODGING

THE LADY MACDONALD COUNTRY INN

1201 Bow Valley Trail, Canmore, 403-678-3665, 800-567-3919;
www.ladymacdonald.com

12 rooms. Complimentary full breakfast. $

RESTAURANT

★★CHEZ FRANCOIS

1604 Second Ave., Canmore, 403-678-6111; www.restaurantchezfrancois.com

French menu. Breakfast, brunch. Closed January 2-10. Outdoor seating. $$$

EDMONTON

As the capital of a province whose economic mainstays are petroleum and agriculture, Edmonton has all the brash confidence of a major supplier of one of the world's most sought-after resources. Yet at its heart, this northern stalwart is rooted in a practical sensibility.

Established as a fort of operations during the fur-trade era, Edmonton came into itself in the 1890s as a major supply depot for the Yukon gold rush—the highlight of the All-Canadian Route to the Klondike. Thousands of men stopped for days, weeks, or months before making the final 1,500-mile (2,400-kilometer) push for gold. Many decided to stay, transforming a quiet village into a prosperous city. Each July the city celebrates this era with Klondike Days.

Edmonton is a beautifully green city, with more park area per capita than any other city in Canada, primarily along the banks of the North Saskatchewan River. Visitors enjoy a

★
★
★
★
★

perfectly Albertan blend of outdoor adventure, shopping, sports, arts, culture, dining, recreation and a wide variety of world-class attractions. Canada's "Festival City" also offers a calendar full of annual events and festivals celebrating jazz, folk, symphony, theatre, dance, visual arts, street performers, food and fun for every member of the family.
Information: www.edmonton.ca

WHAT TO SEE AND DO
ART GALLERY OF ALBERTA
100-10230 Jasper Ave., Edmonton, 780-422-6223; www.artgalleryalberta.com
More than 5,000 works of contemporary and historical art from around the world live here, the largest art museum and longest-running cultural institution in Alberta. Open daily.

CAPITAL CITY RECREATION PARK
95th Street and 97th Avenue, Edmonton, 780-496-7275; www.edmonton.ca
Winding through the city's river valley, this is one of Canada's most extensive park systems. Bicycle, walking and cross-country ski trails link the major parks featuring barbecue and picnic facilities and food concessions.

CITADEL THEATRE
9828 101 A Ave., Edmonton, 780-425-1820; www.citadeltheatre.com
This five-theater complex located in downtown Edmonton is one of Canada's finest centers for the performing arts. Glass-enclosed atrium area; waterfall. Three theater series. September-May.

COMMONWEALTH STADIUM
11000 Stadium Road, Edmonton, 780-944-7400
Built for the 11th Commonwealth Games and now home of the Canadian Football League's Edmonton Eskimos. The Stadium Recreation Centre houses a gym, weights and racquetball and squash courts.

DEVONIAN BOTANIC GARDEN
Highway 60 and Garden Valley Road, Devon, 6 miles (9.6 kilometers) west via Yellowhead Highway 16, then 9 miles (14 kilometers) south on Highway 60, 780-987-3054; www.discoveredmonton.com/devonian
An enormous, lush retreat including alpine and herb gardens, a peony collection and native plants, an extraordinary five-acre (two hectare) Japanese garden, nature trails, aspen and jack pine forests, a lilac garden, a butterfly pavilion and an orchid greenhouse. Open April-October.

EDMONTON OILERS (NHL)
Rexall Place,11230-110 St., Edmonton, 780-451-4000, 866-414-4625; www.oilers.nhl.com
Professional hockey team.

THE EDMONTON QUEEN RIVERBOAT
9734-98 Ave., Edmonton, 780-424-2628; www.edmontonqueen.com
This riverboat runs along the North Saskatchewan River, which travels through many local parks. Packages include Sunday brunch, dinner or cruise only.

23

ALBERTA

★
★
★
★
★

FORT EDMONTON PARK

Whitemud and Fox Drives, Edmonton, 780-496-8787; www.fortedmontonpark.ca

Canada's largest historical park encompasses Fort Edmonton, the Hudson's Bay Company Trading Post that gave the city its name. Demonstrations, artifacts and costumed interpreters as well as steam trains and streetcar rides. Daily 10 a.m.-6 p.m.

FRANCIS WINSPEAR CENTRE FOR MUSIC

4 Sir Winston Churchill Square, Edmonton, 780-428-1414, 800-563-5081; www.winspearcentre.com

Home of the Edmonton Symphony Orchestra.

JOHN JANZEN NATURE CENTRE

7000 143 St., Edmonton, 780-496-2910

Nestled in the heart of the river valley, the John Janzen Nature Centre offers programs, events, exhibits and information to encourage awareness and understanding of nature in an urban setting.

MUTTART CONSERVATORY

9626 96A St., Edmonton, 780-496-8755; www.muttartconservatory.ca

Glass pyramid house controlled growing environments: tropical, arid and temperate. A fourth pyramid is a floral showcase, which is refreshed every few weeks.

ODYSSIUM

11211 142nd St., Coronation Park, Edmonton, 780-452-9100; www.odyssium.com

An entertainment hub with a 275-seat IMAX theater, dome theater, Star Theater and six exhibit galleries featuring the latest discoveries in science, astronomy and space exploration. Artifacts (moon rock, telescopes) and space flight simulation.

OLD STRATHCONA FARMERS' MARKET

10310-83 Ave., Edmonton, 780-439-1844; www.osfm.ca

This is Alberta's biggest and best farmers market. Shop for produce and local crafts at this indoor market. Saturday 8 a.m.-3 p.m.

ROYAL ALBERTA MUSEUM

12845 102nd Ave., Edmonton, 780-453-9100; www.royalalbertamuseum.ca

Excellent displays reflecting the many aspects of Alberta's heritage. Exhibits on natural and human history include information about aboriginal peoples, wildlife, geology, live insects, dinosaurs and ice age mammals.

RUTHERFORD HOUSE

11153 Saskatchewan Drive, Edmonton, 780-427-3995; www.tprc.alberta.ca

This Jacobean Revival home was the residence of Alberta's first premier and has been restored and refurnished to reflect the lifestyle of the post-Edwardian era. Costumed interpreters re-enact life in 1915 with activities such as woodstove baking, historical dramas, craft demonstrations and musical performances. May-September, 9 a.m.-5 p.m.; September-April, 12 p.m.-5 p.m.; closed Monday.

VALLEY ZOO

13315 Buena Vista Road, Edmonton, 780-496-6911; www.valleyzoo.ca

Features a wide variety of birds and mammals, fish and reptiles. Train, merry-go-round, pony and camel rides.

WEST EDMONTON MALL

8882 170 St., Edmonton, 780-444-5308, 800-661-8890; www.westedmontonmall.com

Canada's largest shopping and entertainment complex features more than 800 stores and services, 110 eating establishments, 26 movie theaters, an aquarium, dolphin shows, a replica of a Spanish galleon, four submarines, a water park with wave pool and water slides, bungee jumping, ice-skating rink, casino, the Galaxyland amusement park with a 14-story looping rollercoaster, 18-hole miniature golf course and an IMAX Theatre.

SPECIAL EVENTS

CANADIAN FINALS RODEO

Rexall Place, 7424 118th Ave. N.W., Edmonton, 780-471-7210;
www.canadianfinalsrodeo.ca

Professional indoor rodeo to decide the national championships. Mid-November.

EDMONTON INTERNATIONAL STREET PERFORMERS FESTIVAL

7 Sir Winston Churchill Square, Edmonton, 780-425-5162;
www.edmontonstreetfest.com

Performances by more than 60 international street acts at more than 1,000 free outdoor shows. July.

EDMONTON'S KLONDIKE DAYS

Rexall Place, 7424 118th Ave. N.W., Edmonton, 780-471-7210

Entertainment, exhibits, midway, parade; events include the Sourdough Raft Race, Sunday promenade, band extravaganza and chuck wagon races. Mid-late July.

FOLK MUSIC FESTIVAL

10115-97a Ave., Edmonton, 780-429-1899; www.edmontonfolkfest.org

Three days of music at Alberta's largest outdoor music festival. Mid-August.

FRINGE THEATRE FESTIVAL

10330-84 Ave., Edmonton, 780-448-9000; www.fringetheatreadventures.ca

Dance, music, plays, mime, mask, street entertainers. Over 1,200 performances of 140 productions on 30 stages in the parks and on the streets. Mid-late August.

HERITAGE FESTIVAL

10125-157 St., Edmonton, 780-488-3378; www.heritage-festival.com

More than 70 cultures show Alberta's multicultural heritage in pageantry of color and music. Music, dance, displays and demonstrations at 50 outdoor pavilions, plus arts and crafts and international cuisine. Early August.

JAZZ CITY INTERNATIONAL MUSIC FESTIVAL

Edmonton, 780-432-7166; www.allaboutjazz.com

Jazz concerts, workshops, outdoor events. Late June-early July.

HOTELS

★★BEST WESTERN CEDAR PARK INN
5116 Gateway Blvd., Edmonton, 780-434-7411, 800-780-7234; www.cedarparkinn.com
190 rooms. Restaurant, bar. Pets accepted. Exercise room. Pool. $

★★★DELTA EDMONTON CENTRE SUITE HOTEL
10222-102nd St., Edmonton, 708-429-3900, 800-661-6655; www.deltahotels.com
This hotel is located inside the Edmonton City Centre West shopping mall, and it's connected to City Hall and the Shaw Conference Centre. Rooms have contemporary furnishings and complimentary Internet access. Cocoa's Restaurant features Continental cuisine with regional specialties and serves breakfast, lunch, dinner, Sunday brunch and late-night snacks. 169 rooms. Restaurant, bar. Pets accepted. Fitness room. Business center. $$

★★★THE FAIRMONT HOTEL MACDONALD
10065 100th St., Edmonton, 780-424-5181, 800-540-4468;
www.fairmont.com/MacDonald
This glorious château overlooks the scenic North Saskatchewan River Valley. From its formal high tea to its distinguished guest rooms and suites, this hotel recalls the charm of the Victorian period. Inventive nouveau cuisine is highlighted at Harvest Room, which also serves a Sunday brunch, and the Confederation Lounge is a nice spot for sipping a cocktail while soaking up the clubby atmosphere. 198 rooms. Restaurant, bar. Pets accepted, some restrictions; fee. Fitness room. Pool. Business center. $$

★★★THE SUTTON PLACE HOTEL
10235 101st St., Edmonton, 780-428-7111, 866-378-8866;
www.edmonton.suttonplace.com
Connected by a walkway to Edmonton Centre, this hotel is also located near the Edmonton International Airport, the Space and Science Center, and many other area attractions. Within walking distance is the Sir Winston Churchill Square and the Edmonton Art Gallery. Enjoy dinner at the Sutton Place's Capitals Restaurant with its à la carte menu or sip a drink or two at the open-air atrium of Central Park Lounge. 313 rooms. Restaurant, bar. Pets accepted, some restrictions; fee. Fitness room. Pool. Business center. $$

★RAMADA
5359 Calgary Trail, Edmonton, 780-434-3431, 800-661-9030; www.ramada.ca
122 rooms. Complimentary full breakfast. Restaurant, bar. Exercise room. Pool. $

★★★THE WESTIN EDMONTON
10135 100th St., Edmonton, 780-426-3636, 800-937-8461;
www.thewestinedmonton.com
Conveniently located in downtown Edmonton, this hotel has a pedestrian walkway that connects to area attractions such as Edmonton Art Gallery, Shaw Conference Center and the Citadel Theater. Unwind at the gym or swim in the heated indoor pool. Pradera Café, the Westin's restaurant, focuses on regional and international cuisine. 416 rooms. Restaurant, bar. Children's activity center. High-speed Internet access. Pets accepted. Exercise room. Pool. Business center. $$

ALBERTA

★
★
★
★
☆

RESTAURANTS

★★COCOA'S

10222-102nd St. N.W., Edmonton, 708-423-9650; www.deltahotels.com

French menu. Breakfast, lunch, dinner, Sunday brunch. $$$

★CREPERIE

10220-103rd St., Edmonton, 780-420-6656; www.thecreperie.com

French bistro menu. Lunch, dinner. Reservations recommended. $$

★FIORE

8715-109th St., Edmonton, 780-439-8466; fiorecantina.com

Italian menu. Breakfast, dinner. Outdoor seating. $$

★★★THE HARVEST ROOM

10065 100th St., Edmonton, 780-429-6424, 800-540-4468; www.fairmont.com

Located in the historic chateau-style Hotel MacDonald, this elegant dining room features contemporary Canadian cuisine using fresh, local ingredients such as Alberta beef and veal, farm-raised game and free-range poultry. The outdoor terrace overlooks the North Saskatchewan River Valley. Seafood, steak menu. Breakfast, lunch, dinner. Casual attire. Reservations recommended. $$$

★★LA BOHEME

6427 112th Ave., Edmonton, 780-474-5693; www.laboheme.ca

French menu. Breakfast, lunch, dinner, Sunday brunch. Outdoor seating. $$$

★★★LA RONDE

10111 Bellamy Hill, Edmonton, 780-428-6611; www.chateaulacombe.com/laronde.php

This restaurant sits on the rooftop of the Crowne Plaza Hotel Chateau Lacombe. The revolving room has incredible views of the surrounding city, and the cuisine makes good use of local ingredients. Dishes include bison ribeye with sage spatzle, and maple-glazed arctic char. Seafood, steak menu. Dinner, Sunday Brunch. Reservations recommended. $$$

FORT MACLEOD

From a distance, Fort Macleod looks like any other town—but its rich history and national significance are apparent as soon as visitors wander through its streets. It is at a crossroads that once hosted Indian encampments, wagon trails and buffalo grazing grounds, in view of the Porcupine Hills that front the Rocky Mountains. Once known as Blackfoot Crossing, Fort Macleod became a North West Mounted Police barracks and trading post in 1874. From the fort spread the fame of the "men in red" who stamped out the illegal whiskey trade and kept rowdy gold miners in check—and who eventually became known as the Canadian RCMP.

The town gradually took shape alongside the Oldman River, named for the grandfather of Blackfoot mythology, and within easy view of the mountains. Fort Macleod draws you into a time when the North West Mounted Police, Blackfoot Indians and pioneer settlers were the only inhabitants. Main Street is dotted with gift shops, antique stores and restaurants that recapture this spirit.

Information: www.fortmacleod.com

FORT MUSEUM

219 25th St., Fort Macleod, 403-553-4703; www.nwmpmuseum.com

Experience the rich history of Fort Macleod, the first outpost in the Canadian West. Witness the history of the North West Mounted Police (the precursor to the national RCMP), plains tribes and pioneer life and enjoy the spectacle of the Mounted Patrol Musical Ride. July-September, four times daily.

HEAD-SMASHED-IN BUFFALO JUMP INTERPRETIVE CENTRE

Highways 2 and 785, Fort Macleod, 403-553-2731; 800-310-0000;
www.head-smashed-in.com

This UNESCO World Heritage Site celebrates 6,000-year-old Native American hunting techniques as interpreted by members of Blackfoot Nation, built into the cliff where buffaloes were herded to jump to their death.

REMINGTON CARRIAGE MUSEUM

623 Main St., Cardston, 403-653-5139; www.remingtoncarriagemuseum.com

Displays one of the largest collections of horse-drawn vehicles in North America, with over 200 carriages, wagons and sleighs. Gallery has interactive displays, multimedia productions and a carriage factory.

SPECIAL EVENTS

POWWOW AND TIPI VILLAGE

Head-Smashed-In Buffalo Jump, Highways 2 and 785, Fort Macleod, 403-553-2731;
www.head-smashed-in.com/info.html

Celebration features open tepee village, traditional native dances, games, food. Third weekend in July.

SANTA CLAUS PARADE AND FESTIVAL

Third Avenue and 24th Street, Fort Macleod, 403-553-2500;

One of the oldest and largest Santa Claus parades west of Toronto. Last Saturday in November.

JASPER

Everywhere you turn in the resort town of Jasper, dramatic peaks crown the horizon. Established in 1907 in the heart of the Canadian Rockies, Jasper is one of Canada's largest and most scenic national parks—and unique in that the town of the same name is at its center, jointly governed by a municipal government and Parks Canada. In more than 4,200 square miles (10,878 square kilometers) are waterfalls, lakes, canyons, glaciers and wilderness areas filled with varied forms of wildlife. The park has year-round interpretive programs, trips and campfire talks as well as guided wilderness trips, a sky tram, skating, skiing, ice climbing and rafting and cycling trips. While driving through Jasper, be prepared to be awestruck at every turn. Keep your camera poised—all the better if you've got a wide-angle lens for unmatched panoramas.

Information: jasper-alberta.com

WHAT TO SEE AND DO

THE ICEFIELDS PARKWAY

www.icefieldsparkway.ca

One of the most famous mountain highways in the world, the Icefields Parkway travels between Lake Louise and Jasper along the crown of the Canadian Rockies. The scenery is phenomenal: soaring peaks still under the bite of glaciers, turquoise green lakes surrounded by deep forests, roaring waterfalls and at the very crest of the drive, the Columbia Icefield, the largest non-polar icecap in the world. Lakeside lodges offer canoe rentals, short horseback trail rides, whitewater rafting trips and excursions onto the Columbia Icefield in specially designed snowcoaches. Just off the highway, by the Athabasca Glacier, the Columbia Icefield Center provides information on the ice field and the glaciers (May-mid-October). Wildlife is also abundant: mountain goats, mountain sheep, elk, moose and bears are frequently sighted.

JASPER TRAMWAY

Highway 93 and Whistler Mountain Road, 780-852-3093; www.jaspertramway.com

Two 30-passenger cars take 1¼-mile (2 kilometer) trips up Whistler's Mountain. Vast area of alpine tundra at summit; hiking trails, picnicking; restaurants, gift shops. April-mid-October, daily.

MALIGNE TOURS

Highway 16 and Maligne Road, Jasper, 780-852-3370,
866-625-4463; www.malignelake.com

Narrated boat cruise on Maligne Lake to world-famous Spirit Island (May-mid-October, daily). Fishing supplies and boat rentals. Whitewater raft trips.

MARMOT BASIN

Highway 93 A and Marmot Basin Road, Jasper, 780-852-3816,
866-952-3816; www.skimarmot.com

Quad, triple, three double chairlifts, two T-bars; patrol, school, rentals, repair shop; nursery, three cafeterias, bar. Vertical drop 3,000 feet (897 meters). Early December-late April.

MIETTE HOT SPRINGS

Miette Road and Highway 16, Jasper, 780-866-3939, 800-767-1611;
www.parkscanada.gc.ca/hotsprings

Pool uses natural hot mineral springs. Mid-May-early October.

HOTELS

★ALPINE VILLAGE

Highway 93A N., Jasper, 780-852-3285; www.alpinevillagejasper.com

37 rooms. Closed mid-October-April. $

★★★CHATEAU JASPER

96 Geikie St., Jasper, 780-852-5644, 888-852-7737; www.mpljasper.com

This comfortable hotel is an ideal base for active travelers who enjoy skiing, snow-boarding, snowshoeing and ice skating during the winter, and hiking and guided nature tours during the summer. Spacious rooms feature lovely views, while the hotel's

ALBERTA

★
★
★
★
★

in-town location makes it perfect for dining and shopping. 119 rooms. Restaurant, bar. Pool. $$$

★★★THE FAIRMONT JASPER PARK LODGE

Old Lodge Road, Jasper, 780-852-3301, 866-540-4454; www.fairmont.com/jasper

The Fairmont Jasper Park Lodge is the sophisticated alternative in the Canadian Rocky Mountains. This rustic retreat consists of a series of cedar chalets and log cabins, with luxurious accommodations, fine dining and exceptional services. 446 rooms. Restaurant, bar. Children's activity center. Pets accepted, some restrictions; fee. Fitness room. Pool. Golf. Tennis. $$

★★LOBSTICK LODGE

94 Geikie St., 780-852-4431, 888-852-7737; www.mpljasper.com

139 rooms. Restaurant, bar. Wireless high-speed Internet access. Pets accepted, fee. Pool. $

★★MARMOT LODGE

86 Connaught Drive, Jasper, 780-852-4471, 888-852-7737; www.mpljasper.com

107 rooms. Restaurant, bar. Pets accepted, fee. Pool. $$

★★SAWRIDGE INN & CONFERENCE CENTER

82 Connaught Drive, Jasper, 780-852-5111, 888-729-7343; www.sawridgejasper.com

153 rooms. Restaurant, bar. Wireless Internet access. Pool. $$

RESTAURANTS

★★★EDITH CAVELL DINING ROOM

Old Lodge Road, Jasper, 708-852-6052, 800-441-1414; www.fairmont.com

The gourmet fare, vintage wines and attentive service of Jasper Park Lodge's dining room are all eclipsed by breathtaking lake and mountain views. Settle in for a grilled steak or locally caught mountain trout and take in the scenery. French menu. Jacket required. $$$

★L & W

Hazel and Patricia streets, Jasper, 780-852-4114

American, Greek menu. $$

★SOMETHING ELSE

621 Patricia St., Jasper, 780-852-3850

Italian, Greek menu. Outdoor seating. $$

★★TONQUIN PRIME RIB VILLAGE

100 Juniper, Jasper, 780-852-4966; www.tonquininn.com

Steak menu. Outdoor seating. $$$

LAKE LOUISE

The blue-green glacial lake reflects a mirror image of the Victoria Glacier when the sun hits it at the right point. At the shore, nestled at the base of the mountain, sits the Chateau Lake Louise, one of the most elegant and classic hotel landmarks on the continent.

Lake Louise is the third in the must-visit trinity of Banff and Jasper. Its central Rocky Mountain location, longstanding history and lively resort atmosphere make it both an exciting and scenic destination. During the summer, the sightseeing gondola takes visitors high over the town to Mount Whitehorn, where a lodge serves as alpine home base for hiking, picnicking and exploration. Summer or winter, take in the fresh mountain air equipped with canoe, mountain bike, skis, snowboard, climbing rope or horse.

Information: www.banfflakelouise.com

WHAT TO SEE AND DO
LAKE LOUISE GONDOLA

877-253-6888; www.lakelouisegondola.com

Ascend to 6,810 feet (2,075 meters) in 14 minutes to view Lake Louise Victoria Glacier and The Great Divide. Restaurant, cafeteria, deli bar; hiking trails, nature programs. Summer operation runs June-September.

LAKE LOUISE SKI AREA

403-522-3555, 800-258-7669; www.skilouise.com

Canada's largest ski area with over 100 runs on four mountain faces across more than 4,200 acres (1,700 hectares) of skiing. Top elevation 8,650 feet (3,636 hectares); vertical drop 3,257 feet (993 meters). Four high-speed quads, one quad, one triple chair, two double chairs, one expert platter, one T-bar, one beginner rope tow, one magic carpet. Four restaurants, three cafeterias, three bars; rental shop, ski and snowboard school. Early November-mid-May.

MORAINE LAKE AND VALLEY OF THE TEN PEAKS

7½ miles (12 kilometers) east of Lake Louise

Towering mountain peaks frame the emerald green lake. Hiking trails, canoe rental.

HOTELS
★★BAKER CREEK CHALETS

Highway 1A, Bow Valley Parkway, Lake Louise, 403-522-3761; www.bakercreek.com

35 rooms. Restaurant, bar. $$

★★DEER LODGE

109 Lake Louise Lodge, Lake Louise, 403-522-3991, 800-661-1595; www.crmr.com

73 rooms. Restaurant, bar. Former trading camp. Closed early October-early December. Business center. $$

★★★EMERALD LAKE LODGE

1 Emerald Lake Road, Field, 250-343-6321, 800-663-6336;
www.crmr.com/emerald-lake-lodge.php

Located on 13 acres in Yoho National Park, the lodge has a formal dining room, reading and sitting rooms, conference facilities and a games room. The onsite restaurant, Mount Burgess Dining Room, serves rustic California cuisine with Native American influences and offers award-winning Canadian wines. There are plenty of activities from hiking and fishing in summer to skiing and ice fishing in winter. 25 cabin-style buildings, 85 rooms. Restaurant, bar. Exercise room. Business center. $$

ALBERTA

★
★
★
★
★

★★★THE FAIRMONT CHATEAU LAKE LOUISE

111 Lake Louise Drive, Lake Louise, 403-522-3511, 800-441-1414;
www.fairmont.com/LakeLouise

This grand resort offers its guests a front-row seat to Banff National Park while overlooking the sparkling water of Lake Louise. Stunning panoramas are matched only by the sophistication and comfort offered inside, where European flair blends with Canadian hospitality. 550 rooms. Restaurant, bar. Ski in/ski out. Pets accepted, fee. Exercise room. Pool. Skiing. Business center. $$$

★★★POST HOTEL

200 Pipestone Road, Lake Louise, 403-522-3989, 800-661-1586; www.posthotel.com

This historic alpine lodge shares the finer things with guests who savor gourmet European cooking, sip award-winning wines and sleep in total luxury. One of Canada's best ski areas is just a few minutes from the hotel. 96 rooms. Closed mid-October-mid-December. Restaurant, bar. Ski in/ski out. Pool. Skiing. Business center. $$$

RESTAURANTS

★★★FAIRVIEW DINING ROOM

111 Lake Louise Drive, Lake Louise, 403-522-3511, 800-441-1414; www.fairmont.com

This historic dining room, Chateau Lake Louise's original, is housed in a breathtaking Canadian Rockies location. One of several restaurants at the resort, the dining room serves classic continental cuisine during the summer months amidst original, 1913 grandeur. Continental menu. Breakfast, lunch, dinner. Reservations recommended. Casual attire. $$$

★★★★POST HOTEL DINING ROOM

200 Pipestone Road, Lake Louise, 403-522-3989, 800-661-1586; www.posthotel.com

Tucked into the foothills of the Canadian Rockies is this gem of a dining experience. Set in one of Banff National Parks remaining historic log lodges, the Post Hotel Dining Room achieves an easy sense of old-fashioned charm with majestic mountain views and a blazing stone fireplace. The exceptional cuisine is matched by a highly acclaimed wine list with more than 28,500 bottles and more than 1,500 selections. Canadian menu. Dinner. Closed late October-mid-December. Reservations recommended. Casual attire. $$$$

★★WALLISER STUBE

111 Lake Louise Drive, Lake Louise, 403-522-3511, 800-441-1414; www.fairmont.com

French menu. Dinner. Reservations recommended. Casual attire. $$$

LETHBRIDGE

Lethbridge is one of the warmest and sunniest cities in Canada—and not just in terms of the weather. The community's pride for its recreation-driven lifestyle makes for a friendly, spirited and active community.

Originally known to the Blackfoot as Sik-okotoks or "place of black rocks," Lethbridge transformed from a coal-producing town to a lush parkland with gardens such as the Brewery Gardens at the western edge of town; Indian Battle Park, site of the last battle between Native American nations in North America and Henderson Lake Park. In 1869, traders from the United States came north and built so-called "whiskey forts" in and around the future city site, the most notorious of which was Fort Whoop-Up. The arrival of the North West Mounted Police in 1874 soon stamped out this illegal whiskey trade and brought order to this rambunctious corner of the west. The rebuilt fort now steeps visitors in this wily heritage, and the flag that signaled the arrival of the latest load of whiskey is now the city's official flag.

Information: www.lethbridgecvb.com

WHAT TO SEE AND DO

ALBERTA BIRDS OF PREY CENTER

403-345-4262, 800-661-1222; www.burrowingowl.com

Living museum featuring hawks, owls, falcons and other birds of prey from Alberta and around the world. Interpretive center has educational displays, wildlife art. Daily flying demonstrations; picnicking. May-mid-October, daily, weather permitting.

FORT WHOOP-UP

Third Avenue, South and Scenic Drive, Lethbridge, Indian Battle Park, 403-329-0444; www.fortwhoopup.com

Step into southern Alberta history at this replica of a booming, circa 1870s whiskey trading post. Interpretive gallery, theater, tours. Mid-May-September, daily; rest of year, Tuesday-Friday, Sunday afternoons.

NIKKA YUKO JAPANESE GARDEN

Henderson Lake Park, Mayor Magrath Drive and Ninth Avenue South, Lethbridge, 403-328-3511; www.nikkayuko.com

Built to commemorate Canada's centennial in 1967, the authentic garden is a symbol of Japanese-Canadian friendship. The garden is an art form of peace and tranquility.

SIR ALEXANDER GALT MUSEUM

502–First Street S., Lethbridge, 403-320-3898, 866-320-3898; www.galtmuseum.com

Displays relate to early development of area. Featured exhibits include indigenous culture, pioneer life, civic history, coal mining, farming history, irrigation, ethnic displays. May 15-August: 10 a.m.-6 p.m. daily; September-May 14: Monday-Saturday 10 a.m.-4:30 p.m.; Sunday and holidays 1-4:30 p.m.

WATERTON LAKES NATIONAL PARK

Highways 5 and 6, Waterton Park, 403-859-2224, 800-661-8888; www.pc.gc.ca

Waterton is a rare gem tucked into the southwest corner of Alberta where the great Rocky Mountains rise suddenly out of the rolling prairies. Amid the peaks are the lakes of Waterton, carved out of the rock by ancient glaciers and forming a blend of unusual geology, mild climate, rare flowers and abundant wildlife. In 1932 Waterton Lakes National Park was linked with neighboring Glacier National Park in Montana—the cross-border area is now known as Waterton-Glacier International Peace Park. This park contains 203 square miles (526 square kilometers) on the eastern slope of the Rocky Mountains, just north of the U.S.-Canadian border. Travelers from the United States can reach the park via the Chief Mountain Highway along the east edge of Glacier National Park (mid-May-mid-September). The trails are well maintained and

33

ALBERTA

★
★
★
★
★

afford an introduction to much of the scenery that is inaccessible by car. The Red Rock Parkway goes from the town of Waterton Park to Red Rock Canyon after branching off Alberta Highway 5. A buffalo paddock is located on Highway 6, just inside the northeastern park boundary. Also from the town of Waterton Park, you can drive to Cameron Lake via the Akamina Parkway.

SPECIAL EVENTS

AG EXPO AND THE NORTH AMERICAN SEED FAIR

Exhibition Park, 3401 Parkside Drive South, Lethbridge, 403-328-4491;
www.exhibitionpark.ca
This annual event presents the latest in agricultural technology to the public and also includes a fashion show and Aggie Days for kids. Late February.

INTERNATIONAL AIR SHOW

Highway 5 S. and McNally Road, Lethbridge, 800-661-1222; www.albertaairshow.com
The Canadian Forces Snowbirds are the highlight of this two-day air-show that includes several Canadian and international acts. August.

WHOOP-UP DAYS

3401 Parkside Drive S., Lethbridge, 403-328-4491;
www.exhibitionpark.ca/whoopup.htm
Fair, exhibitions, rodeo, grandstand show. Mid-August.

HOTELS

★★BEST WESTERN HEIDELBERG INN

1303 Mayor Magrath Drive, Lethbridge, 403-329-0555, 800-791-8488;
www.bestwestern.com
65 rooms Restaurant, bar. Complimentary continental breakfast. High-speed Internet access. Fitness center. Business center. $

★★★THE KILMOREY LODGE

117 Evergreen Ave., Waterton Lakes National Park, 403-859-2334, 888-859-8669;
www.kilmoreylodge.com
This historic lodge can be found on the lakeshore at Emerald Bay, tucked between mountain peaks in Waterton Lake. It offers uniquely decorated and well-furnished rooms featuring fine antiques and other treasures from the past. 23 rooms. Restaurant, bar. $

★★LETHBRIDGE LODGE

320 Scenic Drive, Lethbridge, 403-328-1123, 800-661-1232; www.lethbridgelodge.com
190 rooms. Restaurant, bar. Pets accepted, fee. Pool. $

★★PRINCE OF WALES

117 Evergreen Ave., Waterton Lakes National Park, 403-859-2231;
www.princeofwaleswaterton.com
81 rooms. Closed mid-September-early June. Restaurant, bar. $$

ALBERTA

★
★
★
★
★

★★★COCO PAZZO

1264 Third Ave. S., Lethbridge, 403-329-8979

One of the trendiest spots in the area, this restaurant offers guests the best in Italian food in a casual, cafe atmosphere. With a variety of pasta dishes to suit every taste, fantastic red wine and a fun crowd, it is a delightful dining experience. Italian menu. Dinner. Outdoor seating. **$$$**

MEDICINE HAT

Despite its industrious roots, Medicine Hat is the ideal environ for natural bounty and beauty. Rich in clays and natural gas, the area was a natural site for brick, tile and petrochemical plants—but its hot summer temperatures make it ideal for beautiful market gardens and greenhouses.

The name Medicine Hat is a translation of the Blackfoot name Saamis, meaning "headdress of a medicine man." Natural gas was discovered here in 1883, and in 1909 the huge Bow Island gas field was founded, sending the town on a production frenzy that lasted for generations—the gas fields inspired the British poet Rudyard Kipling to refer to the settlement as "the town with all hell for a basement."

Information: www.city.medicine-hat.ab.ca

WHAT TO SEE AND DO

CYPRESS HILLS INTERPROVINCIAL PARK

East from Medicine Hat on Trans-Canada Highway 1, then south on Highway 41, 403-893-3777

This park is an oasis of mixed deciduous and coniferous forests in the middle of a predominantly grassland region. At a maximum elevation of 4,810 feet (1,466 meters) above sea level, the hills are the highest point in Canada between the Rocky Mountains and Labrador. The area offers a swimming beach, boating, canoeing and fishing; camping, golf course, hiking trails and nature interpretive programs.

35

ALBERTA

★
★
★
★
☆

DINOSAUR PROVINCIAL PARK

Approximately 25 miles (40 kilometers) west of Medicine Hat on Highway 1, then north on Highway 884, west on Highway 544, 403-378-4342; www.gov.ab.ca

Discoveries of extensive fossil concentrations in this area in the late 1800s led to the designation of this area as a provincial park and UNESCO World Heritage Site. More than 300 complete skeletons have been recovered and are now displayed in museums worldwide. The 22,000-acre (8,903 hectares) park consists mainly of badlands; large areas have restricted access and can be seen only on interpretive tours. Facilities include canoeing, fishing; interpretive trails, dinosaur displays (at the actual discovery site) along a public loop drive. Camping. Guided tours and hikes, amphitheater events and talks.

MEDICINE HAT MUSEUM AND ART GALLERY

1302 Bomford Crescent S.W., Medicine Hat, 403-502-8580; www.highway3.ca

Displays depict the history of the Canadian West, featuring pioneer items, local fossils, relics and Native artifacts. The archives contain a large collection of photographs and manuscripts. Monday-Friday 9 a.m.-5 p.m., weekends and holidays 1-5 p.m.

EXHIBITION AND STAMPEDE

Stampede Park, 2055 21st Ave. S.E., Medicine Hat, 403-527-1234, 888-647-6336;
www.mhstampede.com

Cattle and horse shows, professional rodeo, midway rides. Late July.

HOTELS

★BEST WESTERN INN

722 Redcliff Drive, Medicine Hat, 403-527-3700, 888-527-6633; www.bestwestern.com

122 rooms. Complimentary continental breakfast. Pets accepted, fee. Business center.
Fitness center. Pool. $

★★MEDICINE HAT LODGE

1051 Ross Glen Drive S.E., Medicine Hat, 403-529-2222, 800-661-8095;
www.medhatlodge.com

223 rooms. Restaurant, bar. High-speed Internet access. Fitness center. Business center. Pets accepted, fee. Pool. $

RED DEER

Midway between Calgary and Edmonton is Red Deer, beautifully positioned in the lush, green parkland of central Alberta. A wealth of recreation and cultural programs keep visitors charmed, including famed dinner theatres by Central Alberta Theatre. Attend rodeos and authentic agricultural exhibitions alongside world-class sporting events such as the Canadian Open Figure Skating Championship and the Scott Tournament of Hearts (curling).

In the early 1870s, the Calgary-Edmonton Trail crossed the river at Red Deer Crossing. With the coming of the railway, traffic increased, and a trading post and stopping place were established. When the Northwest Rebellion broke out in 1885, a small regiment was stationed at Fort Normandeau, which still stands on the outskirts of the city. The river was originally called Was-ka-soo See-pi, the Cree word for elk, because of the abundance of these animals in the area. Early Scottish fur traders thought the elk was related to the red deer of their native land, hence the present name for the river and city.

Information: www.city.red-deer.ab.ca

WHAT TO SEE AND DO

CANYON SKI AREA

Ross St., Red Deer, 403-346-7003; www.canyonski.net

Triple, double chairlifts, two T-bars, handle tow, Nordic jump; patrol, school, rentals, snowmaking; day lodge, bar. Vertical drop 500 feet (164 meters). Cross-country skiing. November-March, daily.

FORT NORMANDEAU

The C & E Trail and 32nd St., Red Deer, 403-346-2010;
www.waskasoopark.ca/ftnorm.htm

Rebuilt 1885 army fort and interpretive center with displays of cultural history. Slide program, living history interpreters. Picnic area, canoe launch. May-September, daily.

36

ALBERTA

★
★
★
★
★

RED DEER AND DISTRICT MUSEUM

4525 47 A Ave., Red Deer, 403-309-8405; www.museum.red-deer.ab.ca

This museum tells the story of the area, from the early First Nations settlements to the present. Also located here are Heritage Square and Red Deer and District Archives.

WASKASOO PARK

49th St. and 48th Ave., Red Deer, 403-342-8159; www.waskasoopark.ca

Large River Valley Park extending throughout city. Includes 47 miles (75 kilometers) of bicycle and hiking trails, equestrian area, fishing, canoeing, water park, 18-hole golf course, camping. Natural and cultural history interpretive centers; other attractions also located within park.

SPECIAL EVENTS
FORT NORMANDEAU DAYS

Fort Normandeau, Range Road 280 and 32nd Street, Red Deer,
403-346-2010, www.waskasoopark.ca/ftnorm.htm

Native American ceremonies and dances, parade, children's activities. Late May.

HIGHLAND GAMES

Westerner Exposition Park, 4847 19th St., Red Deer; www.reddeerhighlandgames.ca

The annual games began in 1947 and feature highland dancing, piping and drumming and shortbread baking competitions. Last Saturday in June.

WESTERNER DAYS

4847 A-19th St., Red Deer, 403-343-7800; www.westerner.ab.ca/events.htm

Fair and exhibition, midway, livestock shows, chuck wagon races. Mid-July.

HOTELS
★★★CAPRI CONFERENCE CENTRE

3310 50th Ave., Red Deer, 403-346-2091, 800-662-7197; www.capricentre.com

Although this full-service hotel is primarily booked by convention travelers, there are diversions for leisure travelers, too. Various types of rooms and suites are available. The hotel has a heated outdoor pool and deck, a whirlpool, a shopping concourse and the Capri Centre Spa & Health Club. Barbero's Restaurant is a great choice for a business lunch or quiet dinner, and guests can kick up their heels at Billy Bob's Country Music Dance Hall or take a breather at Bellini's Lounge. 219 rooms. Restaurant, bar. Wireless Internet access. Pets accepted, some restrictions; fee. Pool. $

★★HOLIDAY INN

6500 67th St., Red Deer, 403-342-6567, 888-465-4329; www.ichotelsgroup.com

142 rooms. Complimentary continental breakfast. Restaurant, bar. High-speed Internet access. Pets accepted, fee. Fitness center. Spa. Pool. Business center. $

★HOLIDAY INN EXPRESS

2803 50th Ave., Red Deer, 403-343-2112, 800-465-4329; www.ichotelsgroup.com

92 rooms. Complimentary continental breakfast. High-speed Internet access. Pets accepted, fee. Fitness center. Spa. Pool. Business center. $

ALBERTA

★
★
★
★
★

BRITISH COLUMBIA

BRITISH COLUMBIANS LIVE IN A CORNER OF CANADA THAT SEES AN EXPLOSION OF DAFFODILS and cherry blossoms while the rest of the country is still shoveling snow. In this westernmost province, life is enormous—from 1,000-year-old trees and everyday mountain vistas to towering city sunflowers.

Five diverse regions make up the whole of the province, each pulling tourists a hundred different ways each day: Vancouver Island, Vancouver Coast and Mountains, Thompson Okanagan, the Kootenay Rockies, the Cariboo Chilcotin Coast and the vast Northern region.

Vancouver Island has one of the world's most diverse ecosystems: rainforests, marshes, meadows, beaches, mountains, oceans, rivers and lakes create habitats for multitudes of wildlife species. It all adds up to one of the world's premier locations for golf, whale watching, birding and salmon and trout fishing. The island is blanketed in rare, old-growth rainforest and dramatic mountain ranges, picturesque cities and towns, and smaller island groups that invite ferry-bound adventures at an island pace.

Vancouver Coast and Mountains, slated to host the 2010 Olympic Games, is a phenomenal mountainous city—a mecca of peaks, ocean, lakes, rivers and beaches encircling a cosmopolitan gem that rivals the most spectacular cities in the world. Revel in the four season resort town of Whistler, famed worldwide for skiing, great shopping and fine restaurants. Visitors and residents cycle, hike, camp, kayak, golf, ski and snowboard year-round—in fact, the mild climate is such that a "West Coast Special" is an everyday option: ski in the morning, then golf or sail in the afternoon.

The Thompson Okanagan region is as famous for its pastoral orchards and vineyards as it is for its wildly varied landscape—the highest mountain in the Canadian Rockies is here, as well as a waterfall twice the height of Niagara Falls and Canada's only true desert. The heart of BC's wine-growing region is located just a four-hour drive east of Vancouver, where more than 40 wineries are within a 150-mile (241-kilometer) range.

The Kootenays are a purer mountain play, a vast wilderness of rivers, lakes, waterfalls, beaches, mineral hot springs, alpine meadows and snow-capped mountains. Adventure connoisseurs tackle some of the world's most intense mountain biking, fishing, windsurfing, whitewater rafting and kayaking. Golfers come here for world-class courses with unbeatable scenery, and city slickers turn cowboy at dude and guest ranches that offer authentic cattle rides. You can visit restored heritage towns, thriving art communities and gold rush boomtowns, and in winter, take in the continent's finest powder skiing and snowboarding.

FUN FACTS British Columbia is Canada's third-largest province after Quebec and Ontario. There are only 30 nations in the world and one U.S. state (Alaska), larger in surface area than British Columbia.

Thousands of lakes and rivers, plus a magnificent stretch of Pacific Ocean coastline, make the Cariboo Chilcotin Coast, which harkens back to the adrenaline-pumping gold rush era, a top destination for fishing, boating, camping, swimming and kayaking. This is a region whose rich, fascinating history is perhaps only rivaled by its captivating present day—complete with cowboys riding off into the sunset. Roam endless gentle trails or hike, ride and canter strenuous backcountry routes. Tramp through the volcanic mountains of Tweedsmuir Provincial Park, stand at the ancient hoodoos and shifting sand dune of Farwell Canyon and drive the original Cariboo Waggon Road on the historic Gold Rush Trail, taking in famed local rodeos and stampedes.

Northern BC's vast wilderness comprises more than half the province, a land of jagged mountain peaks, roaring rivers, serene lakes, green valleys, rugged coastlines and ancient island archipelagos. The region is known for its magnificent freshwater and saltwater fishing, canoeing, kayaking, whitewater rafting and in the winter, powder skiing. A wondrous system of national and provincial parks provides habitats and sanctuary for wildlife. The Queen Charlotte Islands are a living mystery within this region, an untamed, old-growth land rich in Haida culture and with distinct island flora and fauna that have evolved over thousands of years.

Provincial Capital: Victoria. Information: www.hellobc.com

KAMLOOPS

With more than 2,000 hours of annual sunshine, Kamloop is a top destination for fishing, and its trout are world famous and bountiful in over 200 lakes within an hour's drive of the city. Balmy summers encourage rapid plant and fish growth, making the area widely recognized as a freshwater fishing hotspot. In addition to hundreds of lakes, there are many areas of dry forest, hilly areas that are largely treeless (and well tracked-up by enthusiastic mountain bikers) and grasslands that support several endangered species.

Information: www.adventurekamloops.com

WHAT TO SEE AND DO

KAMLOOPS MUSEUM AND ARCHIVES

207 Seymour St., Kamloops, 250-828-3576; www.kamloops.ca/museum

This museum features exhibits depicting the frontier history of Kamloops. Self-guided walking tours, bicycle tours and cemetery tours are also available.

KAMLOOPS WILDLIFE PARK

9077 E. Dallas Drive, Kamloops, 250-573-3242; www.kamloopswildlife.org

More than 300 animals, both native and imported. Nature trail, miniature railroad, park.

SECWEPEMC NATIVE HERITAGE PARK

355 Yellowhead Highway, Kamloops, 250-828-9779; www.secwepemc.org

Located on the Kamloops Reserve, this park interprets culture and heritage of the Secwepemc people. Includes archaeological site, full-scale winter village model, indoor museum exhibits and native arts and crafts.

HOTELS

★★ACCENT INN KAMLOOPS

1325 Columbia St. W., Kamloops, 250-374-8877, 800-663-0298; www.accentinns.com

83 rooms. Restaurant. Pets accepted, fee. Pool. $

★
★
★
★
☆

★★★THE COAST CANADIAN INN

339 St. Paul St., Kamloops, 250-372-5201; www.coasthotels.com

This hotel is located in downtown Kamloops, the center of the Thompson Valley recreation area. The hotel is ideal for business travelers, with complimentary high-speed Internet connection in each room. Enjoy a pint or two at Seargent O'Flaherty's Pub or a light dinner at Pronto Grill. 98 rooms. Restaurant, bar. Pets accepted, fee. Exercise room. Pool. Business center. $

★★RAMADA INN

555 W. Columbia St., Kamloops, 250-374-0358, 800-663-2832;
www.ramadainn.kamloops.com

88 Rooms. Restaurant, bar. Pets accepted, fee. Pool. $

KELOWNA

Kelowna is located on the shores of the vast Okanagan Lake, 80 miles (128 kilometers) north of the U.S. border. The name Kelowna is a corruption of an indigenous word for grizzly bear, and the city dates back to the fur brigades in the 19th century. A mission founded here in 1858 birthed apple orchards that established one of the most prosperous fruit-growing districts in Canada. With legendarily steady weather, any day of the year is the right time to visit. Swim and stroll the beaches or catch the famous Regatta. Tour the orchards when they're in full bloom, or pick the freshest, juiciest fruit during harvest time. For golfers, Kelowna offers one of the longest and driest seasons in Canada.

Information: www.tourismkelowna.org

SPECIAL EVENTS

KELOWNA REGATTA

24-436 Bernard Ave., Kelowna, 250-860-0529, 877-973-4288;
www.kelownaregatta.com

Dating back to 1906, the Kelowna Regatta features many family-oriented land and water activities including a parade, rowing competitions, hydroplane races, waterskiing and an air show. Mid-July.

OKANAGAN WINE FESTIVALS

1527 Ellis St., Kelowna, 250-861-6654; www.owfs.com

Wine tasting at various locations around the Okanagan Valley. May and October.

HOTELS

★★ACCENT INN KELOWNA

1140 Harvey Ave., Kelowna, 250-862-8888, 800-663-0298; www.accentinns.com

101 rooms. Restaurant. Pets accepted, fee. Exercise room. Pool. $

★★BEST WESTERN INN-KELOWNA

2402 Highway 97N., Kelowna, 250-860-1212, 888-860-1212;
www.bestwestern.com/ca/innkelowna

147 rooms. Complimentary breakfast. Restaurant, bar. High-speed Internet access. Pool. Tennis. Fitness center. Pets accepted. $

★★★COAST CAPRI HOTEL

1171 Harvey Ave., Kelowna, 250-860-6060, 800-663-1144; www.coasthotels.com

Surrounded by mountains and orchards, this Kelowna landmark is located near golf courses, water sports and Lake Okanagan. Enjoy the year-round heated outdoor pool, hot tub and fitness center. End the evening with a visit to Bluelines Sport and Comedy Club for some fun. 85 rooms. Restaurant, bar. Pets accepted, fee. Pool. Business center. $

★★SANDMAN HOTEL KELOWNA

2130 Harvey Ave., Kelowna, 250-860-6409, 888-526-1988; www.sandmanhotels.com

120 rooms. Restaurant, bar. Pets accepted, fee. Pool. $

NANAIMO

Nanaimo is located on Vancouver Island across the strait of Georgia from Vancouver, a main entry port for ferries from Vancouver and Horseshoe Bay. Because of its location, it serves as a fine starting point to visit other attractions on the island, as well as being a vacation highlight in itself. A thriving art, culture and sports scene kicks off your island adventure, a perfect mix of big city amenities with small-town charm.
Information: www.tourismnanaimo.com

WHAT TO SEE AND DO

BASTION

Front and Bastion streets, Nanaimo

Built in 1853 as a Hudson's Bay Company fort. Now restored as a museum; cannon firing ceremony (summer months at noon).

NANAIMO ART GALLERY AND EXHIBITION CENTRE

900 Fifth St., Nanaimo, Malaspina College campus, 250-755-8790;
www.nanaimoartgallery.com

Gallery with changing exhibits of art, science and history.

NANAIMO DISTRICT MUSEUM

100 Museum Way, Nanaimo, 250-753-1821; www.nanaimomuseum.ca

Walk-in replica of a coal mine; turn-of-the-century shops, restored miner's cottage; dioramas; Chinatown display; changing exhibits. Daily 10 a.m.-5 p.m.

PETROGLYPH PARK

990 Island Highway S., Nanaimo, 250-391-2300; www.britishcolumbia.com/parks

This park contains ancient indigenous rock carvings.

QUEEN ELIZABETH PROMENADE

Front and Bastion streets, Nanaimo

Named to commemorate the vessel and landing of the first miner-colonists in the area; boardwalk offers pleasant view of waterfront and tidal lagoon.

★
★
★
☆

SPECIAL EVENTS

BOXING DAY POLAR BEAR SWIM

Departure Bay Road, Nanaimo, 250-756-5200; www.nanaimo.ca

Each Boxing Day, hardy souls take a dip in the frigid waters at Departure Bay Beach. All participants receive prizes as well as free ice cream, bananas and suntan lotion. December 26.

NANAIMO MARINE FESTIVAL & INTERNATIONAL BATHTUB RACE

Front Street and Terminal Avenue, Nanaimo, 250-753-7223;
www.nanaimoinformation.com

A festival highlighted by a 34-mile bathtub race (third or fourth Sunday in July) across the Strait of Georgia to Vancouver. The festival begins one week prior to race day.

VANCOUVER ISLAND EXHIBITION

2300 Bowen Road, Nanaimo, 250-758-3247; www.viex.ca

For over 100 years this annual fair has attracted tens of thousands of visitors each year for beautiful artwork, baked goodies and prize-winning livestock. Early or mid-August.

HOTELS

★★★COAST BASTION INN

11 Bastion St., Nanaimo, 250-753-6601; www.coasthotels.com

This downtown high-rise hotel offers views of Nanaimo Harbor and nearby islands from every guest room. Its location is convenient to harbor-front shops, galleries, restaurants and the BC Ferry terminal. After a busy day, Minnoz restaurant is a great place for a delicious meal, and the menu offers traditional West Coast cuisine. The bar also offers a light tapas menu. 179 rooms. Restaurant, bar. Wireless Internet access. Pets accepted, fee. Exercise room. $$

★★★CROWN ISLE RESORT

399 Clubhouse Drive, Courtenay, 250-703-5050; www.crownisle.com

The Crown Isle course meets the needs and playing levels of both novice and seasoned golfers. Accommodations include fairway rooms, one- and two-bedroom villas and loft villas. The resort is close to the nearby Aquatics Centre and Fifth Street shopping district as well as beaches and hiking. 56 rooms. Restaurant, bar. Exercise room. Golf. Airport transportation available. $$

★★FAIRWINDS SCHOONER COVE RESORT & MARINA

3521 Dolphin Drive, Nanoose Bay, 250-468-5364, 800-663-7060; www.fairwinds.bc.ca

31 rooms. Restaurant. Pets accepted, fee. Pool. Tennis. Golf. $$

★★★KINGFISHER OCEANSIDE RESORT & SPA

4330 S. Island Highway, Courtenay, 250-338-1323, 800-663-7929;
www.kingfisherspa.com

Located on wooded grounds in Comox Valley, the Kingfisher has a heated outdoor pool, a sauna, canoe and kayak rentals and nearby golf. The spa offers many services. For a quiet dinner, guests can head to the resort's dining room, the Kingfisher

Restaurant, where West Coast cuisine is served and accented by views of Hartley Bay. 64 rooms. Restaurant, bar. Pets accepted, fee. Exercise room. Pool. Golf. Tennis. Business center. Spa. **$**

RESTAURANT
★★THE MAHLE HOUSE RESTAURANT
2104 Hemer Road, Nanaimo, 250-722-3621; www.mahlehouse.ca
International menu. Reservations recommended. **$$$**

PENTICTON
Situated between the beautiful Okanagan and Skaha lakes on fertile orchard lands and rolling hills, this valley town is famous for summer heat, beaches, lakes, spectacular natural scenery, Canada's beast of legend Ogopogo, and the Ironman Canada Triathlon.
Information: www.penticton.ca

WHAT TO SEE AND DO
DOMINION RADIO ASTROPHYSICAL OBSERVATORY
717 White Lake Road, Penticton, 250-493-2277; www.drao.nrc.ca
Guided tours (August). Visitor center, daily.

PENTICTON MUSEUM
785 Main St., Penticton, 250-490-2451; www.penticton.ca
Collection of Salish artifacts; taxidermy, ghost town and pioneer exhibits. Changing exhibits. At 1099 Lakeshore Drive West are two historic 1914 steamships: *SS Sicamous,* a 200-foot (61-meter) sternwheeler and *SS Naramata,* a 90-foot (27-meter) steam tug. September-June, Tuesday-Saturday, July-August, Monday-Saturday, 10 a.m.-5 p.m.

SUMMERLAND RESEARCH STATION ORNAMENTAL GARDENS
4200 Highway 97 Summerland, 250-494-7711;
www.summerlandornamentalgardens.org
Beautiful display of ornamental gardens; canyon view; picnicking. Picnic grounds May-September, 8 a.m.-8 p.m.; shorter hours October-April; museum daily 1-4 p.m.

SPECIAL EVENTS
IRONMAN CANADA CHAMPIONSHIP TRIATHLON
416 Westminster Ave., Penticton; www.ironman.ca
Qualifier for Hawaiian Ironman. Late August.

MIDWINTER BREAKOUT
553 Railway Ave., Penticton, 250-493-4055; www.tourismpenticton.com
This winter festival celebrates the season with many events and activities, including ice carving and the Polar Bear Dip. Second and third weeks of February.

★
★
★
★
★

OKANAGAN WINE FESTIVALS

1304 Ella St., Penticton, 250-861-6654; www.owfs.com

Wine tasting, grape stomping, seminars and dinners. Various locations around the Okanagan Valley. Late April-early May; late September-mid-October.

PACIFIC NORTHWEST ELVIS FESTIVAL

Okanagan Lake Park, Penticton, 800-663-5052; www.pentictonelvisfestival.com

Tribute shows, judged performances, impromptu entertainment, souvenir booths and more. Late June.

PEACH FESTIVAL

Gyro Park, Main Street and Lake Shore Drive, Penticton, 800-663-5052;
www.peachfest.com

This five-day event celebrating the peach harvest has been taking place since 1947. Festivities include a parade, live entertainment, a fireworks display and arts and crafts exhibits. Families especially love Kiddies Day, which features events and activities created especially with youngsters in mind. Mid-August.

PENTICTON JAMBOREE

553 Railway St., Penticton, King's Park, 250-493-4055; www.tourismpenticton.com

Dancing under the stars on what is perhaps North America's largest outdoor board floor. Early August.

HOTELS

★★BEST WESTERN INN AT PENTICTON

3180 Skaha Lake Road, Penticton, 250-493-0311, 800-668-6746;
www.bestwestern.com

67 rooms. High-speed Internet access. Complimentary breakfast. Restaurant. Pool. Pets accepted. $

★★★PENTICTON LAKESIDE RESORT AND CONFERENCE CENTER

21 Lakeshore Drive W., Penticton, 250-493-8221, 800-663-9400; www.rpbhotels.com

This resort and conference center is located on the southern shore of Lake Okanagan. The hotel is close to local attractions and offers outdoor packages. Onsite is the Barking Parrot, a waterfront bar and club. 204 rooms. Restaurant, bar. Pets accepted, fee. Exercise room. Pool. $$

VANCOUVER

Surrounded by the blue waters of the Strait of Georgia and backed by the mile-high peaks of the Coast Range, the most mundane of Vancouver moments elicits a gasp at the view—on public transit crossing one of many bridges or from the window of a hotel room, snow-capped peaks tower over the skyline with rainforest adventure and urban escape a short drive away. Aside from having a natural setting unsurpassed on this continent, Vancouver is one of Canada's largest cities—a major seaport, cultural center, tourist spot and gateway to Asia. Vancouver's downtown area is a peninsula on a peninsula that juts out from the rest of the city into Burrard Inlet, making for plentiful urban beaches and marinas.

Information: www.tourismvancouver.com

ARTS CLUB THEATRE COMPANY

1585 Johnston St., Vancouver, 604-687-5315; www.artsclub.com

Having helped launch the careers of actors Michael J. Fox and Brent Carver, The Arts Club Theatre steals the Vancouver stage spotlight. In addition to its four annual main stage productions at Stanley Theatre (Granville and 12th streets), the company mounts four productions at the Granville Island Stage.

BALLET BRITISH COLUMBIA

677 Davie St., Vancouver, 604-732-5003; www.balletbc.com

With a strong company of 14 dancers, this reigns as Vancouver's top dance troupe. Directed by John Alleyne, former dancer with the Stuttgart Ballet and the National Ballet of Canada, the company's repertoire includes dances by famed choreographers such as William Forsythe and John Cranko and commissioned works by Canadian talents. Ballet BC's home stage is the Queen Elizabeth Theatre (Hamilton at Dunsmuir). November-May.

BC FERRIES

1112 Fort St., Victoria, 250-386-3432; www.bcferries.bc.ca

Trips to Nanaimo (two hours) or to Swartz Bay near Victoria (1½ hours); both destinations are on Vancouver Island. Terminals at Horseshoe Bay, north of Vancouver via Trans-Canada Highway 1 and Tsawwassen near U.S. border, south of Vancouver via Highway 99.

BC LIONS (CFL)

45

777 Pacific Blvd., Vancouver, 604-589-7627; www.bclions.com

Professional football team.

BITES-ON SALMON CHARTERS

200-1128 Hornby St., Vancouver, Granville Island, 604-688-2483; www.bites-on.com

Coho, sockeye and chinook salmon school in the waters around Vancouver, which is convenient for urban-bound fishing fans. Granville Island-based Bites-On offers day trips of five or eight hours, during which you can sink a line into the Strait of Georgia on a yacht up to 40 feet (12 meters) long. The charters serve parties of up to 12 people. Peak fishing months are April-October, although charters operate year-round. Boat trips also allow fishermen to spot sea lion, porpoise and whale populations.

BURNABY VILLAGE MUSEUM

6501 Deer Lake Ave., Vancouver, 604-293-6500; www.burnabyvillagemuseum.ca

Living museum of the period before 1925 with costumed attendants; more than 30 full-scale buildings with displays and demonstrations. Closed January-April.

CAPILANO SUSPENSION BRIDGE

3735 Capilano Road, Vancouver, 604-985-7474; www.capbridge.com

The 136-meter Capilano Suspension Bridge towers precariously 230 feet (70 meters) above the Capilano River gorge. Originally constructed in 1889 and rebuilt in 1956, the wooden bridge is engineered of wire rope cemented at either end. In addition to

★
★
★
★
★

the bridge, the surrounding park provides walking trails, gardens, a totem pole collection and audiences with First Nations carvers at work. Arrive early in high season.

THE CENTRE IN VANCOUVER FOR PERFORMING ARTS

777 Homer St., Vancouver, 604-602-0616; www.centreinvancouver.com

Acclaimed Canadian architect Moshe Safdie designed the dramatic Centre in Vancouver with an arched glass façade and, punctuating the entry, a spiraling glass cone. The auditorium seats 1,800, accommodating major Broadway tours.

CHAN CENTRE FOR THE PERFORMING ARTS

University of British Columbia, 6265 Crescent Road, Vancouver, 604-822-9197;
www.chancentre.com

Located in the University of British Columbia district, the Chan houses three venues for theater and music, all of which share the same light-flooded lobby. Built in 1997, the distinctive zinc-clad cylindrical building stands out amid the verdant campus. With superior acoustics, this is one of the best spots in town to hear concerts by touring soloists, UBC musicians and the Vancouver Symphony.

CHINATOWN

East Pender and Gore streets, Vancouver

This downtown area is the nucleus of the third-largest Chinese community in North America (behind San Francisco and New York). At the heart lies the Chinese Market where 100-year-old duck eggs may be purchased; herbalists promise cures with roots and powdered bones. The Dr. Sun Yat-Sen Classical Chinese Garden provides a beautiful centerpiece. Chinese shops display a variety of items ranging from cricket cages to cloisonné vases. Offices of three Chinese newspapers and one of the world's narrowest buildings are located within the community's borders. Resplendent Asian atmosphere offers fine examples of Chinese architecture, restaurants and nightclubs.

CN IMAX THEATRE

201-999 Canada Place, Vancouver, 604-682-2384; www.imax.com/vancouver

Under the white sails that distinguish waterfront Canada Place, CN IMAX screens wide-format documentary films on subjects ranging from space travel to wildlife conservation. Several shows are screened throughout the day, with a new film starting approximately every hour.

THE COMMODORE BALLROOM

868 Granville St., Vancouver, 604-739-4550; www.hob.com

It's been swinging since the big band era, and the Commodore flaunts its age with brass chandeliers and polished wood stairs. A renovation in 1999 restored its elegance (and kept the spring-loaded dance floor) while modernizing its stage wizardry. U.S.-based House of Blues now programs the acts that come through the ballroom, ranging primarily from rock to blues with a smattering of world talent. HOB also operates a kitchen on site.

★
★
★
★
★

CYPRESS MOUNTAIN

Cypress Bowl and Highway 1, Vancouver, 604-419-7669; www.cypressmountain.com

Covering two mountains with 34 runs and five lifts, Cypress Mountain claims the region's biggest vertical drop at 1,750 feet (533 meters). But the ski area's bigger claim to fame are its cross-country skiing facilities, which span 12 miles (19 kilometers) of groomed trails, nearly five of which are lit for night gliding. The region's most popular Nordic destination also offers private and group lessons as well as rental equipment. Snowshoers can tramp on designated trails solo or take a guided tour.

DR. SUN-YAT-SEN CLASSICAL CHINESE GARDEN

578 Carrall St., Vancouver, 604-662-3207; www.vancouverchinesegarden.com

Unique to the Western Hemisphere, this garden was originally built in China circa 1492 and transplanted to Vancouver for Expo '86.

ECOMARINE OCEAN KAYAK CENTRE

1668 Duranleau St., Vancouver, Granville Island, 604-689-7575; www.ecomarine.com

To get the full impact of Vancouver's magnificent setting on the coast, troll the waterways under paddle power with a kayak from Ecomarine. The outfitter rents both single and double kayaks at its Granville Island headquarters and at an outpost on Jericho Beach (Jericho Sailing Center, 1300 Discovery Street), where first-timers can take a three-hour lesson before getting started. Navigate from placid False Creek to more rugged inlets up the shore.

FORT LANGLEY NATIONAL HISTORIC SITE

23433 Mavis Ave., Fort Langley, 604-513-4777; www.pc.gc.ca

Originally one of a string of the Hudson's Bay Company trading posts across Canada, the Fraser Valley's Fort Langley became the birthplace of modern-day British Columbia with the Crown Colony Proclamation, an act of protection by the British against an American gold rush influx, which was read there in 1858. In addition to preserving the restored buildings, Fort Langley is garrisoned by costumed re-enactors who demonstrate pioneer activities such as blacksmithing and open-fire cooking.

GALLERY AT CEPERLEY HOUSE

6344 Deer Lake Ave., Vancouver, 604-297-4422; www.burnabyartgallery.ca

Monthly exhibitions of local, national and international artists. Collection of contemporary Canadian works on paper. Housed in Ceperley Mansion, overlooking Deer Lake and the surrounding gardens. Open Tuesday-Friday 10 a.m.-4:30 p.m., Saturday, Sunday 12 p.m.-5 p.m.

GASTOWN

145-332 Water St., Vancouver, 604-683-5650; www.gastown.org

Vancouver's historic nucleus consists of a series of Victorian buildings rehabbed to shelter an array of shops, clubs and eateries. Among the highlights, the Gastown Steam Clock pipes up every 15 minutes and the Vancouver Police Centennial Museum covers the most notorious local crimes. To fully appreciate the neighborhood, show up for a free tour sponsored by the Gastown Business Improvement Society in Maple Tree Square (2 p.m. daily in summer).

BRITISH COLUMBIA

★ ★ ★ ★ ★

GRANVILLE ISLAND

Beneath the South end of the Granville Street Bridge, Vancouver, 604-666-5784; www.granvilleisland.bc.ca

A former industrial isle, Granville Island is an urban renewal case study, with markets, shops, homes and entertainment fashioned out of decaying wharf warehouses beginning in the 1970s. Its hub is the Public Market, a prime picnic provisioner teeming with fishmongers, produce vendors, butchers, cheese shops, bakeries and chef demonstrations. A specialized kids' market and a free outdoor water park (May-September) appeal to children. The Maritime Market on the southwest shore serves as a dock for boat owners as well as those looking to hire a fishing charter, hop on a ferry or rent a kayak. Three Granville Island museums showcase miniature trains, ship models and sport fishing. Dozens of bars and restaurants, many with views back across the water to the downtown skyline, drive the after-dark trade. An art school, artists' studios and several galleries lend bohemian flare to the Granville, abetted by several theaters and street musicians.

GRANVILLE ISLAND KIDS' MARKET

1496 Cartwright St., Vancouver, 604-689-8447; www.kidsmarket.ca

Vancouver's open food market turns its third floor into something kids can enjoy—beyond pastries on the market floor. Twenty-five children's shops, including eight selling toys and another seven selling clothes, take aim at junior consumers, many of whom, of course, prefer Kids' Market's indoor play area. Strolling clowns and face-painters amplify the carnival-like setting. Daily 10 a.m.-6 p.m.

GREATER VANCOUVER ZOO

5048-264th St., Aldergrove, 604-856-6825; www.greatervancouverzoo.com

Explore 120 acres housing more than 700 animals. Miniature train ride; bus tour of North American Wild exhibit.

GROUSE MOUNTAIN

6400 Nancy Greene Way, North Vancouver, 604-984-0661; www.grousemountain.com

For skiing in winter, hiking in summer and sightseeing year-round, Grouse Mountain draws legions of visitors to Vancouver's North Shore. The area's first ski mountain is still its most convenient, with ski and snowboard runs that overlook the metropolis, as well as a skating rink and sleigh rides available. Hikers have loads of trails to choose from, but the one to boast about is the Grouse Grind, a 1.8-mile (2.9 kilometers) hike straight up the 3,700-foot (1,128-meter) peak. Look for mountain bike trails on the back side of the slopes. The Skyride Gondola takes the easy route up in an eight-minute ride. At the top, all-season attractions include Theater in the Sky, a high-definition aerial film and several panoramic-view restaurants starring the Strait of Georgia and the twinkling lights of Vancouver.

HASTINGS PARK

453 West 12th Ave., Vancouver, 604-871-6845; www.vancouver.ca/pnepark

Approximately 66-hectares (162 acres). Concert, convention, entertainment facilities. Thoroughbred racing (late spring-early fall) and Playland Amusement Park (April-June, weekends; July-October, daily; also evenings).

HASTINGS PARK RACECOURSE

Renfrew and Dundas streets, Vancouver, 604-254-1631, 800-677-7702;
www.hastingspark.com

Thoroughbreds run in Vancouver at Hastings Park on the city's east side. Although the lengthy racing season runs late April-November, most races are held on Saturday and Sunday, with extra meets scheduled for major holidays like Canada Day and Labor Day. Two-dollar-bet minimums encourage cheap dates, while self-service betting terminals patiently acquaint you with the track lingo.

HR MACMILLAN SPACE CENTRE

1100 Chestnut St., Vancouver, 604-738-7827; www.hrmacmillanspacecentre.com

One of several museums in Vanier Park tucked between Kitsilano Beach and Granville Island, the MacMillan Space Centre appeals to would-be astronauts with a space flight simulator, planetarium and interactive games. After hours, laser light shows depart from the scientific, dramatizing music by the likes of Pink Floyd and Led Zeppelin.

INUIT GALLERY OF VANCOUVER

206 Cambie St., Vancouver, 604-688-7323; www.inuit.com

Immerse yourself in the rich artistic tradition of coastal natives with soapstone sculptures, native prints, ceremonial masks and bentwood boxes. One of Vancouver's best sources for First Nations art, Inuit represents tribes up and down the Pacific Northwest. In the Gastown district, Inuit is a short walk from the convention center and cruise ship terminal. Monday-Saturday, 10 a.m.-6 p.m.; Sunday and holidays 11 a.m.-5 p.m. (winter), 10 a.m.-5 p.m. (summer).

THE LOOKOUT AT HARBOR CENTRE

555 W. Hastings St., Vancouver, 604-689-0421; www.vancouverlookout.com

Glass elevators take you to a 360-degree viewing deck 553 feet (167 meters) above street level; multimedia presentation, historical displays, tour guides.

MUSEUM OF ANTHROPOLOGY AT THE UNIVERSITY OF BRITISH COLUMBIA

6393 N.W. Marine Drive, Vancouver, 604-822-3825; www.moa.ubc.ca

Built to reference a First Nations longhouse, the glass and concrete Museum of Anthropology makes a fitting shrine for the art and artifacts of West Coast natives. The Great Hall surrounds visitors with immense totem poles, canoes and feast dishes of the Nisgaa, Gitksan and Haida people, among others. An outdoor sculpture garden sets tribal houses and totem poles, many carved by the best-known contemporary artists, against a backdrop of sea and mountain views. In its mission to explore all the cultures of the world, the Anthro also catalogs 600 ceramics works from 15th- to 19th-century Europe.

OLD HASTINGS MILL

1575 Alma Road, Vancouver, 604-734-1212

One of the few buildings remaining after the fire of 1886, the structure now houses indigenous artifacts and memorabilia of Vancouver's first settlers. Tuesday-Sunday 11 a.m.-4 p.m. (summer); Saturday, Sunday, 1-4 p.m. (winter)

★
★
★
★
★

QUEEN ELIZABETH PARK

Cambie Street and West 33rd Avenue, Vancouver, 604-257-8570;
www.city.vancouver.bc.ca/parks
Observation point affords a view of the city, harbor and mountains; Bloedel
Conservatory has more than 100 free-flying birds, plus tropical, desert and seasonal
displays.

QUEEN ELIZABETH THEATRE & PLAYHOUSE & ORPHEUM THEATRE

649 Cambie St., Vancouver, 604-665-3050; www.city.vancouver.bc.ca/theatres
A symphony orchestra, an opera company and many theater groups present produc-
tions around town, especially at the Queen Elizabeth Theatre and Playhouse and
Orpheum Theatre.

ROBSON STREET

The epicenter of Vancouver's street chic, Robson makes a nice window-shopping
stroll. A string of shops and sidewalk cafés runs several blocks in either direction
from the intersection of Robson and Burrard streets. Retailers range from the posh
Giorgio Armani and Salvatore Ferragamo to the playful Benetton on down to the
divine ice cream at Cows. Jewelry stores, chocolatiers and craft galleries round out
the offerings.

ROYAL CITY STAR RIVERBOAT CASINO

788 Quayside Drive, New Westminster, 604-519-3660; www.royalcitystar.bc.ca
The late-model paddle wheeler *Queen of New Orleans*, once stationed on the Mississippi, is now docked on the Fraser River as the *Royal City Star*. Games of chance
include Pai Gow poker, mini baccarat, blackjack, roulette and Caribbean stud poker.
Several bars, a deli and a restaurant feed and water patrons. Between May and October, the boat schedules regular sailings.

SAMSON V MARITIME MUSEUM

New Westminster, moored on the Fraser River at the Westminster Quay Market,
604-522-6891; www.nwpl.new-westminster.bc.ca
The last steam-powered paddle wheeler to operate on the Fraser River now functions
as a floating museum. Displays focus on the various paddle wheelers and paddle
wheeler captains that have worked the river and on river-related activities.

SCIENCE WORLD BRITISH COLUMBIA

1455 Quebec St., Vancouver, 604-443-7443; www.scienceworld.bc.ca
The massive, golf ball-shaped Science World attracts both architecture and museum
fans. Modeled on the geodesic domes of F. Buckminster Fuller, the aluminum ball
was erected for Expo '86 and now houses a science center devoted to interactive
exhibits on nature, invention, ecology and optical illusions. A play space with a water
table and giant building blocks engages the 3-to-6 set, while the dome-projection
Omnimax theater entertains the whole brood.

SPOKES BICYCLE RENTALS

1789 W. Georgia St., Vancouver, 604-688-5141; www.vancouverbikerental.com

Located just across from the Stanley Park entrance on Georgia Street, this cycle shop rents from a vast fleet that includes cruisers, tandems, mountain bikes and hybrid models. Spokes also offers bike tours of the Stanley Park perimeter (1½ hours) and Granville Island (3½ hours). Daily 9 a.m.-6 p.m.

STANLEY PARK

2099 Beach Ave., Vancouver, 604-257-8400; www.seestanleypark.com

One thousand acres of unspoiled British Columbia in the heart of the city, Stanley Park, the largest city park in Canada, is a green haven with few peers. Towering forests of cedar, hemlock and fir spill onto sand beaches, immersing visitors and residents alike in the wild just minutes from the civilized. Parkgoers recreate along forest hiking trails, on three beaches and along the 5½-mile (8.9-kilometer) 1920s vintage seawall, where in-line skaters, runners and cyclists admire skyline and ocean views. Man's hand distinguishes the park in gardens devoted to roses and rhododendrons and in a vivid stand of First Nations totem poles. Providing an appeal for every interest, Stanley Park also hosts the Vancouver Aquarium, Children's Farmyard, Miniature Railway, Theatre Under the Stars and several restaurants.

UBC BOTANICAL GARDEN

6804 S.W. Marine Drive, Vancouver, 604-822-9666; www.ubcbotanicalgarden.org

Seven separate areas include Asian, physick, native, alpine and food gardens. Nitobe Garden, authentic Japanese tea garden located behind Asian Centre.

VANCOUVER AQUARIUM MARINE SCIENCE CENTRE

845 Avison Way, Stanley Park, Vancouver, 604-659-3474; www.vanaqua.org

With inviting, hands-on exhibits, Vancouver Aquarium in sylvan Stanley Park explores the undersea world from Amazon to Arctic, assembling 300 species of fish. For all its globetrotting interests, the aquarium is a top spot to study the local environment as well. In outdoor pools, graceful beluga whales, frisky sea lions and playful otters prove comfortable with the changeable Pacific Northwest climate (private encounters with the belugas and dolphins run $125 to $175 per parent/child pair). Progeny of salmon released by the aquarium in 1998 from a park river return each winter, roughly November to February, illustrating BC's rich salmon-spawning waterways. Behind-the-scenes tours with trainers (an extra $15 to $20) provide visitors a glimpse of the marine mammal rescue and rehab program for which the aquarium is lauded.

VANCOUVER ART GALLERY

750 Hornby St., Vancouver, 604-662-4719; www.vanartgallery.bc.ca

Most visitors bound up to the Vancouver Art Gallery's fourth floor for a look at the largest collection of works by British Columbia's best-known painter Emily Carr. The other galleries in Western Canada's largest art museum, housed in an early 20th-century courthouse, are fantastic—subjects range from Group of Seven landscapes to photo conceptual art.

BRITISH COLUMBIA

★
★
★
★
☆

VANCOUVER CANADIANS

Nat Bailey Stadium, 4601 Ontario St., Vancouver, 604-872-5232;
www.canadiansbaseball.com
A-level Minor League Baseball in Northwest League. Mid-June-early September.

VANCOUVER CANUCKS (NHL)

800 Griffiths Way, Vancouver, 604-280-4400; www.canucks.com
Professional hockey team.

VANCOUVER MARITIME MUSEUM

1905 Ogden Ave., Vancouver, 604-257-8300; www.vancouvermaritimemuseum.com
Built around the *St. Roch*, the first ship to navigate Canada's Inside Passage from
west to east, Vanier Park's Maritime Museum lets seafaring fans explore the 1928
supply ship from wheelhouse to captain's quarters. In addition to the series of historic
model ships housed inside the museum, several historic craft are tethered outside its
waterfront Heritage Harbor, including two tugs, a rescue boat and the 1927 seiner
once featured on Canada's $5 bill.

VANCOUVER MUSEUM

1100 Chestnut St., Vancouver, 604-736-4431; www.vanmuseum.bc.ca
Keeper of city history and another Vanier Park attraction, Vancouver Museum takes a
sweeping view of civilization, collecting everything from Egyptian mummies to local
vintage swimming togs. In addition to the urban story, told in lifelike re-creations
of an Edwardian parlor, ship's berth and trading post, the museum examines First
Nations artifacts, the contributions of Asian Rim cultures and world history.

VANCOUVER OPERA

835 Cambie St., Vancouver, 604-683-0222; www.vancouveropera.ca
Vancouver Opera stages four productions annually. Established in 1958, the company
has hosted a roster of greats, including guest singers Placido Domingo, Joan Suther-
land and Marilyn Horne. Performances take place at the Queen Elizabeth Theatre.

VANCOUVER POLICE CENTENNIAL MUSEUM

240 E. Cordova St., Vancouver, 604-665-3346; www.city.vancouver.bc.ca
For fans of the macabre, the Vancouver Police Centennial Museum in Gastown not
only supplies the gruesome details of the city's most lurid crimes (such as bodies
found in Stanley Park and the man who tried to murder his wife with arsenic-laced
milkshakes) but also dramatizes them, crime-scene style. Run by the city's police
department, the museum tells the history of local lawkeeping and ushers visitors into
an eerie mock-forensics laboratory in the former city morgue.

VANCOUVER RAVENS (NATIONAL LACROSSE LEAGUE)

800 Griffiths Way, Vancouver; www.vancouverravens.com
Professional lacrosse team.

VANCOUVER SYMPHONY ORCHESTRA

601 Smithe St., Vancouver, 604-684-9100; www.vancouversymphony.ca

Canada's third-largest orchestra, the Vancouver Symphony presents more than 140 concerts annually, most of them at the ornate Orpheum Theatre. The symphony's featured programs broadly encompass classical, light classical, pops and children's works. Most concerts are on weekends with family-oriented matinees. September-June.

VANCOUVER TROLLEY COMPANY LTD

875 Terminal Ave., Vancouver, 604-801-5515; www.vancouvertrolley.com

Narrated trolley tours to top attractions and neighborhoods throughout the city. Get on and off at designated stops throughout the day.

VANDUSEN BOTANICAL GARDEN

5251 Oak St., Vancouver, 604-878-9274; www.vandusengarden.org

Approximately 55 acres (22 hectares) of flowers and exotic plants. Seasonal displays, mountain views, restaurant.

WHITECAPS F.C.

Kingsway and Boundary roads, Burnaby, 604-669-9283; www.whitecapsfc.com

Professional soccer team in United Soccer League's first division. April-October.

WINDSURE WINDSURFING SCHOOL

1300 Discovery St., Vancouver, 604-224-0615; www.windsure.com

Head to Jericho Beach to catch the offshore drafts in English Bay aboard a windsurfer. Windsure Windsurfing School, operating out of the Jericho Sailing Center, rents both boards and wetsuits, including rigs suitable for children. May-Labor Day, 9 a.m.-8 p.m.

THE YALE HOTEL

1300 Granville St., Vancouver, 604-681-9253; www.theyale.ca

Built in 1889 as a hotel for rough-and-tumble miners, fishermen and loggers, The Yale, prizes its working-class roots and makes a fitting home for the city's best blues club. Past headliners include John Lee Hooker, Clarence "Gatemouth" Brown, Jeff Healey and Jim Byrnes.

YALETOWN

From False Creek to Burrard Inlet on the northwest and Georgia Street on the northeast

A former rail yard, Yaletown once held the world record for the most bars per acre. With time and prosperity the redevelopment grew, and the warehouse district is now one of Vancouver's hippest, drawing urban dwellers with an arty bent. The former loading docks along Hamilton and Mainland teem with cafés with umbrella-shaded tables onto concrete terraces. Tucked in between are a slew of shops, galleries and clothiers.

BRITISH COLUMBIA

★★★★★

SPECIAL EVENTS

ALCAN INTERNATIONAL DRAGON BOAT FESTIVAL

110 Keefer St., Vancouver, 604-688-2382; www.dragonboatbc.ca

Vancouver's considerable Asian community imports an eastern rite in dragon boat racing, the traditional Chinese rain ceremony that is equal parts pageant and competition. But don't tell that to the 100 or so crews that enter the False Creek event paddling boats with dragon figureheads representing the Asian water deity. Bring loads of film to the colorful event, which, in addition to racing, features a Taoist blessing of the fleet and on land, Asian entertainment, crafts and food. Mid-June.

BARD ON THE BEACH SHAKESPEARE FESTIVAL

301-601 Cambie St., Vancouver, 604-739-0559; www.bardonthebeach.org

The works of Shakespeare take the outdoor stage at Vanier Parks permanent seasonal theater, Bard on the Beach. Elizabethan-style tents cover the audience and actors, who play against an open backdrop of coastal landscape. The company mounts approximately three plays each summer, performed in repertory with several shows slated daily on two stages. June-September.

CARIBBEAN DAYS FESTIVAL

Waterfront Park, North Vancouver, 604-515-2400; www.caribbeandaysfestival.com

The Trinidad and Tobago Cultural Society of BC throws the province's biggest island jump-up at this North Vancouver park. Its highlight parade kicks off Saturday morning with a slow, carnival-like promenade of bands and costumes, drawing crowds of pan-Caribbean expats. Head to the park festival grounds for calypso, steel drum, soca and reggae music, as well as island food and crafts. Late July.

HSBC POWER SMART CELEBRATION OF LIGHT

English Bay, Vancouver, 604-641-1193; www.celebration-of-light.com

On four nights spread over two weeks, pyrotechnic fans gasp as the world's best fireworks designers compete for bragging rights in Vancouver's Celebration of Light. Teams from China, Canada and Spain have competed on the basis of originality, rhythm, musical synchronization and color, leading up to the grand finale night on which all competitors restage their shows. For best viewing, park your beach towel along English Bay at Stanley or Vanier parks, Kitsilano or Jericho beaches. Come prepared for very large crowds, especially for the finale. Late July-early August.

HYACK FESTIVAL

First and Third avenues, New Westminster, 12 miles (19 kilometers)
south of Vancouver via Highway 1A, 604-522-6894; www.hyack.bc.ca

Commemorates the birthday of Queen Victoria, held yearly since 1971; 21-gun salute; band concerts, parade, carnival, sports events. Ten days in mid-May.

PACIFIC NATIONAL EXHIBITION ANNUAL FAIR

Exhibition Park, 2901 E. Hastings St., Vancouver, 604-253-2311; www.pne.bc.ca

Second-largest fair in Canada. Hundreds of free exhibits, major theme events, concerts, thrill shows, world championship timber show; petting zoo, thoroughbred horse racing, commercial exhibits, roller coaster, agricultural shows, horse shows, livestock competitions, horticultural exhibits. Mid-August-early September.

THEATRE UNDER THE STARS

Stanley Park, Malkin Bowl, 2099 Beach Ave., Vancouver, 604-687-0174; www.tuts.ca

Theatre Under the Stars puts the outdoors in outdoor theater. Towering forests of Douglas fir surround the 1,200-seat open-air Malkin Bowl theater in Stanley Park, binding art and nature in nightly performances. The short summer season generally presents two shows in every-other-night rotation, an annual repertory that hews to comedies and musicals. July-August.

VANCOUVER FRINGE FESTIVAL

1402 Anderson St., Vancouver, 604-257-0350; www.vancouverfringe.com

From comedies to musical acts to full-on drama, Vancouver Fringe trains the spot-light on fledgling theater troupes who come from around the globe to participate in the 11-day annual arts festival. Modeled on the oft-copied fringe festival in Edinburgh, Scotland, the Canadian organization mounts about 100 productions in a variety of venues including theaters, garages and even an Aquabus. Early-mid-September.

VANCOUVER INTERNATIONAL CHILDREN'S FESTIVAL

402-873 Beatty St., Vancouver, 604-708-5655; www.childrensfestival.ca

Though the 7-day slate of events programmed by the annual Children's Festival aims at school group audiences, its talent warrants broader attention. In a program ranging from music to theater, the performance lineup for young audiences might include Japanese dancers, Australia's teen troupe Flying Fruit Fly Circus, Aboriginal story-tellers and clown companies. Aside from show time, the festival engages kids with more than two dozen hands-on art activities. Mid-May.

VANCOUVER INTERNATIONAL JAZZ FESTIVAL

Coastal Jazz and Blues Society, 316 W. Sixth Ave., Vancouver, 604-872-5200;
www.vancouverjazz.com

The Coastal Jazz and Blues Society run this annual jazz festival over a 10-day span in several venues, climaxing in the headlining stage at the Orpheum Theatre. Past performers range from greats such as Dizzy Gillespie to New Age interpreters such as Pat Metheny to crooners such as Diana Krall. In addition to the main event, CJBS also sponsors 40 concerts between September and May each year (its 24-hour jazz hotline delivers a useful "what's-on-now" club report year-round). June.

HOTELS

★★BEST WESTERN DOWNTOWN VANCOUVER

718 Drake St., Vancouver, 604-669-9888, 800-780-7234;
www.bestwesterndowntown.com

143 rooms. Restaurant, bar. Complimentary wireless Internet access. Children's activity center. Pets accepted, fee. Exercise room. Business center. $$

★★BEST WESTERN SANDS

1755 Davie St., Vancouver, 604-682-1831, 800-663-9400; www.bestwesternbc.com

124 rooms. Restaurant, bar. High-speed Internet access. Pets accepted, fee. Exercise room. $$

BRITISH COLUMBIA

★
★
★
★
★

★★★COAST PLAZA SUITE HOTEL

1763 Comox St., Vancouver, 604-688-7711, 806-716-6199; www.coasthotels.com

This tower hotel is located just blocks from Stanley Park in Vancouver's West End, overlooking English Bay. Because of the range of amenities offered here, this hotel is a nice choice for the business or leisure traveler. It also offers many suites with kitchenettes, and there is a mall on the lower floors of the building. 269 rooms. Restaurant, bar. Complimentary high-speed Internet access. Pets accepted, fee. Exercise room. Pool. Business center. $$$

★★DAYS INN VANCOUVER DOWNTOWN

921 W. Pender St., Vancouver, 604-681-4335; www.daysinnvancouver.com

85 rooms. Restaurant. Complimentary wireless Internet access. Two bars. Business center. $$

★★★DELTA VANCOUVER SUITES

550 W. Hastings St., Vancouver, 604-689-8188, 888-890-3222;
www.deltavancouversuites.ca

This high-rise, all-suite hotel is located in the middle of downtown Vancouver and just minutes from Gastown, Yaletown, Chinatown, Robson Square, Canada Place, Stanley Park and Kitsilano Beach. 225 rooms, all suites. Complimentary high-speed Internet access. Restaurant, bar. Pets accepted, fee. Exercise room. Pool. Business center. $$$

★★★ENGLISH BAY INN

1968 Comox St., Vancouver, 604-683-8002, 866-683-8002; www.englishbayinn.com

This relaxing, 20th-century Tudor-style escape is a short walk from the West End's Stanley Park and shops and restaurants on Denman Street. All guest rooms feature Ralph Lauren linens, featherbeds, antiques, reproductions, and some rooms have fireplaces. Take some time to lounge in the back garden. Six rooms. Complimentary full breakfast. $$

★★★THE FAIRMONT HOTEL VANCOUVER

900 W. Georgia St., Vancouver, 604-684-3131, 800-441-1414;
www.fairmont.com/hotelvancouver

The Fairmont Hotel echoes the vibrancy of its home city. Grand and inviting, it has been a local favorite since 1939, when it opened to celebrate the royal visit of King George VI and Queen Elizabeth. The décor gives a nod to the past, but the dining and entertainment venues are cutting edge. The building is also home to high-end boutiques such as Louis Vuitton and St. John. 556 rooms. Restaurant, bar. High-speed Internet access. Pets accepted, fee. Exercise room. Pool. Spa. Business center. $$

★★★THE FAIRMONT VANCOUVER AIRPORT

3111 Grant McConachie Way, Vancouver, 604-207-5200, 800-676-8922;
www.fairmont.com/vancouverairport

This stylish hotel is located inside the airport and features contemporary rooms and suites. Airport dining is elevated to new levels at the Globe@YVR, where you can watch approaching and departing jets while enjoying cosmopolitan cuisine. 392 rooms. Restaurant, bar. Pets accepted, fee. Exercise room. Pool. Spa. Business center. $$

★★★THE FAIRMONT WATERFRONT

900 Canada Way, Vancouver, 604-691-1991, 800-441-1414;
www.fairmont.com/Waterfront

With state-of-the-art conference facilities, a comprehensive health club and fine dining, this hotel offers just about everything a business or leisure traveler would need. It is located beside an enclosed walkway to the Vancouver Convention and Exhibition Center, the Cruise Ship Terminal, and is within walking distance from Stanley Park and Gastown. 489 rooms. Restaurant, bar. High-speed Internet access. Pets accepted, fee. Exercise room. Pool. Business center. $$$

★★★★FOUR SEASONS HOTEL VANCOUVER

791 W Georgia St., Vancouver, 604-689-9333; www.fourseasons.com/vancouver

Located downtown in the commercial and cultural hub of the city, the Four Seasons Hotel Vancouver is a home-away-from-home for both business and leisure travelers. Families are welcome—children will love the indoor/outdoor pool and the in-room PlayStations. In addition to 24-hour room service, the hotel has three dining options: Chartwell restaurant, headed by executive chef Rafael Gonzalez, The Garden Terrace and the Terrace Bar. Chartwell, named after Churchill's summer home, is famous for its exemplary service and West Coast cuisine. 372 rooms. High-speed Internet access. Restaurant, bar. Fitness room. Pools, spa. Pets accepted, some restrictions. Business center. $$$

★★GOLDEN TULIP GEORGIAN COURT HOTEL

773 Beatty St., Vancouver, 604-682-5555, 800-663-1155; www.georgiancourt.com

180 rooms. Restaurant, bar. Pets accepted, fee. Exercise room. $$

★★HAMPTON INN & SUITES

111 Robson St., Vancouver, 604-602-1008, 877-602-1008;
www.hamptoninnvancouver.com

132 rooms. Restaurant, bar. Complimentary wireless Internet access. Children's activity center. Exercise room. $$

★HAMPTON INN VANCOUVER AIRPORT

8811 Bridgeport Road, Richmond, 604-232-5505, 800-426-7866;
www.hamptoninn-vancouver.com

111 rooms. Complimentary continental breakfast. Complimentary wireless Internet access. Exercise room. Business center. $

★★★HILTON VANCOUVER METROTOWN

6083 McKay Ave., Burnaby, 604-438-1200, 800-445-8667; www.hiltonvancouver.com

The Hilton Vancouver Metrotown is located in suburban Burnaby, a 20-minute drive from downtown and the airport, in the Metrotown Shopping Mall complex. A skytrain light rail station is across the street and offers high-speed travel to downtown. After a busy day, head to the hotel's small outdoor area with an outdoor lap pool, children's

BRITISH COLUMBIA

★
★
★
★
☆

pool, whirlpool and sundeck for some relaxation. 283 rooms. Restaurant, bar. High-speed Internet access. Pets accepted, fee. Exercise room. Business center. **$$**

★★★HYATT REGENCY VANCOUVER

655 Burrard St., Vancouver, 604-683-1234, 800-233-1234; www.vancouver.hyatt.com

This hotel is located within the Royal Centre shopping complex, which also includes two levels of shops, restaurants and a Skytrain station. After checking in, take a dip in the indoor pool, or get a bite to eat in one of the three restaurants. Then, relax in the guest rooms which all feature pillow-top mattresses and flat-screen televisions. 644 rooms. Restaurant, bar. High-speed Internet access. Exercise room. Pool. Business center. **$$**

★★★LE SOLEIL HOTEL & SUITES

567 Hornby St., Vancouver, 604-632-3000, 877-632-3030; www.lesoleilhotel.com

In the heart of the city's financial and business districts sits this charming boutique hotel. The lobby boasts 30-foot gilded ceilings and a Louis XVI-style collection of imported Italian furniture. Complimentary bottled water and fruit upon arrival are welcome surprises, and the property's restaurant offers an eclectic Asian-Mediterranean cuisine. 119 rooms. Restaurant, bar. Pets accepted, fee. Spa. Business center. **$$**

★★★METROPOLITAN HOTEL

645 Howe St., Vancouver, 604-687-1122; www.metropolitan.com/vanc

Located in the heart of Vancouver's downtown, the hotel is convenient to local sightseeing. The guest rooms are modern and spacious, with marble washrooms, down duvets and Frette linens and some have Juliet balconies. Enjoy a dinner at the Diva at the Met, with its international and Pacific Northwest-influenced cuisine. 197 rooms. Complimentary full breakfast. Pets accepted, fee. **$**

★★★OPUS HOTEL

322 Davie St., Vancouver, 604-642-6787, 866-642-6787; www.opushotel.com

This hip boutique hotel blends contemporary design with great service. Located in the Yaletown area, it is close to all local attractions. The guest rooms have unique décor that's modern and minimalist without losing warmth and comfort. The hotel is home to both the modern bistro, Elixir, and the hot spot, Opus Bar. 96 rooms. Restaurant, bar. Pets accepted, fee. Exercise room. Spa. Business center. **$**

★★★PACIFIC PALISADES HOTEL

1277 Robson St., Vancouver, 604-688-0461, 800-663-1815;
www.pacificpalisadeshotel.com

This hotel underwent a total makeover in 2001 and now earns its reputation as one of the trendiest home bases on the legendary Robson Street. Fitness-minded guests can take advantage of complimentary yoga kits and a designated yoga channel, with personal trainers available for private yoga and Pilates sessions. 232 rooms. Complimentary high-speed Internet access. Restaurant, bar. Pets accepted. Exercise room. Spa. Pool. Business center. **$$$**

★
★
★
★
★

★★★PAN PACIFIC VANCOUVER

300-999 Canada Place, Vancouver, 604-662-8111, 800-937-1515; www.panpacific.com

Awe-inspiring waterfront views take center stage at Vancouver's Pan Pacific Hotel, located minutes from some of the best shopping in the city. Luxurious guest rooms look out over unobstructed mountains and ocean and some rooms even feature private balconies. Four distinctive restaurants offer sushi, Italian and other international cuisine. 504 rooms. Three restaurants, bar. High-speed Internet connection. Exercise room. Spa. Pool. Business center. Pets accepted, fee. **$$$**

★★RAMADA PLAZA VANCOUVER AIRPORT CONFERENCE RESORT

10251 St. Edwards Drive, Richmond, 604-207-9000, 800-272-6232; www.ramada.com

438 rooms. Restaurant, bar. Children's activity center. Pets accepted, fee. Exercise room. Pool. Tennis. Business center. **$$**

★★★RENAISSANCE VANCOUVER HARBORSIDE HOTEL

1133 W. Hastings, Vancouver, 604-689-9211, 800-905-8582;
www.renaissancevancouver.com

Located on the waterfront and close to local attractions, this is a great spot for both leisure and business travelers. Some rooms offer a balcony and all rooms have duvets and feather pillows along with Internet access. Enjoy a meal and the views at Patina Restaurant or dinner and a drink at the Coal Harbour Bar. 437 rooms. High-speed Internet access. Restaurant, bar. Children's activity center. Pets accepted, fee. Exercise room. Pool. Business center. **$$**

★★SHERATON GUILDFORD HOTEL

15269 104th Ave., Surrey, 604-582-9288; www.sheraton.com

279 rooms. Restaurant. Internet access. Exercise room. Business center. **$**

★★★★THE SUTTON PLACE HOTEL - VANCOUVER

845 Burrard St, Vancouver, 604-682-5511; www.vancouver.suttonplace.com

Located in the business and shopping core of downtown Vancouver, the hotel offers guest rooms that exude a European flavor, while the dining and lounge areas feature comforting old-world décor. Business travelers are pampered with the business center that was renovated to provide state-of-the-art technology. The hotel offers a serene spa, indoor swimming pool under a big sunroof, and a fitness center. 396 rooms. High-speed Internet access. Restaurant, bar. Pets accepted, some restrictions; fee. Fitness room, fitness classes available, spa. Pool. Business center. **$$$**

★★★WEDGEWOOD HOTEL

845 Hornby St., Vancouver, 604-689-7777, 800-663-0666; www.wedgewoodhotel.com

Tradition abounds at this independent boutique hotel, which features rooms decorated with classic furnishings and luxurious fabrics. Bacchus, the onsite restaurant, offers a full menu plus sumptuous weekend brunch menus and traditional high tea is served from 2 to 4 p.m. daily. 83 rooms. Restaurant, bar. Complimentary Internet access. Exercise room. Business center. **$$$**

★★★THE WESTIN GRAND

433 Robson St., Vancouver, 604-602-1999, 888-680-9393;
www.westingrandvancouver.com

All of Vancouver is within reach of the Westin Grand. Sleek and stylish, this property introduces visitors to the hip side of this western Canadian city. Guests never leave behind the comforts of home here, where all rooms feature well-stocked kitchenettes. The hotel caters to the sophisticated, and many services are offered 24 hours daily. Guests can dine on Pacific Rim dishes at the Aria Restaurant & Lounge. 219 rooms. Restaurant, bar. Complimentary wireless Internet access. Spa. Exercise room. Pool. Business center. Pets accepted, fee. $$

SPECIALITY LODGINGS

BARCLAY HOUSE IN THE WEST END

1351 Barclay St., Vancouver, 604-605-1351, 800-971-1351; www.barclayhouse.com

Six rooms. Children over 12 years only. Complimentary full breakfast. Wireless Internet access. $$

O CANADA HOUSE

1114 Barclay St., Vancouver, 604-688-0555, 877-688-1114; www.ocanadahouse.com

Seven rooms. Children over 11 years only. Complimentary full breakfast. Wireless Internet access. $$

WEST END GUEST HOUSE

1362 Haro St., Vancouver, 604-681-2889, 888-546-3327;
www.westendguesthouse.com

Nine rooms. Children over 11 years only. Complimentary full breakfast. Wireless Internet access. $$

RESTAURANTS

★★AQUA RIVA

200 Granville St., Vancouver, 604-683-5599; www.aquariva.com

Pacific Northwest menu. Reservations recommended. $$$

★★★BACCHUS

845 Hornby St., Vancouver, 604-608-5319, 800-663-0666; www.wedgewoodhotel.com

This luxurious restaurant is adorned with richly upholstered furniture, décor from Venice and of course, a large canvas depicting Bacchus, Greek god of wine and revelry. The menu spotlights local ingredients, including salmon with braised leeks and red wine sauce, or herb crusted smoked cod. French menu. Dinner. Reservations recommended. $$$

★★★BEACH HOUSE

150 25th St., West Vancouver, 604-922-1414; www.atthebeachhouse.com

Originally built in 1912, this waterfront restaurant affords diners beautiful views of Burrard Inlet. The rustic wood shingled building provides a cozy setting where diners can sample dishes such as seared tuna with black truffle and red wine sacue, and pan roasted sablefish with honey and soy glaze. Seafood menu. Dinner. Reservations recommended. Outdoor seating. $$$

★
★
★
★
★

★★★★BISHOP'S
2183 W. Fourth Ave., Vancouver, 604-738-2025; www.bishopsonline.com
Intimate, modern and airy, with a loft-like yet upscale feel, this chic duplex restaurant is known for West Coast continental cuisine and has a menu that emphasizes seasonal, organic produce and locally-sourced seafood. It isn't uncommon to spy celebrities nibbling on these delicious culinary gems. For those who like to sample lots of different wines with dinner, Bishop's offers a nice selection of wines by the glass and an outstanding range of wines by the half-bottle. In addition to being a visionary chef, owner John Bishop is a gracious host. International menu. Dinner. Bar. Reservations recommended. Outdoor seating. $$$

★★★C RESTAURANT
Z-1600 Howe St., Vancouver, 604-681-1164; www.crestaurant.com
Located along the boardwalk running under the Granville Building and overlooking the marina, this contemporary seafood house offers a raw bar, an enclosed patio area and more than 900 wines. The sleek, modern décor is a nice complement to the inventive presentations of the fresh, inventive cuisine. Sample dishes such as lobster with slow-cooked sunchokes and heirloom tomato jam, or grilled tuna with black truffle Caesar dressing and potatoes. Seafood menu. Dinner. Reservations recommended. Outdoor seating. $$$

★★CAFE DE PARIS
751 Denman St., Vancouver, 604-687-1418; www.cafedeparisbistro.com
French bistro. Dinner. Reservations recommended. $$$

★★THE CANNERY
2205 Commissioner St., Vancouver, 604-254-9606, 877-254-9606;
www.canneryseafood.com
Seafood menu. Lunch, dinner. Reservations recommended. $$$

★★★CINCIN RISTORANTE
1154 Robson St., Vancouver, 604-688-7338; www.cincin.net
Located upstairs in a two-story building on trendy Robson Street, this Italian dining room has a mellow Tuscan atmosphere. A wood-fired brick oven emits a wonderful aroma throughout the restaurant and the extensive wine list offers the perfect complement to any meal. Italian menu. Reservations recommended. Outdoor seating. $$$

★★CLOUD 9
1400 Robson St., Vancouver, 604-687-0511, 800-830-6144; www.cloud9restaurant.ca
Seafood, steak menu. Reservations recommended. $$$

★★DELILAH'S
1789 Comox St., Vancouver, 604-687-3424; www.delilahs.ca
Continental, Dinner. tapas menu. Reservations recommended. $$$

★★DOCKSIDE BREWING COMPANY
1253 Johnston St., Vancouver, 604-685-7070; www.docksidebrewing.com
Seafood menu. Lunch, dinner. Reservations recommended. Outdoor seating. $$$

★★★FISH HOUSE IN STANLEY PARK

8901 Stanley Park Drive, Vancouver, 604-681-7275, 877-681-7275;
www.fishhousestanleypark.com

This Vancouver landmark seafood restaurant favored by both locals and tourists is located in Vancouver's West End at the south entrance to beautiful Stanley Park. The leafy setting is a relaxing spot to tuck into steamed mussels, maple-glazed salmon or cedar planked arctic char. Seafood menu. Lunch, dinner, brunch. Reservations recommended. Outdoor seating. $$$

★★★FIVE SAILS

410-999 Canada Place, Vancouver, 604-844-2855, 800-937-1515;
www.dinepanpacific.com

Exceptional views of the harbor and neighboring mountains, a talented kitchen that produces creative Northwest/Asian fusion food and good service make this restaurant a favorite destination among locals. The affable staff can make recommendations for local or international wines to pair with the fresh seafood on the menu. International menu. Dinner. Reservations recommended. $$$$

★★★GOTHAM STEAKHOUSE AND COCKTAIL BAR

615 Seymour St., Vancouver, 604-605-8282; www.gothamsteakhouse.com

It's worth the splurge for truly excellent steaks, smooth, friendly service and a sleek crowd at this downtown destination. The dining room, a converted bank, is modern and opulent with main floor and balcony dining. Steak menu. Dinner. Reservations recommended. Outdoor seating. $$$

★★★HART HOUSE ON DEER LAKE

6664 Deer Lake Ave., Burnaby, 604-298-4278; www.harthouserestaurant.com

Known as having some of the best steaks in the Vancouver area, the Hart House Restaurant also offers one of the most charming dining atmospheres. The imaginative menu takes its inspiration from the flavors native to countries around the globe. In pleasant weather, the outdoor patio opens up to let diners enjoy the fresh air and views of Deer Lake. International menu. Dinner. Reservations recommended. Outdoor seating. $$

★★★IL GIARDINO DI UMBERTO RISTORANTE

1382 Hornby St., Vancouver, 604-669-2422; www.umberto.com

This rustic room, housed in a historic Victorian building, transports its young, established fans to a Tuscan villa. Come for the fresh pastas, grilled steaks and transcendent desserts, but linger over the elegant atmosphere and attentions of the polished staff. Italian menu. Lunch, dinner. Reservations recommended. Outdoor seating. $$$

★★IMPERIAL CHINESE SEAFOOD RESTAURANT

355 Burrard St., Vancouver, 604-688-8191; www.imperialrest.com

Cantonese, Chinese menu. Dinner. Reservations recommended. $$$

★★★★LA BELLE AUBERGE

4856 48th Ave., Ladner, 604-946-7717; www.labelleauberge.com

If you crave the glorious food of France's best kitchens, opt for a 30-minute drive from Vancouver to Ladner and enjoy dinner at La Belle Auberge. Set in a charming 1902 country inn, the restaurant is an intimate, five antique-filled salon-style dining rooms. The kitchen, led by chef/owner Bruno Marti, a masterful culinary technician, offers spectacular, authentic French cuisine. French menu. Dinner. Reservations recommended. Outdoor seating. **$$$**

★★★LA TERRAZZA

1088 Cambie St., Vancouver, 604-899-4449; www.laterrazza.ca

This Italian restaurant feels like a classic villa with burnt-sienna walls, murals, massive windows and vaulted ceilings, as well as an impressive wine cellar. The menu features classic Italian dishes, from freshly-made pappardelle with boar ragu to veal scallopine with marsala sacue. Italian menu. Reservations recommended. Outdoor seating. **$$$**

★★★LE CROCODILE

100-909 Burrard St., Vancouver, 604-669-4298; www.lecrocodilerestaurant.com

A wonderful dress-up place, this downtown French bistro is worth a trip for the food alone. Clasically trained chef Michel Jacob creates classic dishes such as Dover sole with beurre blanc, and pan-seared sweetbreads with black truffle-foie gras cream sauce. The extensive wine list spotlights French bottles that pair perfectly with the menu. French menu. Lunch, dinner. Reservations recommended. Outdoor seating. Closed Sunday. **$$$**

63

LUMIERE

2551 W. Broadway, Vancouver, 604-739-8185; www.lumiere.ca

Lumiere has made a name for itself for being a stunning and elegant restaurant that offers European-style dining of the most divine order. However, it is scheduled to reopen in late 2008 after undergoing renovations and forgoing a new partnership with Chef Daniel Boulud, and it will be rated again in the near future. French menu. Reservations recommended. Outdoor seating. **$$$$**

★★MONK MCQUEENS

601 Stamps Landing, Vancouver, 604-877-1351; www.monkmcqueens.com

Seafood menu. Lunch, dinner, brunch. Reservations recommended. Outdoor seating. **$$$**

★★PROVENCE MEDITERRANEAN GRILL

4473 W. 10th Ave., Vancouver, 604-222-1980; www.provencevancouver.com

Casual Mediterranean bistro. Reservations recommended. Outdoor seating. **$$**

BRITISH COLUMBIA

★★★QUATTRO ON FOURTH

2611 W. Fourth Ave., Vancouver, 604-734-4444; www.quattrorestaurants.com

This popular suburban Italian restaurant, located in the heart of Kitsilano near downtown, has an excellent selection of Italian entrées paired with fantastic wines. Sample fresh-made pastas and traditional grilled meats in an elegant setting. Italian, Mediterranean menu. Reservations recommended. Outdoor seating. $$$

★★★RAINCITY GRILL

1193 Denman St., Vancouver, 604-685-7337; www.raincitygrill.com

Located in Vancouver's West End, this eclectic, fine dining restaurant has views across a small park to English Bay. The delicious à la carte and chef's tasting menus draw almost exclusively on organic, regional sources. Don't miss brunch on Saturday and Sunday. International menu. Dinner, brunch. Reservations recommended. Outdoor seating. $$$

★★★SAVEUR

850 Thurlow St., Vancouver, 604-688-1633

Located a block off Robson in downtown Vancouver, this warm and intimate French restaurant is the perfect spot for a special-occasion celebration. A French West Coast menu is served for lunch and dinner. French menu. Lunch, dinner. Reservations recommended. $$$

★★★SEASONS HILL TOP BISTRO

33rd Avenue and Cambie Street, Vancouver, 604-874-8008, 800-632-9422; www.vancouverdine.com/seasons/home.html

This restaurant was the site of a Clinton-Yeltsin summit in 1993—come for the history and stay for the incredible international menu (and the view). Located on top of a hill in beautiful Queen Elizabeth Park in suburban Vancouver, there are magnificent views from the tiered dining room and attractive heated terrace. International menu. Reservations recommended. Outdoor seating. $$$

★★SEQUOIA GRILL

7501 Stanley Park Drive, Vancouver, 604-669-3281; www.sequoiarestaurants.com

West Coast eclectic menu. Lunch, dinner, brunch. Reservations recommended. Outdoor seating. $$$

★★SHIJO JAPANESE RESTAURANT

1926 W. Fourth Ave., Vancouver, 604-732-4676; www.shijo.ca

Japanese menu. Dinner. Reservations recommended. $$$

★★STAR ANISE

1485 W. 12th Ave., Vancouver, 604-737-1485; www.restaurant.ca

International menu. Reservations recommended. $$$

★★SUN SUI WAH SEAFOOD RESTAURANT

3888 Main St., Vancouver, 604-872-8822, 866-872-8822; www.sunsuiwah.com

Chinese menu. Lunch, dinner. Reservations recommended. $$

★TAPASTREE

1829 Robson St., Vancouver, 604-606-4680; www.tapastree.ca

Spanish, tapas menu. Reservations recommended. Outdoor seating. **$$**

★★TOJO'S

1133 W. Broadway, Vancouver, 604-872-8050; www.tojos.com

Japanese menu. Dinner. Reservations recommended. Outdoor seating. **$$**

★★TOP OF VANCOUVER

555 W. Hastings St., Vancouver, 604-669-2220; www.topofvancouver.com

International menu. Lunch, dinner, brunch. Reservations recommended. **$$$**

★TRUE CONFECTIONS

866 Denman St., Vancouver, 604-682-1292; www.trueconfections.ca

Desserts. Lunch, dinner, late-night. **$**

★★★VILLA DEL LUPO

869 Hamilton St., Vancouver, 604-688-7436; www.villadellupo.com

Tiny white lights and sparkling bay windows attract attention at this classic Italian restaurant housed in a charming, turn-of-the-century home. The menu highlights different regions of Italy, using fresh, local ingredients in dishes such as osso bucco with risotto Milanese. Italian menu. Dinner. Reservations recommended. **$$$**

★★★★WEST

2881 Granville St., Vancouver, 604-738-8938; www.westrestaurant.com

West is one of those sleek, heavenly spots that make sipping cocktails for hours on end an easy task. It is an ideal choice for gourmets in search of an inventive, eclectic meal, as well as those who crave local flavor and seasonal ingredients. Located in Vancouver's chic South Granville neighborhood, West offers diners the chance to sample the vibrant cuisine of the Pacific Northwest region. Stunning, locally sourced ingredients are on display here thanks to the masterful kitchen. International menu. Dinner. Reservations recommended. **$$$**

VANCOUVER ISLAND

The largest of the Canadian Pacific Coast Islands, Vancouver Island stretches almost 300 miles (480 kilometers) along the shores of Western British Columbia. It is easily accessible by ferry from the city of Vancouver on the mainland as well as from other parts of the province and the state of Washington. With most of its population located in the larger cities on the eastern coast, much of the island remains a wilderness and is very popular with outdoor enthusiasts.

The Vancouver Island Mountain Range cuts down the middle of the island, providing spectacular snowcapped scenery, fjords and rocky coastal cliffs. The southern portion of the island contains more than half the island's total population and includes Victoria, British Columbia's capital. Here, countryside resembles rural Britain with its rolling farmland, rows of hedges and colorful flower gardens. Travelers go island-hopping among the Gulf Islands, located in the sheltered waters of the Strait of Georgia between the big island and the mainland. These beautiful, isolated islands are a mecca for artists, cottagers and tourists alike.

BRITISH COLUMBIA

Nanaimo is the dominant town, an area known for excellent sandy beaches and beautiful parks. In the center of the island is the Alberni Valley, which includes several parks with excellent swimming and fishing and one of the tallest waterfalls found in North America (Della Falls). From Port Alberni, the mountain highway winds its way to the peaceful fishing village of Tofino, the rugged northern boundary of the Long Beach section of the Pacific Rim National Park.

Information: www.seetheislands.com

WHAT TO SEE AND DO

BC FOREST MUSEUM

40 miles (64 kilometers) north of Victoria on Hwy 1, near Duncan, 250-715-1113; www.bcforestmuseum.com

Logging museum; old logging machines and tools, hands-on exhibits, logging camp, 1½ miles (2.4 kilometers) steam railway ride, sawmill, films, nature walk. May-September, daily.

WHALE WATCHING

Vancouver Island is known as one of the best places to view migrating and resident whales. Whale-watching tours leave from Victoria and other large city centers on the island. View migrating gray whales during March and April, while Orca (killer) whales are best observed between May and October, with July and August as the key months for sightings. Three Orca pods totaling more than 80 whales make their home in the waters off of Victoria. North of Vancouver Island, a resident community of 217 whales, patrol the Johnstone Strait in 16 pods. Other whales and marine mammals that can be seen off of Vancouver Island include humpback whales, minke whales, otters, seals, sea lions and dolphins.

HOTELS

★★★★THE AERIE RESORT

600 Ebedora Lane, Malahat, 250-743-7115, 800-518-1933; www.aerie.bc.ca

Built into the mountains on 85 acres above the southern part of Vancouver Island, the Aerie Resort attracts travelers with its casual sophistication and incredible views. Persian and Chinese carpets, goose-down comforters and wood-burning fireplaces make the rooms cozy and comfortable. A multitude of activities, from biking and sailing to hiking and fishing are available. The fantastic Aerie Spa and Wellness Centre offers everything from facials to massage and body wraps. The resort's dining room is a sophisticated spot bathed in tones of cream and white with views of the mountains, and the Asian-influenced cuisine is equally alluring. 29 rooms. Complimentary full breakfast. Wireless Internet access. Restaurant, bar. Pool. $$$

★★★MALAHAT MOUNTAIN INN

265 Trans-Canada Highway, Malahat, 250-478-1979, 800-913-1944; www.malahatmountaininn.com

Just a short drive from Victoria brings guests to this inn's five ocean-view rooms and five ocean-view lofts. Take in dramatic views of the ocean and Saanich Inlet while dining on the outdoor patio. 10 rooms. Complimentary full breakfast. Restaurant, bar. $$

★★★★WICKANINNISH INN

500 Osprey Lane, Tofino, 250-725-3100, 800-333-4604; www.wickinn.com

Famous for its storm-watching events (the luxurious resort is perched on the edge of a particularly volatile stretch of Pacific Ocean), this three-story cedar inn is a rustic retreat on a remote stretch of Vancouver Island. Floor-to-ceiling windows frame dazzling views of the crashing surf. Furnishings crafted from recycled fir, cedar, and driftwood add a unique touch in the comfortable accommodations, as do fireplaces, oversized tubs and private balconies. Beach comb with your pet in tow on Chesterman Beach, and then stop by the pet shower station to freshen up. The superb onsite spa takes its cues from botanicals from the nearby ancient rainforest. The sea is the focus at the Pointe Restaurant, where the ocean's bounty is highlighted. 75 rooms. Restaurant, bar. Pets accepted, fee. Exercise room. Business center. $$$$

SPECIALITY LODGING

CLAYOQUOT WILDERNESS RESORT & SPA

390 Main St., Tofino, 250-726-8235, 888-333-5405; www.wildretreat.com

Tucked within the secluded inlets of Clayoquot Sound, this all-inclusive resort treats guests to luxurious accommodations amid snowcapped mountains, lush forests and pristine waters. 16 rooms. Restaurant, bar. Exercise room. Pool. Business center. $$$

RESTAURANTS

★★★★AERIE DINING ROOM

600 Ebedora Lane, Malahat, 250-743-7115, 800-518-1933; www.aerie.bc.ca

Spectacular views of snowy mountaintops are among the many highlights of an evening at The Aerie Dining Room. The Aerie's kitchen is known for its use of superb local produce, sourcing its ingredients from a network of 60 small farms. The kitchen is loyal to classic French technique but brings plates to modern life with Pacific accents. The result is straightforward, yet innovative and sophisticated, fare. A lengthy wine list features Vancouver's own, in addition to wines of the Pacific Coast. French menu. Dinner. Closed 10 days in January. Reservations recommended. Outdoor seating. $$$

★★★THE POINTE RESTAURANT

500 Osprey Lane, Tofino, 250-725-3106, 800-333-4604; www.wickinn.com

Perched above the crashing waves of Vancouver Island's west shore is the Pointe Restaurant at the Wickaninnish Inn. The cedar-beamed, circular dining room features a breathtaking 240-degree view of the Pacific Ocean. The adjoining On the Rocks Bar & Lounge is a perfect spot for a pre- or post-dinner cocktail, with a variety of wines by the glass and an extensive selection of single-malt scotches. Seafood menu. Dinner. Reservations recommended. $$$

SPA

★★★★ANCIENT CEDARS SPA

500 Osprey Lane, Tofino, 250-725-3100; www.wickinn.com

Resting on a rocky promontory jutting into the Pacific Ocean with an old-growth rainforest in the background, this is truly a one-of-a-kind hideaway. The interiors have been designed to bring the outdoors in, with slate tiles, dark colors and cedar

★
★
★
★

decorating this serene space. The treatment menu focuses on relaxation and renewal. Thai, lomi lomi and hot stone massage are among the bodywork therapies available, or try the signature sacred sea treatment, which uses the renowned Bouvier Hydrotherapy tub. $$

VICTORIA

One of Canada's most temperate and eminently walkable cities, British Columbia's capital has a distinctly British flavor, yet is a heartland of Pacific Northwest indigenous culture. This city of lush parks and gardens literally bursts with beauty in early spring, when even the five-globed Victorian lampposts are decorated with baskets of flowers. Take a horse-drawn carriage or double-decker bus tour through many historic and scenic landmarks and wander through the bistros, boutiques and colorful alleys of a delightfully compact downtown and Chinatown district that sparkles with history.
Information: www.tourismvictoria.com

WHAT TO SEE AND DO

ART GALLERY OF GREATER VICTORIA

1040 Moss St., Victoria, 250-384-4101; www.aggv.bc.ca

This gallery is said to have the finest collection of Japanese art in Canada; it includes major holdings of Asian ceramics and paintings. Also housed here are collections of Canadian and European art, with a focus on prints and drawings and decorative arts. The gallery is home to the only Shinto shrine outside of Japan and is the site of many lectures, film screenings and concerts.

BEACON HILL PARK

Douglas Street and Dallas Road, Victoria, 250-361-0370; www.beaconhillpark.ca

Approximately 180 acres (75 hectares) with lakes, wildfowl sanctuary, children's petting farm, walks and floral gardens, cricket pitch; world's second-tallest totem pole; beautiful view of the sea.

BUTCHART GARDENS

800 Benvenuto Ave., Victoria, 250-652-4422; www.butchartgardens.com

At approximately 50 acres (20 hectares), the Sunken Garden was created in the early 1900s by the Butcharts on the site of their depleted limestone quarry with topsoil brought in by horse-drawn cart. Already a tourist attraction by the 1920s, the gardens now include the rose, Japanese and Italian gardens; also Star Pond, Concert Lawn, Fireworks Basin, Ross Fountain and Show Greenhouse. The gardens are subtly illuminated at night (mid-June-mid-September) and on Saturday evenings in July and August, visitors enjoy firework displays.

CARR HOUSE

207 Government St., Victoria, 250-383-5843; www.emilycarr.com

Italianate birthplace, built in 1863, of famous Canadian painter/author Emily Carr. Ground floor restored to period. May-October, daily; rest of year, by appointment.

CHINATOWN

Chinese immigrants, employed for railroad labor, established Canada's oldest Chinatown in 1858. Two key attractions are Fan Tan Alley, the narrowest street in North

★
★ ★
★ ★
★

America and the Gate of Harmonious Interest, guarded by hand-carved stone lions from Suzhou, China. Visit shops with exotic merchandise and restaurants.

CRAIGDARROCH CASTLE
1050 Joan Crescent, Victoria, 250-592-5323; www.craigdarrochcastle.com
Historic house museum, constructed in 1890, with beautifully crafted wood, stained glass; furnished with period furniture and artifacts.

CRAIGFLOWER FARMHOUSE & SCHOOLHOUSE HISTORIC SITE
2709 Manor and Schoolhouse, Victoria, 250-383-4627; www.conservancy.bc.ca
This farmhouse was built in 1856 in simple Georgian style. The adjoining 1854 schoolhouse is the oldest in Western Canada. Some original furnishings.

CRYSTAL GARDEN
613 Pandora Ave., Victoria, 250-953-8800; www.crystalgarden.bcpcc.com
Glass building formerly housed the largest saltwater pool in the British Empire. Tropical gardens, waterfall, fountain, aviary, monkeys, free-flying butterflies, exotic fish pool; restaurant, shops.

DOMINION ASTROPHYSICAL OBSERVATORY
5071 W. Saanich Road, Victoria, 250-363-0001; www.hia-iha.nrc-cnrc.gc.ca
The observatory contains three telescopes, two of which are used for research by professional astronomers. The 72-inch Plaskett Telescope is used for public viewing on Saturday nights during "Star Parties" (April-October, 7-11 p.m.). Interactive exhibits, film presentations and other special programs are designed to entertain visitors while educating them about the universe.

FORT RODD HILL & FISGARD LIGHTHOUSE NATIONAL HISTORIC SITE
603 Fort Rodd Hill Road, Victoria, 250-478-5849; www.fortroddhill.com
A coastal artillery fort from 1895 to 1956; casemated barracks, gun and searchlight positions, loop-holed walls. Historic lighthouse is adjacent.

HATLEY CASTLE
2005 Sooke Road, Colwood, 250-391-2600; www.hatleycastle.com
Once the private estate of James Dunsmuir, former Lieutenant Governor of British Columbia. Buildings are noted for their beauty, as are the grounds, with their Japanese, Italian and rose gardens.

HELMCKEN HOUSE
10 Elliot Square, Victoria, 250-356-7226
Second-oldest house in British Columbia, built in 1852; most furnishings are original. Extensive 19th-century medical collection.

MARITIME MUSEUM
28 Bastion Square, Victoria, 250-385-4222; www.mmbc.bc.ca
Depicts rich maritime heritage of the Pacific Northwest from early explorers through age of sail and steam; Canadian naval wartime history; large collection of models of ships used throughout the history of British Columbia. The Tilikum, a converted

BRITISH COLUMBIA

dugout that sailed from Victoria to England during the years 1901 to 1904, is here. Captain James Cook display.

NATIONAL GEOGRAPHIC IMAX THEATRE

675 Belleville St., Victoria, 250-480-4887 www.imaxvictoria.com
Visit this theater to view science and nature-related IMAX films.

PACIFIC UNDERSEA GARDENS

490 Belleville St., Victoria, 250-382-5717; www.pacificunderseagardens.com
Underwater windows for viewing of more than 5,000 marine specimens; scuba diver shows.

POINT ELLICE HOUSE MUSEUM

2616 Pleasant St., Victoria, 250-380-6506; www.victorialodging.com/pointellice
Original Victorian setting, furnishings. Afternoon tea served in restored garden.

ROYAL BRITISH COLUMBIA MUSEUM

675 Belleville St., Victoria, 250-356-7226, 888-447-7977; www.royalbcmuseum.bc.ca
Three-dimensional exhibits include natural and human history, indigenous history and art; also a re-creation of a turn-of-the-century town. In the natural history gallery, the "Living Land-Living Sea" exhibit depicts the natural history of British Columbia from the Ice Age to the present.

THUNDERBIRD PARK

675 Belleville St., Victoria; www.thunderbirdpark.com
Collection of authentic totem poles and indigenous carvings, representing the works of the main Pacific Coastal tribes. Indigenous carvers may be seen at work in the Carving Shed. May-September.

WHALE-WATCHING TOURS

950 Wharf St., Victoria
Whale-watching boats line both the Wharf Street waterfront and Inner Harbor. Half-day tours display marine life, including orcas, sea lions, seals and porpoises. Victoria Marine Adventures (250-995-2211) and Prince of Whales (250-383-4884) operate tours.

HOTELS

★★★ABIGAIL'S HOTEL

906 McClure St., Victoria, 250-388-5363, 866-347-5054; www.abigailshotel.com
This colorfully painted inn consists of an historic Tudor mansion and converted carriage house. The quiet setting belies the inn's location just three blocks from Victoria's Inner Harbor and main tourist attractions. A full gourmet breakfast is served overlooking the patio and English-style gardens. 23 rooms. Children over 10 years only. Complimentary full breakfast. Pets. $$$

★★★BEACONSFIELD INN

998 Humboldt St., Victoria, 250-384-4044, 888-884-4044; www.beaconsfieldinn.com

This three-story Edwardian mansion on Victoria's south side is a Registered Heritage Property. The gardens are kept in the English style, and high tea and sherry are served each afternoon. Each guest room boasts unique features such as canopied beds, beamed ceilings, stained-glass windows and wood-burning fireplaces. Nine rooms. Children over 11 years only. Complimentary full breakfast. $$$

★★★BEACON INN AT SIDNEY

9724 Third St., Sidney, 250-655-3288, 877-420-5499; www.beaconinns.com

Located in the center of Book Town, this elegant Edwardian-inspired property is the perfect romantic getaway. A complimentary gourmet breakfast in the breakfast room (or on the front patio) starts each day. However, for guests who want pure relaxation, the Ocean Palm Spa is just a few minutes from the inn. Nine rooms. Complimentary full breakfast. Wireless Internet access. $$

★★BEDFORD REGENCY HOTEL

1140 Government St., Victoria, 250-384-6835, 800-665-6500;
www.bedfordregency.com

40 rooms. Restaurant, bar. Wireless Internet access. $$

★★BEST WESTERN CARLTON PLAZA HOTEL

642 Johnson St., Victoria, 250-388-5513, 800-663-7241; www.bestwesterncarlton.com

103 rooms. Restaurant. High-speed Internet access. Exercise room. Pets accepted, fee. $$

★★★COAST HARBORSIDE HOTEL & MARINA

146 Kingston St., Victoria, 250-360-1211, 800-716-6199; www.coasthotels.com

This location can't be beat. The hotel has an inner harbor spot with a 42-slip private marina and it's close to Victoria International Airport. All rooms have balconies or terraces, some with marina side views, and complimentary high-speed Internet access. Guests can relax in one of the two pools or hot tub and enjoy a seafood dinner at the Blue Crab Bar & Grill. 132 rooms. Restaurant, bar. Pets accepted, fee. Exercise room. Pool. Business center. $$

★★CHATEAU VICTORIA HOTEL AND SUITES

740 Burdett Ave., Victoria, 250-382-4221, 800-663-5891; www.chateauvictoria.com

177 rooms Restaurant, bar. Pets accepted, fee. Exercise room. Pool. $$

★★★DELTA VICTORIA OCEAN POINTE RESORT AND SPA

45 Songhees Road, Victoria, 250-360-2999, 800-667-4677; www.deltahotels.com

Located on a point between Victoria's Inner and Upper harbors, this elegant, modern hotel offers wonderful views of the waterfront, Parliament Buildings and the Royal BC Museum. Take advantage of the resort experience by participating in fitness classes, booking a tee time on a nearby golf course and playing tennis on one of the hotel's two lighted courts. 239 rooms. Restaurant, bar. Pets accepted, fee. Exercise room. Pool. Tennis. Business center. $$

BRITISH COLUMBIA

★★★ENGLISH INN & RESORT
429 Lampson St., Victoria, 250-388-4353, 866-388-4353; www.englishinnresort.com
This unique resort was built to echo an English country village, and its buildings are set amidst five acres of beautifully landscaped English-style gardens. Rooms are spacious and streamlined, with contemporary furnishings and some with fireplaces or spa tubs. 30 rooms. Restaurant, bar. Spa. **$$$**

★★EXECUTIVE HOUSE HOTEL
777 Douglas St., Victoria, 250-388-5111, 800-663-7001; www.executivehouse.com
181 rooms. Restaurant, bar. Pets accepted, fee. Exercise room. **$$**

★★★THE FAIRMONT EMPRESS
721 Government St., Victoria, 250-384-8111, 800-441-1414; www.fairmont.com
The Fairmont Empress is one of Victoria's most cherished landmarks. Nearly a century old, this storybook castle resting on the banks of Victoria's Inner Harbor enjoys a legendary past, sparkling with royals, celebrities and a bygone era. Afternoon tea at The Fairmont Empress is a must for all visitors to Victoria. 477 rooms. Two restaurants, bar. Pets accepted, fee. Exercise room. Pool. Business center. **$$$**

★★★★HASTINGS HOUSE
160 Upper Ganges Road, Salt Spring Island, 250-537-2362, 800-661-9255;
www.hastingshouse.com
Snuggled on Salt Spring Island, the Tudor-style Hastings House captures the essence of the English countryside. Scattered throughout the lovely grounds, the rooms and suites are housed within ivy-covered garden cottages and the timber-framed barn. High Tea and pre-dinner cocktails are served daily in the lounge. Hastings House boasts one of the most accomplished kitchens in British Colombia. Longtime executive chef Marcel Kauer and his brigade have the great fortune to draw on British Columbia's Pacific Northwest bounty. The wine list, although international in scope, features a slate of reds and white from B.C.'s Okanagan Valley. 18 rooms. Closed mid-November-mid-March. Restaurant. **$$$$**

★★HARBOR TOWERS HOTEL & SUITES
345 Quebec St., Victoria, 250-385-2405, 800-663-5896; www.harbourtowers.com
195 rooms Restaurant, bar. Children's activity center. Pets accepted, fee. Exercise room. Pool. Business center. **$$**

★★★HOTEL GRAND PACIFIC
463 Belleville St., Victoria, 250-386-0450, 800-663-7550; www.hotelgrandpacific.com
Located at the southern tip of Vancouver Island, this hotel offers serene water views and easy access to historic Old Town and area businesses. The rooms and suites are light and airy. Fine dining is one of Victoria's hallmarks, and this hotel is no exception. The Pacific Northwest cuisine at The Pacific is a standout, while The Mark's regionally influenced dishes are equally delicious. 304 rooms. Three restaurants, bar, spa. Pets accepted, fee. Exercise room. Pool. Business center. **$$**

★★★LAUREL POINT INN

680 Montreal St., Victoria, 250-386-8721, 800-663-7667; www.laurelpoint.com

Every room of this hotel has a balcony and a fabulous view of either the Inner or the Upper Harbor. The grounds include a Japanese-style garden and the Asian influence is felt in the décor. Relax in the cozy piano lounge, the fragrant garden or the outdoor patio. 200 rooms. Restaurant, bar. High-speed Internet access. Pets accepted, fee. Pool. Business center. $$$

★★★MAGNOLIA HOTEL AND SPA

623 Courtney St., Victoria, 250-381-0999, 877-624-6654; www.magnoliahotel.com

This luxury boutique hotel one block from the Inner Harbor provides comfort and pampering throughout. The spa offers a full range of beauty and relaxation regimens and prides itself on using natural products from renewable resources. 63 rooms. Complimentary continental breakfast. Restaurant, bar. Pets accepted. Exercise room. $$$

★★★MIRALOMA ON THE COVE

2306 Harbour Road, Sidney, 250-656-6622, 877-956-6622; www.miraloma.ca

This luxurious seaside property is located just 20 minutes from downtown Victoria and five minutes from ferries and the airport. Guests can choose from studios, one-bedroom suites or two-bedroom suites. Each guest room also includes pillow-top mattresses, a balcony or patio, spa tubs and heated towel bars. Guests can enjoy a number of amenities such as hot chocolate, cookies, use of mountain bikes and a complimentary continental breakfast buffet. 22 rooms. Pets accepted, fee. Exercise room. $$

★★OAK BAY BEACH AND MARINE RESORT

1175 Beach Drive, Victoria, 250-598-4556, 800-668-7758; www.oakbaybeachhotel.com

49 rooms. Complimentary continental breakfast. Restaurant, bar. Spa. Pets accepted, fee. $$

★★ROYAL SCOT SUITE HOTEL

425 Quebec St., Victoria, 250-388-5463, 800-663-7515; www.royalscot.com

178 rooms. Restaurant, bar, children's activity center. Exercise room. Pool. $

★★★SOOKE HARBOR HOUSE

1528 Whiffen Spit Road, Sooke, 250-642-3421, 800-889-9688;
www.sookeharbourhouse.com

Located on Vancouver Island by the sea, this bed and breakfast features beautifully designed guest rooms with fireplaces and spectacular ocean views. Guests can enjoy area activities such as hiking, whale-watching and cross-country skiing. 28 rooms Closed three weeks in January. Complimentary continental breakfast. Wireless Internet access. Restaurant. Pets accepted, fee. $$$

★★★SWANS SUITE HOTEL

506 Pandora Ave., Victoria, 250-361-3310, 800-668-7926; www.swanshotel.com

Built in 1913, this hotel holds 30 one- and two-bedroom suites. Most of the guest rooms have a loft that contributes a spacious feeling, and some have skylights and private patios. All rooms boast full kitchens, duvets and original artwork. It's a lively place with its own brewery and two popular eating and drinking establishments.

BRITISH COLUMBIA

29 rooms, all suites. Complimentary continental breakfast. Wireless Internet access. Restaurant, bar. $$

★★TRAVELODGE

229 Gorge Road East, Victoria, 250-388-6611, 800-565-3777;
www.travelodgevictoria.com
73 rooms. Restaurant, bar. Pets accepted, fee. Exercise room. Pool. Business center. $

SPECIALITY LODGINGS

ANDERSEN HOUSE

301 Kingston St., Victoria, 250-388-4565, 877-264-9988; www.andersenhouse.com
Four rooms. Children over 11 years only. Complimentary full breakfast. Wireless Internet access. $$

GATSBY MANSION B&B

309 Belleville St., Victoria, 250-388-9191, 800-563-9656; www.gatsbymansion.com
20 rooms. Complimentary full breakfast. Restaurant. Spa. $$

HATERLEIGH HERITAGE INN

243 Kingston St., Victoria, 250-384-9995, 866-234-2244; www.haterleigh.com
Seven rooms, all suites. Children over 9 years only. Complimentary full breakfast. $$$

PRIOR HOUSE B&B INN

620 St. Charles St., Victoria, 250-592-8847, 877-924-3300; www.priorhouse.com
Six rooms. Complimentary full breakfast. $$$

ROSEWOOD VICTORIA INN

595 Michigan St., Victoria, 250-384-6644, 866-986-2222; www.rosewoodvictoria.com
17 rooms. Complimentary full breakfast. $$

RESTAURANTS

★★BLUE CRAB BAR AND GRILL

146 Kingston, Victoria, 250-480-1999; www.bluecrab.ca
Seafood menu. Reservations recommended. $$$

★★★CAFE BRIO

944 Fort St., Victoria, 250-383-0009; www.cafe-brio.com
This award-winning restaurant is located in downtown Victoria and offers West Coast/Continental cuisine featuring an abundance of fresh wild fish. The daily menu also offers local, seasonal, organic foods. For an exceptional value, come for the early prix fixe menu. International menu. Closed first two weeks in January. Reservations recommended. Outdoor seating. $$$

★★CAMILLE'S

45 Bastion Square, Victoria, 250-381-3433; www.camillesrestaurant.com
International menu. Closed Monday. Reservations recommended. $$$

★★CEDAR DINING ROOM AT TIGH-NA-MARA RESORT

1155 Resort Drive, Parksville, 250-248-2333, 800-663-7373; www.tigh-na-mara.com

International menu. Reservations recommended. **$$**

★★★DEEP COVE CHALET

11190 Chalet Road, Sidney, 250-656-3541; www.deepcovechalet.com

This charming and historic country inn has a great view overlooking the waters of the inside passage. Built in 1914, it was originally a teahouse for a railroad station. French menu. Reservations recommended. Outdoor seating. **$$$**

★★★EMPRESS ROOM

721 Government St., Victoria, 250-995-3615; www.fairmont.com

Dine on classic cuisine in this richly appointed room of tapestries, intricately carved ceilings and live harp music. The 100-year-old hotel's waterfront location is full of European style, a great spot for a romantic meal. International menu. Reservations recommended. **$$$$**

★★GATSBY MANSION

309 Belleville St., Victoria, 250-388-9191, 800-563-9656; www.gatsbymansion.com

International menu. Reservations recommended. Outdoor seating. **$$$**

★★★HERALD STREET CAFE

546 Herald St., Victoria, 250-381-1441; www.emenus.ca/heraldstcaffe

International menu. Reservations recommended. Outdoor seating. **$$**

★★HUGO'S

625 Courtney St., Victoria, 250-920-4846; www.hugosbrewhouse.com

West Coast menu. Reservations recommended. Outdoor seating. **$$$**

★★IL TERRAZZO

555 Johnson St., Victoria, 250-361-0028; www.ilterrazzo.com

Italian menu. Reservations recommended. Outdoor seating. **$$$**

★★JAPANESE VILLAGE STEAK AND SEAFOOD HOUSE

734 Broughton St., Victoria, 250-382-5165; www.japanesevillage.bc.ca

Japanese menu. Reservations recommended. **$$**

★★KINGFISHER RESTAURANT

4330 S. Island Highway, Courtenay, 250-334-9600, 800-663-7929; www.kingfisherspa.com

International menu. Reservations recommended. Outdoor seating. **$$**

★★★LURE

45 Songhees Road, Victoria, 250-360-5873; www.lureatoceanpointe.com

This contemporary, sophisticated seafood restaurant is located inside the Delta Ocean Pointe Resort and offers excellent water and downtown views. Seafood menu. Reservations recommended. Outdoor seating. **$$$**

★★THE MARINA

1327 Beach Drive, Victoria, 250-598-8555; www.marinarestaurant.com

International menu. Reservations recommended. $$

★★OLD HOUSE RESTAURANT

1760 Riverside Lane, Courtenay, 250-338-5406; www.theoldhouse.ca

International menu. Reservations recommended. Outdoor seating. $$

★★★★RESTAURANT MATISSE

512 Yates St., Victoria, 250-480-0883; www.restaurantmatisse.com

Restaurant Matisse is a gem of a dining room that has become a destination for simple, traditional French fare among Victoria's dining elite. While French wines dominate the list, a great selection of California bottles is also included. French menu. Closed Monday-Tuesday and for two weeks in spring. Reservations recommended. $$$

★★SPINNAKER'S BREW PUB

308 Catherine St., Victoria, 250-386-2739, 877-838-2739; www.spinnakers.com

Canada's oldest brew pub. Reservations recommended. Outdoor seating. $$

★★★SOOKE HARBOR HOUSE

1528 Whiffen Spit Road, Sooke Harbor, 250-642-3421, 800-889-9688;
www.sookeharbourhouse.com

Considered one of the most unique restaurants in Canada, the bistro serves local organic seafood, meat and produce, with edible herbs and flowers from the garden. International menu. Closed Monday-Wednesday from December to early February. Reservations recommended. Outdoor seating. $$$

★WHITE HEATHER TEA ROOM

1885 Oak Bay Ave., Victoria, 250-595-8020

Scottish menu, afternoon tea and delicious baked goods. Reservations recommended. $

WHISTLER

The winning combination of Blackcomb and Whistler mountains makes this an internationally famous ski area—yet it's also packed full through the summer, as preppy golfers descend upon the village alongside mud-spattered, hardcore mountain bikers. Five lakes dot Whistler valley, offering ample opportunity to fish, swim, windsurf, canoe, kayak or sail. The alpine slopes for a time give way to extensive hiking and mountain biking trails, but even in summer there is skiing to be found—Whistler is where enthusiasts will find the only lift-serviced, summertime public glacier skiing in North America. Everything in Whistler is larger-than-life: the ideal getaway with opulent food and wine, an infectious party atmosphere and sumptuous accommodations, plus a staging ground for epics that is nothing short of extraordinary.

Information: www.tourismwhistler.com

★
★
★
★

BLACKCOMB SKI AREA

4545 Blackcomb Way, Whistler, 604-687-1032, 866-218-9690;
www.whistlerblackcomb.com

Six high-speed quad chairlifts, three triple chairlifts, three handletows, two T-bars, platter lift, magic car lift. More than 100 runs; longest run seven miles (11 kilometers), vertical drop 5,280 feet (1,609 meters). Glacier skiing (mid-June-August, weather permitting). High-speed gondola.

WHISTLER MUSEUM AND ARCHIVES SOCIETY

4333 Main St., Whistler, 604-932-2019; www.whistlermuseum.com

Discover the rich history of the thriving Whistler community through artifacts, photographs and stories from local community members.

WHISTLER SKI AREA

4545 Blackcomb Way, Whistler, 604-687-1032, 866-218-9690;
www.whistlerblackcomb.com

Six high-speed quad, double, two triple chairlifts; two handletows, two T-bars, platter pull. More than 100 runs; longest run 7 miles (11 kilometers), vertical drop 5,020 feet (1,530 meters). Two high-speed gondolas.

SPECIAL EVENTS

CORNUCOPIA, WHISTLER'S FOOD AND WINE CELEBRATION

www.whistlercornucopia.com

Enjoy wine from more than 70 wineries from the province, neighboring U.S. states and around the world. Food tastings, wine dinners and seminars. Early November.

TELUS WORLD SKI & SNOWBOARD FESTIVAL

www.whistlerblackcomb.com

Ten-day festival features outdoor concert series, action-sports photography and film events, demonstration days and festive parties. Mid-April.

HOTELS

★★BEST WESTERN LISTEL WHISTLER HOTEL

4121 Village Green, Whistler, 604-932-1133, 800-663-5472; www.bwlistelhotel.com

98 rooms. Restaurant, bar. Wireless internet access, Pets accepted, fee. Pool. **$$**

★★CRYSTAL LODGE

4154 Village Green, Whistler, 604-932-2221, 800-667-3363; www.crystal-lodge.com

159 rooms. Restaurant, bar. High-speed Internet access. Pets accepted, fee. Exercise room. Pool. **$**

★★★THE FAIRMONT CHATEAU WHISTLER

4599 Chateau Blvd., Whistler, 604-938-8000, 800-606-8244; www.fairmont.com

The Fairmont Chateau Whistler is a skier's nirvana. During summer, its golf course and David Leadbetter Golf Academy lend the same status for golfers. The Vida Wellness Spa soothes the tired muscles of active visitors. Taste buds are tantalized at the

77

BRITISH COLUMBIA

★
★
★
★
☆

resort's three restaurants. 550 rooms. Restaurant, bar. Ski in/ski out. Pets accepted, fee. Exercise room. Pool. Golf. Skiing. Business center. $$$

★★★★FOUR SEASONS RESORT WHISTLER

4591 Blackcomb Way, Whistler, 604-935-3400, 800-819-5053; www.fourseasons.com

This resort is nestled in the foot of the Blackcomb and Whistler mountains and offers a year-round getaway that features signature Four Seasons service and style. Located at the base of Blackcomb Mountain, the resort is a five-minute walk to the ski lifts and a 10-minute stroll to the village center. The guest rooms are spacious, beautifully furnished and decorated. The dining room and lounge, Fifty Two 80 Bistro, delight with flavorful food and an extensive wine list and specialty cocktails. After a day of activity, retreat to the Spa, where body wraps, hydro-therapy, facials and massages will help you unwind. 273 rooms. Restaurant, bar. Children's activity center (winter only). Spa. Pets accepted, fee. Exercise room. Pool. Business center. $$$$

★★★PAN PACIFIC WHISTLER MOUNTAINSIDE

4320 Sundial Crescent, Whistler, 604-905-2999, 888-905-9995; www.panpacific.com

Nestled at the foot of Whistler and Blackcomb mountains and facing Skier's Plaza, this all-suite boutique resort offers kitchens, fireplaces and balconies with beautiful views of the mountains of Whistler Village. After a day of skiing, retreat to the onsite spa for a hot stone massage, or swim in the heated outdoor pool. 121 rooms, all suites. Two restaurants, bar. Exercise room. Pool. Business center. $$$

★★SUMMIT LODGE & SPA

4359 Main St., Whistler, 604-932-2778, 888-913-8811; www.summitlodge.com

81 rooms. Restaurant, bar. Pets accepted, fee. Pool. $$$

★★★THE WESTIN RESORT AND SPA

4090 Whistler Way, Whistler, 604-905-5000, 888-634-5577; www.westinwhistler.com

Dramatic views are enjoyed from the privacy of airy suites and guests retreat to the comfort of the FireRock Lounge après-ski or the aubergine grille for fresh cuisine. The Avello Spa & Health Club entices visitors with more than 70 treatments and the latest fitness equipment. 419 rooms, all suites. Restaurant, bar. Children's activity center. Pets accepted, fee. Exercise. Pool. Business center. $$$

RESTAURANTS

★★★BEARFOOT BISTRO

4121 Village Green, Whistler, 604-932-3433; www.bearfootbistro.com

Only a hard day of skiing can justify this four-hour, decadent feast for the senses. Each of eight courses is handcrafted from a huge range of rare, high-quality ingredients including caribou and pheasant. Add to this one of the most beautiful locations in North America and the result is a truly standout dining experience. International menu. Reservations recommended. $$$$

★★LA RUA

4557 Blackcomb way, 604-932-5011; www.larua-restaurante.com

Seafood, steak menu. Closed six weeks in October-November. Reservations recommended. Outdoor seating. $$$

★
★
★
★
★

★★RIMROCK CAFE

2117 Whistler Road, Whistler, 604-932-5565; www.rimrockwhistler.com

Seafood menu. Closed late October-mid-November. Reservations recommended. Outdoor seating. $$$

★★★RISTORANTE ARAXI

4222 Village Square, Whistler, 604-932-4540; www.araxi.com

Tables encircle a giant stone urn, the centerpiece of this warm and friendly dining room. A blend of French and Italian culinary styles and fine, regional ingredients have gained this resort town restaurant continent-wide recognition. International menu. Closed two weeks in early May, late October. Reservations recommended. Outdoor seating. $$$

★★SUSHI VILLAGE

4272 Mountain Square, Whistler, 604-932-3330; www.sushivillage.com

Japanese menu. Dinner. $$

★★TRATTORIA DI UMBERTO

4417 Sundial Place, Whistler, 604-932-5858; www.umberto.com

Italian menu. Reservations recommended. Outdoor seating. $$$

★★★VAL D'ISERE

4314 Main St., Whistler, 604-932-4666; www.valdisere-restaurant.com

Impressive for both the food and the charming interior, this fine restaurant is located in the north village plaza. The menu covers a wide range of culinary influences and includes dishes such as venison flank steak with chanterelle sauce and wild salmon baked in a potato crust. French menu. Reservations recommended. Outdoor seating. $$$

★★★WILDFLOWER RESTAURANT

4599 Chateau Blvd., Whistler, 604-938-8000, 800-606-8244; www.fairmont.com

Tucked inside the Chateau Whistler, this restaurant features a local, organic-laden menu with weekly table d'hote signature dishes, an ever-popular coastal market buffet and a "Flavors of Asia" buffet on Friday and Saturday nights. International menu. Reservations recommended. Outdoor seating. $$$

SPAS

★★★THE AVELLO SPA

4090 Whistler Way, Whistler, 604-935-3444; www.whistlerspa.com

The Avello Spa takes a holistic approach in its well-being treatments. Massage accounts for most of the menu, with the signature massage treatments including the Avello hot rock massage, Thai and Chinese therapies. Asian approaches to balance include Reiki, acupuncture, reflexology and shiatsu. A wide variety of hydrotherapy sessions are available, from herbal, milk, mustard, and mud to soaks using salts from the Dead Sea.

79

BRITISH COLUMBIA

★★★★SPA AT FOUR SEASONS WHISTLER

4591 Blackcomb Way, Whistler, 604-935-3400; www.fourseasons.com/whistler/spa

This contemporary spa located inside the Four Seasons Whistler offers a full menu of massages and body treatments designed to sooth and restore sore muscles after a day on the slopes. Chilly feet are wrapped in warm towels while muscles are warmed with hot stones during the après-ski massage. The men's fitness facial restores wind- and sun-burned skin while the British Columbia glacial clay wrap is a great way to warm up at the end of the day. Those who can't pry themselves from the comfort of their rooms can order up an in-room massage.

★
★
★
★
★

MANITOBA

MANITOBA IS LOCATED IN THE LONGITUDINAL CENTER OF THE COUNTRY, THOUGH IT IS CONSIDERED part of Western Canada and is the easternmost of Canada's three prairie provinces. It is renowned for dramatic landscapes with golden fields, granite ridges and sparkling lakes, a lively cultural heritage of fur trade-era voyagers, accessible yet dramatic wildlife and warm, friendly people.

Sand dunes, ancient granite and amazing waterfalls are all crisscrossed by extensive trail networks that attract hikers and bikers to broad valleys and lush Canadian Shield forests. More than 10,000 trophy-sized fish are pulled out of Manitoba's plentiful waters every year, with pristine fly-in as well as road-accessible lodges peppering the north. Arctic grayling, brook trout, lake trout, northern pike and walleye thrive here, and Winnipeg's Red River offers some of the best giant channel cat fishing in the world. Recognized as a birder's paradise, Manitoba attracts two-thirds of Canada's more than 500 species of birds. In spring, the birds fly north in amazing flocks in the hundreds of thousands over lakes, marshes and forests.

In contrast to Manitoba's off-the-beaten-track experiences, Winnipeg is a multicultural city bursting with festivals, art, music and food. Restaurants serve everything from Ukrainian perogies to a fusion of regional and western cuisine.

www.travelmanitoba.com

> ★ **FUN FACTS**
>
> Manitoba's lakes cover approximately 14.5% of its surface area, many with native-inspired names such as Lake Pekwachnamay-koskwaskwaypinwanik.

81

MANITOBA

BRANDON

Brandon, Manitoba's second-largest city, has a rich agricultural heritage and reputation as a prosperous farming community, which it celebrates with the province's largest agricultural fair.

Information: www.tourism.brandon.com

WHAT TO SEE AND DO

COMMONWEALTH AIR TRAINING PLAN MUSEUM

Hangar 1, McGill Field, Brandon, 204-727-2444; www.airmuseum.ca

Display of WWII aircraft, vehicles; photos, uniforms, flags and other mementos of Air Force training conducted in Canada from 1940 to 1945 under the British Commonwealth Air Training Plan. Tours by appointment.

★
★
★
★
★

SPECIAL EVENTS

MANITOBA FALL FAIR

Keystone Centre, 18th Street and Richmond Avenue, Brandon, 204-726-3590;
www.brandonfairs.com

Keystone Centre. Manitoba's largest livestock show and sale; tractor pull, rodeo. November.

MANITOBA SUMMER FAIR

Keystone Centre, 18th Street and Richmond Avenue, Brandon, 204-726-3590;
www.brandonfairs.com

Competitions, children's entertainment, midway, dancing. June.

ROYAL MANITOBA WINTER FAIR

Keystone Centre, 18th Street and Richmond Avenue, Brandon, 204-726-3590;
www.brandonfairs.com

Manitoba's largest winter fair. Equestrian events, heavy horses, entertainment. Late March.

HOTELS

★COMFORT INN

925 Middleton Ave., Brandon, 204-727-6232; www.choicehotels.ca

81 rooms. Pets accepted, fee. High-speed Internet access. Complimentary breakfast. $

★★ROYAL OAK INN & SUITES

3130 Victoria Ave., Brandon, 204-728-5775, 800-852-2709; www.royaloakinn.com

96 rooms. Restaurant, bar. Pets accepted, fee. Exercise room. Pool. Complimentary Wireless Internet connection. $

★★VICTORIA INN

3550 Victoria Ave., Brandon, 204-725-1532; www.vicinn.ca

131 rooms. Restaurant, bar. Pets accepted, fee. Exercise room. Pool. Business center. $

CHURCHILL

Churchill is the only human settlement where visitors can come to see polar bears in the wild. Fast and dangerous at more than 1,300 pounds (590 kilograms) and standing up to 10 feet (3 meters) tall, the bears are a marvel to behold when they frequent the area each fall. Wildlife admirers also come to this area of northern Manitoba to see some of the 250 species of birds that pass through, and in the summer to view beluga whales in the waters of the Churchill River.

Information: www.townofchurchill.ca

WHAT TO SEE AND DO

ESKIMO MUSEUM

242 Laverendrye Ave., Churchill, 204-675-2030; www.museumsmanitoba.com

This museum contains an impressive collection of Inuit carvings and artifacts, considered some of the oldest and finest in the world. Artifacts date from 1700 B.C. to modern times. June-mid-November. Admission by donation.

WAPUSK NATIONAL PARK OF CANADA
204-675-8863; www.pc.gc.ca

This park, southeast of Churchill, is home to one of the world's largest known polar bear denning sights. Wapusk, the Cree word for white bear, is dedicated to protecting the habitat for polar bears, as well as for the hundreds of thousands of birds that nest or migrate here each year. Unescorted visits to the park are not recommended. For the most current list of operators, contact the park office.

WINNIPEG

Winnipeg, the provincial capital, is situated in the heart of the continent and combines the sophistication and friendliness of east and west. Assini-boine, Cree and Ojibwa tribes inhabited the formerly prairie-covered landscape more than 6,000 years ago. These tribes met at the junction of the Assiniboine and Red rivers to trade. Today, Winnipeg, derived from the Cree word for "muddy waters," is home to Canada's largest city-dwelling aboriginal community. A historic gathering place, it is still a destination that foreigners and Canadians alike visit to enjoy a wide range of attractions and cultural offerings. The city offers relaxing cruises on the Assiniboine and Red rivers, Rainbow Stage Summer Theater in Kildonan Park, the Manitoba Theatre Centre, the Winnipeg Symphony, the Manitoba Opera and the renowned Royal Winnipeg Ballet. Sports fans will enjoy the Blue Bombers football team and the Manitoba Moose hockey team.

Information: www.tourism.winnipeg.mb.ca

WHAT TO SEE AND DO
ASSINIBOINE FOREST NATURE PARK
2355 Corydon Ave., Winnipeg, 204-986-3989; www.winnipeg.ca

This park features colorful English and formal gardens, the Leo Mol Sculpture Garden, a conservatory with floral displays, a duck pond, playgrounds, a cricket and field hockey area, a miniature train, bike paths and a fitness trail featuring more than 39 species of mammals and more than 80 species of birds. The Assiniboine Park Zoo has a collection of rare and endangered species, tropical mammals, birds and reptiles; the children's discovery area features a variety of young animals.

ASSINIBOINE PARK CONSERVATORY
Assiniboine Park, Winnipeg, 204-986-5537; www.winnipeg.ca

The longest established conservatory in western Canada gives visitors a chance to view tropical trees and plants, exotic flowers and foliage not indigenous to the country.

BIRDS HILL PROVINCIAL PARK
8 miles (13 kilometers) north of Winnipeg on Highway 59, Winnipeg, 204-222-9151; www.gov.mb.ca

A 8,275-acre (3,350-hectare) park situated on a glacial formation called an esker. The park has a large population of white-tailed deer and many orchid species. Interpretive, hiking, bridle and bicycle trails; in-line skating path; snowshoe, snowmobile and cross-country skiing trails.

83

MANITOBA

★
★
★
★
★

CENTENNIAL CENTRE

555 Main St., Winnipeg, 204-956-1360; www.mbccc.ca

Complex includes concert hall and Manitoba Theatre Centre Building.

DALNAVERT MUSEUM

61 Carlton St., Winnipeg, 204-943-2835; www.mhs.mb.ca

Restored Victorian residence of Sir Hugh John Macdonald, premier of Manitoba, depicts the lifestyle and furnishings of the period.

FORKS

Downtown Winnipeg, 204-943-7752; www.theforks.com

Several key Winnipeg attractions are centered in the general location of what has been a gathering place for people for thousands of years. Come here to shop, dine, explore museums and historic sites, or simply stroll along the Riverwalk.

THE FORKS MARKET

Downtown Winnipeg, 204-942-6302; www.theforks.com

Browse through more than 50 specialty shops for handicrafts, toys, gift items and more and dine on cuisine from around the world and on local specialties.

THE FORKS NATIONAL HISTORIC SITE OF CANADA

401-25 Forks Market Road, Winnipeg, 204-983-6757; www.pc.gc.ca

Situated on 13.6 acres (5.5 hectares). Riverside promenade; walkways throughout. Historical exhibits, playground; evening performances. Special events. Adjacent area open in winter for skating, cross-country skiing.

FORT WHYTE CENTRE FOR FAMILY ADVENTURE AND RECREATION

1961 McCreary Road, Winnipeg, 204-989-8355; www.fortwhyte.org

Hike on self-guided trails through 400 acres (162 hectares) of marshes, lakes and forests that are home to 27 species of birds and mammals. Year-round fishing; canoe and boat rentals. Dine at Buffalo Stone café and shop for souvenirs at The Nature Shop. A 10,000-square-foot (920-square-meter) interpretive center showcases a variety of exhibits. Do not miss the Bison Prairie, with the largest urban-based herd of Plains bison in the country, or the Prairie Dog Exhibit.

LEO MOL SCULPTURE GARDEN

Assiniboine Park, Winnipeg, 204-953-4518; www.partnersinthepark.org

Garden and gallery to view the bronze sculptures and other artwork by this acclaimed local artist. An onsite studio allows visitors to see how bronze sculptures are created.

LYRIC THEATRE

Assiniboine Park, Winnipeg, 204-888-5466; www.partnersinthepark.org

View performances by the Royal Winnipeg Ballet, the Winnipeg Symphony Orchestra and during assorted festivals.

THE MANITOBA CHILDREN'S MUSEUM

45 Forks Market Road, Winnipeg, 204-924-4000; www.childrensmuseum.com

Children explore and create in seven galleries, such as one that enables preschoolers to learn about the habitats of different animal species and to climb on a 17-foot (5.2-meter) oak tree, while older children can surf the Internet. Travel into the past on a 1952 diesel locomotive and passenger coach, or into a fairytale wonderland.

MANITOBA MUSEUM OF MAN AND NATURE

190 Rupert Ave., Winnipeg, 204-956-2830; www.manitobamuseum.ca

Galleries interpret Manitoba's human and natural history. September 2, 2008-May 18, 2009, Tuesday-Friday 10 a.m.-4 p.m., Saturday-Sunday 11 a.m.-5 p.m.; closed Mondays.

MANITOBA OPERA ASSOCIATION

555 Main St.,Winnipeg, 204-942-7479; www.manitobaopera.mb.ca

The strength of character of the Manitoba Opera comes from its ability to attract great international artists such as the Met's Leona Mitchell and La Scala's Eduard Tumagian, and to highlight local talent, such as Tracy Dahl and Phillip Ens. The Manitoba Opera Chorus is supported by Winnipeg Symphony Orchestra under the direction of internationally known conductors. Lavish sets and costumes bring the performances to life, while English subtitles, projected on an overhead screen, make foreign-language operas accessible and comprehensible to everyone.

OAK HAMMOCK MARSH WILDLIFE MANAGEMENT AREA

204-467-3300, 888-506-2774; www.oakhammockmarsh.ca

More than 8,000 acres (3,238 hectares) of marshland and grassland wildlife habitat. Attracts up to 300,000 ducks and geese during spring (April-mid-May) and fall migration (September-October). Nature trails; picnic sites, marsh boardwalk, viewing mounds, drinking water. Conservation center with displays, interpretive programs.

PLANETARIUM

190 Rupert Ave., Winnipeg, 204-956-2830; www.manitobamuseum.ca

Circular, multipurpose audiovisual theater. Wide variety of shows; subjects include cosmic catastrophes and the edge of the universe. Learn about science through hands-on exhibits.

ROSS HOUSE

Joe Zuken Heritage Park, 204-943-3958; www.mhs.mb.ca

Oldest building in the original city of Winnipeg; first post office in western Canada. Displays and period-furnished rooms depict daily life in the Red River Settlement.

ROYAL CANADIAN MINT

520 Lagimodière Blvd., Winnipeg, 204-983-6429;
www.mint.ca/royalcanadianmintpublic

One of the world's most modern mints; striking glass tower, landscaped interior courtyard. Tour allows viewing of coining process; coin museum. May-August, Monday-Friday 9 a.m.-4 p.m.; September-April, Monday-Friday 10 a.m.-2 p.m. Tours by appointment only.

★
★
★
★

ROYAL WINNIPEG BALLET

Centennial Concert Hall, 555 Main St., Winnipeg, 204-956-0183, 800-667-4792;
www.rwb.org

This nationally acclaimed company performs throughout the year in Winnipeg and also presents Ballet in the Park during the summer.

THE SPLASH DASH WATER BUS

204-783-6633; www.splashdash.ca

Explore the river on a half-hour boat tour, rent a canoe, or use the water taxi service to get to downtown locations. May-October.

ST. BONIFACE MUSEUM

494 Tache Ave., Winnipeg, 204-237-4500; www.virtualmuseum.ca

Located in the largest French-Canadian community west of Quebec, where Louis Riel, a founder of Manitoba, was born, this museum is housed in the oldest structure in the city, dating to the days of the Red River Colony; it's the largest oak-log construction in North America.

WINNIPEG ART GALLERY

300 Memorial Blvd., Winnipeg, 204-786-6641; www.wag.mb.ca

Canada's first civic gallery. Eight galleries present changing exhibitions of contemporary, historical and decorative art, plus world's largest public collection of Inuit Art. Free admission Wednesday evening and Saturdays. Programming includes tours, lectures, films, concerts. Restaurant.

WINNIPEG SYMPHONY ORCHESTRA

Centennial Concert Hall, 555 Main St., Winnipeg, 204-949-3999; www.wso.mb.ca

Performances ranging from classical to pop to family-oriented music at Centennial Concert Hall. May-September.

SPECIAL EVENTS

FESTIVAL DU VOYAGEUR

Voyageur Park, Joseph and Messager streets, Winnipeg, 204-237-7692;
www.festivalvoyageur.mb.ca

In St. Boniface, Winnipeg's French Quarter. Winter festival celebrating the French-Canadian voyageur and the fur trade era. Ten days in mid-February.

FOLKLORAMA

183 Kennedy St., Winnipeg, 204-982-6210, 800-665-0234; www.folklorama.ca

Multicultural festival featuring more than 40 pavilions. Singing, dancing, food, cultural displays. August.

RED RIVER EXHIBITION

3977 Portage Ave., Winnipeg, 204-888-6990; www.redriverex.com

Large event encompassing grandstand shows, band competitions, displays, agricultural exhibits, parade, entertainment, midway, petting zoo, shows, food. Late June-early July.

WINNIPEG FOLK FESTIVAL

Birds Hill Provincial Park, 204-231-0096; www.winnipegfolkfestival.ca

More than 60 regional, national and international artists perform; nine stages; children's village; evening concerts. Juried crafts exhibit and sale; international food village. Early July.

WINNIPEG FRINGE THEATRE FESTIVAL

Old Market Square, 174 Market Ave., Winnipeg, 204-956-1340;
www.winnipegfringe.com

More than 100 theater companies perform during North America's second-largest Fringe Festival. July.

HOTELS

★★BEST WESTERN CHARTER HOUSE HOTEL

330 York Ave., Winnipeg, 204-942-0101, 800-782-0175; www.bestwestern.com

86 rooms. Restaurant, bar. Fitness center. High-speed Internet access. **$**

★COMFORT INN

1770 Sargent Ave., Winnipeg, 204-783-5627, 800-228-5150; www.comfortinn.com

81 rooms. Pets accepted, fee. Free high-speed Internet access. **$**

★★DELTA WINNIPEG

350 St. Mary Ave., Winnipeg, 204-942-0051, 888-311-4990; www.deltahotels.com

393 rooms. Restaurant. Exercise room. Pool. High-speed Internet access. **$$**

★★★THE FAIRMONT WINNIPEG

2 Lombard Place, Winnipeg, 204-957-1350, 800-257-7544; www.fairmont.com

The Fairmont Winnipeg's stylish interiors and central location have earned it a loyal following among leisure and business travelers. The city's large historic district, cultural attractions, restaurants, shops and businesses are all within walking distance from this hotel. The Velvet Glove restaurant is an ideal place for business meetings or private dinners with inspired Canadian cuisine and an exceptional wine list. 340 rooms. Restaurant. Exercise room. Business center. High-speed Internet access. **$$**

★★HOLIDAY INN

2520 Portage Ave., Winnipeg, 204-885-4478, 800-465-4329; www.holiday-inn.com

190 rooms. Restaurant, bar. Children's activity center. Exercise room. High-speed Internet access. Pool. Business center. **$$**

★★RADISSON HOTEL DOWNTOWN

288 Portage Ave., Winnipeg, 204-956-0410, 800-333-3333; www.radisson.com

272 rooms. Restaurant, bar. Pets accepted, fee. Exercise room. Pool. Business center. High-speed Internet access. **$**

★★VICTORIA INN HOTEL CONVENTION

1808 Wellington Ave., Winnipeg, 204-786-4801

259 rooms. Restaurant, bar. Pets accepted, fee. Pool. Fitness center. **$**

MANITOBA

★★AMICI

326 Broadway, Winnipeg, 204-943-4997; www.amiciwpg.com

Italian menu. Dinner. **$$$**

★★ICHIBAN JAPANESE STEAKHOUSE AND SUSHI BAR

189 Carlton St., Winnipeg, 204-925-7400; www.ichiban.ca

Japanese menu. Dinner. **$$$**

★★HY'S STEAK LOFT

1 Lombard Place, Winnipeg, 204-942-1000; www.hyssteakhouse.com

Steak menu. Lunch, dinner. **$$$**

NEW BRUNSWICK

TRIUMPH OVER TRAGEDY PERSONIFIES THE GREAT ACADIAN ODYSSEY IN NEW BRUNSWICK—and through the Acadians' difficult historical journey, their "joie de vivre" (joy of life) has sustained them and the spirit of this province for 250 years. This indomitable spirit is celebrated in kitchen parties filled with fiddle music, traditional cuisine, lively dance and storytelling. While not a purely French population, New Brunswick's flavor is Gallic-inspired.

New Brunswick, the largest of Canada's three Maritime provinces, is bursting with the pride and color of the Acadian French (Cajuns' northern cousins). New Brunswick's rich historic past is reflected in major restorations such as the Acadian Historical Village near Caraquet, Kings' Landing Historical Settlement near Fredericton and MacDonald Historic Farm near Miramichi. Despite the number of provinces with French-speaking locals, New Brunswick is Canada's only official bilingual province, with about 33 percent of the people speaking French.

There is much more to New Brunswick than history—including the Bay of Fundy to the south (featuring some of the highest tides in the world and a great variety of whales), the Reversing Falls in Saint John, Magnetic Hill in Moncton, Hopewell Cape Rocks at Hopewell Cape and always the sea. The four seasons of New Brunswick are some of the most vivid in the country. Summers are breezy and hot, with record-breaking tides and the warmest salt water north of Virginia, exposed ocean floors and vast expanses of sand dunes ripe for picnics and exploring. Fall brings brilliant colors and the bounty of the harvest amid some of the best whale-watching in the country. In winter, enjoy endless frozen ponds and lakes, alpine and cross-country skiing and the world's longest network of groomed snowmobile trails. Spring visitors feast on maple syrup and fiddleheads, and anglers are drawn to the world-famous Atlantic salmon river, Miramichi, for the opening of the fishing season.

EDMUNDSTON

Known as the Gateway of the Maritimes, Edmundston is in northwest New Brunswick, a few minutes from the province of Quebec, on the border of Maine and at the doorstep of Atlantic Canada. Acadian culture predominates in this cheerful and active town, with almost all of the population speaking French and English.

Information: www.ville.edmunston.nb.ca

 FUN FACTS

The inventor of the ice cream cone was born in Sussex Corner, the dairy capital of Canada, midway along the Fundy Coastal Drive. Locals tell the story of baker Walter Donelly, who made a bad batch of dough. He was at a loss with what to do with his hard, crispy pastry. So he ran next door to the ice-cream parlor,... and the rest, as they say, is history.

The world's largest covered bridge was completed in Hartland in 1899. It is 1,282 feet (390 meters) long and spans the Saint John River.

WHAT TO SEE AND DO

ANTIQUE AUTO MUSEUM

35 Principale St., Edmundston, 506-735-2637; www.tourismenouveau-brunswick.ca

This museum houses an extensive display of vintage vehicles and mechanical marvels of the past 70 years. Mid-June-Labor Day.

GRAND FALLS

81 Burgess St., Grand Falls, 506-475-7717; www.grandfalls.com

At 75 feet (23 meters) high, this is one of largest cataracts east of Niagara. Fascinating gorge and scenic lookouts along trail; museum. Stairs to bottom of gorge. Late May-October.

LES JARDINS DE LA REPUBLIQUE PROVINCIAL PARK

5 miles (8 kilometers) north of Edmundston, via Trans-Canada Highway 2, 506-735-2525

Park of 107 acres (43 hectares) overlooking the Madawaska River. Amphitheater, scene of music and film performances; 20-acre (8-hectare) botanical garden. Heated swimming pool, boat dock, launch; tennis, volleyball, softball, horseshoes, bicycling, playground.

MONT FARLAGNE

360 Mont Farlagne Road, Saint-Jacques, 506-739-7669; www.montfarlagne.com

Twenty trails open to downhill skiing and snowboarding, with five chair lifts, a snow park, restaurant and bar. December-March, weather permitting.

NEW BRUNSWICK BOTANICAL GARDEN

15 Main St., Saint-Jacques, 506-737-4444; www.umce.ca/jardin

Conceived and designed by a team from the prestigious Montreal Botanical Garden, the garden covers more than 17 acres (7 hectares). More than 30,000 annual flowers and 80,000 plants are on display. June-mid-October.

ST. BASILE CHAPEL MUSEUM

321 Main St., St. Basile, 506-263-5971

Parish church; replica of first chapel built in 1786. July-August: daily.

SPECIAL EVENTS

INTERNATIONAL SNOWMOBILERS FESTIVAL

506-737-1866; www.isfim.net

Featuring snowmobile events on both sides of the International Border in Madawaska, Maine and Edmundston. Highlights include a two-day Lucky Run, Fun Night and many more events for Snowmobilers. Sledders from throughout the U.S. and Canada converge on the beautiful St. John Valley for three days of riding top-rated trails. First week in February.

JAZZ FESTIVAL

8 44th Ave., Canada Road and Rue Francois, Edmundston, 506-737-8188; www.jazzbluesedmundston.com

Annual jazz festival held third weekend in June.

L'ACADIE DES TERRES ET FORÊTS EN FÊTE
Republic Provincial Park, Saint-Jacques, 506-739-0919; www.acadiedesterresetforets.com
The performance celebrates 400 years of Acadian history through song, dance and theater. The representations are held on a natural site (covered in the event of rain). Early July-mid-August.

LA FOIRE BRAYONNE
215 Victoria St., Edmundston, 506-739-6608; www.foirebrayonne.com
French heritage festival featuring concerts, crafts, cultural activities and sporting events. Late July-early August.

FREDERICTON

In the 1950s, the patron of this city, the late Lord Beaverbrook, raised Fredericton from a quiet provincial capital to a major cultural center. Born in Ontario, this British newspaper baron maintained a strong loyalty to New Brunswick, the province of his youth. Wander the elm tree-lined streets through the Green, a lovely park along the St. John River, and admire examples of Beaverbrook's generosity. Nestled along the tree-shaded Green sits Christ Church Cathedral, an 1853 example of decorated Gothic architecture. The art gallery that is Beaverbrook's namesake boasts a collection worthy of continent-wide pride.
Information: www.city.fredericton.nb.ca

WHAT TO SEE AND DO
BEAVERBROOK ART GALLERY
703 Queen St., Fredericton, 506-458-8545; www.beaverbrookartgallery.org
Collection includes 18th- to 20th-century British paintings, 18th- and early 19th-century English porcelain, historical and contemporary Canadian and New Brunswick paintings; Hosmer-Pillow-Vaughan Collection of European fine and decorative arts from the 14th to 20th centuries.

HISTORIC GARRISON DISTRICT
Queen Street, Fredericton, between Regent and York streets; www.tourismfredericton.ca
In summer, daily outdoor walking tours. Attractions include the New Brunswick School Days Museum, the York Sunbury Museum, the New Brunswick Sports Hall of Fame, the Guard House and the Casemate Artisans Shops.

KINGS LANDING HISTORICAL SETTLEMENT
20 Kings Landing Road, Kings Landing, 23 miles (37 kilometers) west of Fredericton on Trans-Canada Highway at exit 259, 506-363-4999; www.kingslanding.nb.ca
Settlement of 70 buildings, costumed staff of 100; recalls Loyalist lifestyle of a century ago. Carpenter's shop, general store, school, church, blacksmith shop, working sawmill and gristmill, inn; replica of a 19th-century wood river craft. All restoration and work is done with tools of the period. June-early October.

MACTAQUAC PROVINCIAL PARK
1256 Route 105, Mactaquac, 15 miles (24 kilometers) west of Fredericton, 506-363-4747; www.mactaquacgolf.com
Approximately 1,400 acres (567 hectares) of farmland and forest overlooking the headpond of Mactaquac Dam. Boating (launch, marinas), swimming beaches, fishing;

hiking, camping, golf, picnicking, playgrounds, restaurant, store, laundry. Also in the vicinity are a historic village, a fish culture station and a generating plant.

ODELL PARK

End of Rookwood Avenue, Fredericton, 506-458-8530; www.tourismnewbrunswick.ca

Unique example of the primeval forest of New Brunswick; part of the original land grant. Approximately 400 acres (160 hectares) include lodge, picnicking, play area, walking paths through woods; ski trails; arboretum with $1^3/_4$-mile (2.8-kilometer) trail.

OFFICERS' SQUARE

397 Queen St., Fredericton, 506-460-2129; www.tourismfredericton.ca

Park with Lord Beaverbrook statue; changing of the guard ceremonies (July-Labor Day); band concerts Tuesday and Thursday evenings (late June-August), theater in the park (July-August).

OLD OFFICERS' QUARTERS

397 Queen St., Fredericton; www.tourismfredericton.ca

Typical architecture of Royal Engineers in the Colonial period; stone arches, iron handrails and stone staircase. Older part (circa 1839-1840) near the river has thicker walls of solid masonry and hand-hewn timbers; later end (circa 1851) has thinner walls and sawn timbers.

YORK-SUNBURY HISTORICAL SOCIETY MUSEUM

571 Queen St., Fredericton, 506-455-6041; www.yorksunburymuseum.com.

Permanent and changing exhibits of military and domestic area history; seasonal exhibitions of history, New Brunswick crafts and fine arts.

SPECIAL EVENTS

HARVEST JAZZ AND BLUES FESTIVAL

King and Westmorland streets, Fredericton, 506-454-2583, 888-622-5837;
www.harvestjazzandblues.com

Five days of performances from newer and more established local and international musicians. Mid-September.

NEW BRUNSWICK HIGHLAND GAMES AND SCOTTISH FESTIVAL

Woodstock Road, Fredericton (on the grounds of Old Government House),
506-452-9244, 888-368-4444; www.highlandgames.ca

Immerse yourself in Scottish culture while listening to pipe bands, watching traditional dances, purchasing crafts and more. Last weekend in July.

NEW BRUNSWICK SUMMER CHAMBER MUSIC FESTIVAL

9 Bailey Drive, Fredericton, 506-453-4697; www.cel.unb.ca/music

Classical musicians celebrate chamber music at these outdoor concerts held throughout the downtown. Late August.

★★★DELTA FREDERICTON HOTEL

225 Woodstock Road, Fredericton, 506-457-7000, 888-890-3222; www.deltahotels.com

This brownstone hotel directly fronts the St. John River. The guest rooms are spacious, and the décor reflects a combination of styles. Rooms offer views of the river or surrounding woods, and the onsite bar is a local favorite gathering spot. 222 rooms. Restaurant, bar. Exercise room. Pool. **$$**

MONCTON

The Petitcodiac River and its branches twist and turn through this commercial and cultural center of the Atlantic provinces, becoming a mudflat clustered with sea gulls at the record-breaking low tides. Moncton is an excellent beginning for a tour to the northeast along the coast to beautiful Kouchibouguac National Park. Nearby, Shediac, "Lobster Capital of the World," boasts one of the finest beaches in Canada—Parlee Beach—with endless white sand dunes and the warmest ocean waters north of Virginia. Moncton, a bustling center with great shopping and plentiful amenities, hosts sailing regattas and hydroplane races, festivals, seafood and coastal relaxation.

WHAT TO SEE AND DO

FORT BEAUSEJOUR NATIONAL HISTORIC SITE

111 Fort Beauséjour Road, Aulac, approximately 37 miles (60 kilometers) East of Moncton on Highway 2, exit 550, 506-536-4399; www.pc.gc.ca

Built by the French between 1751 and 1755 during their long struggle with England for possession of Acadia. Attacked in 1755, the fort was captured by the British under Colonel Monckton who renamed it Fort Cumberland. Following its capture, the fort was strengthened and its defenses extended. During the American Revolution in 1776, it withstood an attack by revolutionaries. It was manned by a small garrison during the War of 1812. Three casements and a massive stone curtain wall have been restored; displays on history and the culture of Isthmus of Chignecto; outdoor paintings showing the garrison as it existed in 18th century. Panoramic view of site and surrounding salt marshes. June-mid-October.

FUNDY NATIONAL PARK

8642 Highway, Alma, 506-887-6000; www.pc.gc.ca/fundy

On the coast between Saint John and Moncton sits an extraordinary parcel of land—80 square miles (207 square kilometers) of forested hills and valleys crisscrossed by miles of hiking trails. Cliffs front much of the rugged coastline, home of the highest tides in the world. To view this phenomenon, visit the beaches at Herring Cove, Point Wolfe and the picturesque town of Alma. Since the ocean water is cold enough for only the bravest of souls, swim in the heated saltwater pool or in one of the lakes; golf, tennis, lawn bowling, picnicking, camping (May-October) and cross-country skiing are also available. Amphitheater programs and guided beach walks (June-August).

HOPEWELL ROCKS PROVINCIAL PARK

131 Discovery Road, Hopewell Cape, Albert County, 506-856-2940, 877-734-3429; www.thehopewellrocks.ca

Unique cliffs, caves and flowerpot-shaped pillars of conglomerate rock interspersed with shale and sandstone layers. The tourist information center has interpretive displays; tour guides are available. Visitors are advised to watch for caution signs, avoid loose cliff sections, stay off cliffs and return from the beach by the time posted at the stairs to avoid problems with rising tides. Picnicking, restaurant. May-October: daily.

MAGNETIC HILL ZOO

125 Magic Mountain Road, Moncton, 506-877-7718; www.moncton.org/zoo

Wild animal park and petting zoo; many species represented, including wildfowl. May-October: daily.

PARLEE BEACH PROVINCIAL PARK

45 Parlee Beach Road, Shediac, Pointe-du-Chêne, 506-533-3363; www.tourismnewbrunswick.ca

Parlee Beach boasts some of the warmest salt water north of Virginia, with vast sand dunes and clear swimming waters. Besides supervised swimming, enjoy volleyball, football and sand-sculpture competitions. Onsite are restaurants, a canteen, an amphitheater, showers, washrooms, a playground, picnic area and ample parking. Nearby you'll also find camping facilities, a marina, more restaurants, accommodations and cultural activities.

TIDAL BORE

655 Main St., Moncton, New Brunswick, 506-853-3590; www.moncton.ca

A small tidal wave running upstream to usher in the Bay of Fundy tides on the normally placid Petitcodiac River. The water level rises more than 25 feet in an hour. The bore arrives twice daily.

SPECIAL EVENTS

ATLANTIC SEAFOOD FESTIVAL

506-855-8525; www.atlanticseafoodfestival.com

Enjoy all things seafood while listening to musicians from the Maritime provinces and observing the culinary skills of international celebrity chefs. Mid-August.

SHEDIAC LOBSTER FESTIVAL

Shediac, 506-532-1122; www.shediaclobsterfestival.ca

Shediac hosts five days of fantastic seafood and world-class entertainment. Started in 1949, the Shediac Lobster Festival draws visitors from all over the world to feast on succulent lobster and soak up Acadian and maritime culture. Ride the midway, join in the kids' parade and enjoy daily musical performances. Early July.

HOTEL

★★★DELTA BEAUSEJOUR

750 Main St., Moncton, 506-854-4344, 800-268-1133; www.deltahotels.com

This stylish urban hotel is located in the heart of downtown Moncton, overlooking the Petitcodiac River. The spacious guest rooms feature contemporary décor. Guests can take advantage of bicycle rentals and walking maps available through the hotel. 310 rooms. Restaurant, bar. Pets accepted, fee. Exercise room. Pool. $$

AVALON TERRACE

739 Frampton Lane, Moncton, 506-854-6494, 888-833-7177; www.avalonterrace.com
Four rooms, all suites. Complimentary full breakfast. **$**

SAINT JOHN

The largest and oldest city in the province, this deep sea port was founded by loyalists to the British crown after the American Revolution. Saint John is a vibrant arts and entertainment community with pristine parks, steep, history-lined streets, quality dining, shopping and festivals. The highest tides in the world rise here, where the powerful Saint John River changes its flow at the Reversing Falls—a natural wonder to watch, but even more so to ride in a specially-designed jet boat. Day adventures from the city base include bird-watching, whale-watching, canoeing or kayaking the amazing Bay of Fundy ecosystem. Take a walking tour of the oldest incorporated city in Canada and shop at the historic Old City Market.

Information: www.tourismsaintjohn.com

WHAT TO SEE AND DO

BARBOUR'S GENERAL STORE

King and Water streets, Saint John, Market Slip area of downtown, 506-658-2855; www.tourismsaintjohn.com
This restored general store reflects the period between 1840 and 1940; 2,000 artifacts and a wide selection of old-fashioned grocery items, china, yard goods, farm implements and cooking tools; recreated post office; barbershop with wicker barber's chair; pharmacy with approximately 300 samples of cure-alls, potbellied stove; staff outfitted in period costumes. Mid-June-mid-September: daily.

CARLTON MARTELLO TOWER NATIONAL HISTORIC PARK

454 Whipple St., Saint John, 506-636-4011, 888-773-8888; www.pc.gc.ca
These circular coastal forts were built for the War of 1812 and used in World War II as a fire command post for harbor defenses when a two-story superstructure was added. Restored 1840s powder magazine; barrack room (circa 1865). Panoramic view of the city, harbor and surrounding landscape. Guided tours of the tower. June-mid-October: daily.

FERRY SERVICE TO DIGBY, NOVA SCOTIA

www.bayferries.com
Car and passenger ferry; 45 miles (72 kilometers). Reservations required.

IRVING NATURE PARK

1379 Sand Cove Road and Bleury Street, Saint John, 506-653-7367; www.jdirving.com
Features winding coastal road and hiking trails. Harbor seals, porpoises and many species of migrating birds can be viewed offshore. Picnicking.

95

NEW BRUNSWICK

LOYALIST HOUSE

120 Union St., Saint John, 506-652-3590; www.saintjohn.nbcc.nb.ca

Built by David Daniel Merritt, a United Empire Loyalist from New York. Six generations have lived in the house, a gracious Georgian mansion that remains much as it was when built with excellent craftsmanship in 1810-1817. July-August: daily; June and September: Monday-Friday; also by appointment.

NEW BRUNSWICK MUSEUM

1 Market Square, Saint John, 506-643-2300; www.nbm-mnb.ca

Canada's oldest continuous museum contains everything from international fine art and decorative objects to exhibits detailing the human and natural history of New Brunswick. Exhibits include skeletons of a right whale, a mastodon and a geologic trail through time.

OLD CITY MARKET

47 Charlotte St., Saint John, 506-658-2820; www.tourismsaintjohn.com

This centralized market dating to 1876 sells fresh meats and vegetables as well as indigenous baskets and handicrafts.

REVERSING FALLS

Catherwood Street, Saint John, 506-658-2937; www.tourismsaintjohn.com

As the tides of the Bay of Fundy rise and fall, they cause the water of the St. John River to change the direction of its flow.

TRINITY ROYAL HERITAGE PRESERVATION AREA

115 Charlotte St., Saint John, 506-693-8558; www.trinitysj.com

A 20-block heritage area located in the city center; 19th-century residential and commercial architecture; handicrafts and specialty goods.

HOTELS

★★DELTA BRUNSWICK

39 King St., Saint John, 506-648-1981, 888-890-3222; www.deltahotels.com

254 rooms. Restaurant, bar. Children's activity center. Pets accepted, fee. Exercise room. Pool. $$

★★★HILTON SAINT JOHN

1 Market Square, Saint John, 506-693-8484, 800-561-8282; www.saint-john.hilton.com

Connected by an above ground, sheltered pedway to the Saint John Trade and Convention Center, Market Square shopping mall, New Brunswick Museum, and Canada Games Aquatic Centre, this hotel overlooking the Saint John Harbor and waterfront is centrally located. Guest rooms feature white duvet-covered beds, large-view windows, large work desks and minibars. 197 rooms, Restaurant, bar. Exercise room. Pool. Business center $$

ST. ANDREWS

Dramatic scenery frames this oceanside golf mecca, a playground of the rich and famous through the years and long recognized as one of North America's premier destinations for the game. Much unchanged over the past 100 years, St. Andrews is a town of character and charm, complemented by many historic sites including the Algonquin Hotel, a War of 1812 Blockhouse, the Charlotte County Courthouse and an impressive collection of period homes. The old downtown commercial core is a shopper's paradise, especially renowned for handcrafts and woolen products. The Public Wharf at the center of town acts as the gateway to the abundant recreational water activities of Passamaquoddy Bay. The Fundy Isles dot the bay, the most famous of which is Campobello. Here, Franklin Delano Roosevelt spent his summers from 1905 to 1921 when he was stricken with infantile paralysis. Tours of Roosevelt's cottage in the International Park are available. Nearby, a ferry leaves for Grand Manan Island, a popular vacation destination with picturesque lighthouses and tiny fishing villages nestled in the barren seaside cliffs.

Information: www.townofstandrews.ca

WHAT TO SEE AND DO

ALGONQUIN GOLF COURSES

465 Brandy Cove Road, St. Andrews, 506-529-8165; www.fairmontgolf.com/courses
Opened in 1894, this 18-hole championship course offers wooded glades and beautiful shoreline views. Executive nine-hole woodland course. Late April-late October.

BLOCKHOUSE NATIONAL HISTORIC SITE

Harriet Street and Joe's Point Road, St. Andrews. Centennial Park,
506-529-4270; www.pc.gc.ca
Sole survivor of coastal defenses built during the War of 1812; restored in 1967. Mid-May-mid-October: daily.

HUNTSMAN MARINE SCIENCE CENTER AQUARIUM & MUSEUM

1 Lower Campus, St. Andrews, Brandy Cove Road, 506-529-1202;
www.huntsmanmarine.ca
Displays of coastal and marine environments with many fish and invertebrates found in waters of Passamaquoddy Region; "Touch Tank" allows visitors to handle marine life found on local rocky beaches. Displays of live animals including local amphibians, reptiles and a family of harbor seals. Exhibits on local geology; seaweed collection. May-early October: daily.

KINGSBRAE GARDEN

220 King St., St. Andrews, 506-529-3335, 866-566-8687;
www.kingsbraegarden.com
This garden contains 27 acres (11 hectares) of walking trails that pass more than 45,000 flowers, shrubs and other plants.

ROSS MEMORIAL MUSEUM

188 Montague St., St. Andrews, 506-529-5124; www.townsearch.com/rossmuseum
This museum, housed in a circa-1824 redbrick Georgian mansion, houses the furniture and art collection of a prominent local family.

NEW BRUNSWICK

★
★
★
★
☆

HOTELS

★★★THE FAIRMONT ALGONQUIN

184 Adolphus St., St. Andrews, 506-529-8823, 800-441-1414; www.fairmont.com

This seaside resort overlooks Passamaquoddy Bay, with an area of tidal changes that varies 28 feet between the high and low tides. Guest rooms feature period décor in the main historic building and a more contemporary style in the 1993 Prince of Wales wing. The fourth-floor rooms, originally the servants' quarters, offer the best views of the bay and surrounding countryside. Croquet, shuffleboard, and bocce ball are among the extensive activities offered. 234 rooms. Restaurant, bar. Spa, beach. Exercise room. Pool. Golf. Tennis. $$

★★★★KINGSBRAE ARMS

219 King St., St. Andrews, 506-529-1897; www.kingsbrae.com

Housed in a circa-1897 country house, this intimate inn overlooks the breathtaking Passamaquoddy Bay. Nearby are a renowned golf course, art galleries and the old town. Each suite has a gas fireplace, marble bathroom and a separate living room. The restaurant is popular with locals and visitors alike thanks to its focus on fresh, seasonal and local food, particularly seafood. Settle in for a pre-determined menu of several courses and enjoy a selection from the award-winning cellar. 9 rooms. Closed October-May. Complimentary full breakfast. Restaurant. Pets accepted. Pool. Business center. $$$$

SPECIALITY LODGING

PANSY PATCH

59 Carleton St., St. Andrews, 506-529-3834, 888-726-7972; www.pansypatch.com

Built in 1911 and modeled after a French residence, this turreted cottage and its extensive gardens remain one of the most photographed homes in New Brunswick. The attached gallery showcases works of local artisans, and rates for all rooms include afternoon tea. 9 rooms. Closed mid-October-April. Complimentary full breakfast. Restaurant. Exercise room. Tennis. $$$

RESTAURANTS

★★THE LIBRARY LOUNGE & BISTRO

184 Adolphus St., St. Andrews by the Sea, 506-529-8823; www.fairmont.com

American menu. Reservations recommended. Outdoor seating. $$

★★WINDSOR HOUSE OF ST. ANDREWS

132 Water St., St. Andrews, 506-529-3330, 888-890-9463

Seafood menu. Closed January-March. Reservations recommended. Outdoor seating. $$

★
★
★
★
★

NEWFOUNDLAND AND LABRADOR

NEWFOUNDLAND AND LABRADOR OFFER SO MANY ICONIC SOUNDS AND SCENES, IT'S ALMOST impossible to pick a representative few: thousand-year-old icebergs, multi-colored saltbox houses, fishing villages, fjords, lighthouses, whales, endless pubs and that Irish-origin lilt.

Wake up each day and walk outside, talk to the locals, tell them what mood you're in and see where it takes you. You might plan to tour the coastline by sea kayak one afternoon, but suddenly find yourself in a pub eating pan-fried cod. Or set out to tour a museum one morning and end up shopping along the oldest street in North America.

In Gros Morne National Park, exposed rock has been found that is 1.25 billion years old—as old as the planet itself. The mountains and fjords in this UNESCO World Heritage Site are 20 times older than the Rockies. Travel along some of the 10,500 miles (16,898 kilometers) of coastline to see 10,000-year-old icebergs drifting past or humpback whales in their annual migration to the north. See the Northern Lights from Labrador more than 240 nights a year, where endless wilderness shelters wildlife such as moose, black bears.

Thirty-five million seabirds gather in this province every year. Human visitors hike, bike and kayak, fish for Atlantic salmon and brook trout, dogsled, snowmobile, ski, golf on more than 20 courses and visit archaeological and historic sites.

Information: www.newfoundlandlabrador.com

FUN FACTS

George Street, located in downtown St. John's, is closed to traffic 20 hours a day and is widely understood to have the most pubs per square foot of any street in North America. Newfoundland has its own time zone, which is half an hour later than Atlantic Time.

CORNER BROOK

Corner Brook is nestled among the folded and faulted Long Range Mountains, a continuation of the Appalachian Mountain belt. The landscape of the Corner Brook region is rugged and the scenery is spectacular. The surrounding coastline holds magnificent fjords, jagged headlands, thickly forested areas and many offshore islands. Wildlife, forest and water mingle with the city's borders on all sides and mountains fill the horizon in all directions.

Information: www.cornerbrook.com

WHAT TO SEE AND DO
MARBLE MOUNTAIN
Route 1, Steady Brook, 709-637-7600, 888-462-7253; www.skimarble.com
Some of the best skiing east of the Rockies, and certainly one of the top ski destinations of the Canadian east. 1,600-foot (488-meter) vertical drop. Downhill, cross-country and cat skiing. Lodging.

TNL (THEATRE NEWFOUNDLAND AND LABRADOR)

Corner Brook, 709-639-7238; www.theatrenewfoundland.com

Theatre Newfoundland and Labrador (TNL) is a not-for-profit organization dedicated to creating and producing professional theater.

SPECIAL EVENTS

CORNER BROOK WINTER CARNIVAL

709-632-5343; www.cornerbrookwintercarnival.ca

The Corner Brook Winter Carnival is an annual community festival dedicated to the celebration of winter, fostering of community spirit and pride. Enjoy an enlivening blend of sports, recreation, entertainment and culture within a 'snowfunland' theme. Mid-February.

FESTIVAL 500 SHARING THE VOICES

709-738-6013; www.festival500.com

This international, biennial choral festival features choral groups from around the world and international guest performers. The festival occurs on several summer weekends in various places throughout the province. Mid-May-mid-July.

GRAND FALLS-WINDSOR

With above average temperatures in the summer and beautiful, snow covered winters, this bustling town offers year-round vitality and entertainment. The Town's major event for the year is the Exploits Valley Salmon Festival, held each July and chosen as one the Top 100 Events by the American Bus Association.

WHAT TO SEE AND DO

ANOTHER NEWFOUNDLAND DRAMA COMPANY

Royal Canadian Legion (Branch 12), Queen Street, Grand Falls-Windsor,
877-822-7469; www.andco.nf.ca

This local theater group entertains the town with dinner theater and lunch time shows held at the Royal Canadian Legion.

ATLANTIC SALMON INTERPRETIVE CENTRE

On the banks of the Exploits River, Grand Falls-Windsor, 709-489-7350;
www.asf.ca/interpretive.php

Located at Grand Falls Fishway. Exhibits on history, biology and habitat of the Atlantic Salmon. Underwater viewing windows and other live exhibits. Restaurant and gift shop.

SPECIAL EVENT

EXPLOITS VALLEY SALMON FESTIVAL

Route 1, Grand Falls-Windsor, 709-489-0407; www.salmonfestival.com

The annual Salmon Festival features an outdoor concert, stadium dances, a craft fair, salmon dinner and more. July.

ST. JOHN'S

For more than 500 years, St. John's—the provincial capital and home of Canada's greatest number of per-capita pubs—has been visited by European explorers, adventurers, soldiers and pirates. First discovered in 1497 by John Cabot and later claimed as the first permanent settlement in North America for the British Empire by Sir Humphrey Gilbert, St. John's has a rich and colorful history. St. John's is cradled in a harbor carved from granite and surrounded by hills running down to the ocean. This city is bursting with old world charm, unique architectural, historic and natural attractions and excellent facilities and services. And if that's not enough, a short drive brings visitors to spectacular coastlines, historic villages and a diverse selection of wildlife. *Information: www.stjohns.ca*

WHAT TO SEE AND DO

BOTANICAL GARDENS

306 Mount Scio Road, St. John's, 709-737-8590; www.mun.ca/botgarden
Memorial University's Botanical gardens cover 110 acres (45 hectares) of land close to the heart of St. John's. It is unusual in its dual purposes of botanical garden and natural reserve. The flower gardens include a rock garden, peat and woodland beds, cottage garden, perennial garden, rhododendrons and a display of Newfoundland heritage plants. Five nature trails meander through a managed natural reserve.

CAPE SPEAR NATIONAL HISTORIC SITE

Route 11, Blackhead/Cape Spear, 709-772-5367; www.pc.gc.ca
Just 6 miles (11 kilometers) from St. John's, Cape Spear National Historic Site is situated at the most eastern point in North America. Here, overlooking the North Atlantic, stands the oldest surviving lighthouse in Newfoundland, a World War II coastal defense battery and the place where the light of dawn is first seen in North America. Mid-May-mid-October.

THE FLUVARIUM

Pippy Park, Nagle's Place (North Bank of Long Pond), St. John's, 709-754-3474; www.fluvarium.ca
A unique facility on the shores of Long Pond in the heart of Pippy Park, this structure includes as series of nine panoramic viewing windows gives visitors a chance to see the secret underwater life of a river. This is the only year-round public fluvarium in North America. Exhibits related to freshwater ecology. Guided tours year round.

GRAND CONCOURSE WALKWAYS

439 Allandale Road, St. John's, 709-737-1077; www.grandconcourse.ca
More than 74 ½ miles (120 kilometers) of walkways connecting ponds, lakes and rivers in three municipalities make this one of the best walking networks in Canada.

INSTITUTE FOR OCEAN TECHNOLOGY

Prince Philip Drive, St. John's, 709-772-4939; www. iot-ito.nrc-cnrc.gc.ca
IOT is an innovative research facility for the ship technology and oil and gas industries. Learn how scale model ocean vessels are made and tested. See models of Hibernia and Terra Nova. View the ocean simulated indoors and the world's largest Ice Tank.

JOHNSON GEO CENTRE

175 Signal Hill Road, St. John's, 709-737-7880 , 866-868-7625; www.geocentre.ca
The Johnson Geo Centre tells the story of "Our Earth and Our People" through the remarkable geology of Newfoundland and Labrador. The large, glass-encased entry

NEWFOUNDLAND AND LABRADOR

is the only part of the building above ground. Most of the 33,600 square feet of floor space is underground.

MILE ONE CENTRE & ST. JOHN'S FOG DEVILS
50 New Gower St., 709-758-1111; www.mileonecentre.com
Mile One Centre is a first-class multipurpose sports and entertainment facility located next to City Hall on New Gower Street in the heart of downtown St. John's. It is home to the Quebec Major Junior Hockey League (QMJHL), the St. John's Fog Devils and will host numerous entertainment events, including concerts by top artists from around the world, ice shows, family shows, conventions and local hockey events.

NEWFOUNDLAND SCIENCE CENTRE
5 Beck's Cove, The Murray Premises, 709-754-0823
The Newfoundland Science Centre was created in 1993 to encourage interest and participation in science through informal education programs, interactive science displays and province-wide outreach programs. New exhibits arrive up to three times a year. The Centre also offers birthday parties, overnighters, science buskers, summer camps and more.

OCEAN SCIENCE CENTRE OF MEMORIAL UNIVERSITY
Marine Drive (Route 30), Logy Bay, 709-737-3708; www.mun.ca
The Ocean Sciences Centre is a cold ocean research facility operated in conjunction with Memorial University of Newfoundland. Located in Logy Bay, the Centre houses laboratories where research is conducted on the North Atlantic fishery, aquaculture, oceanography, ecology and physiology. Research is conducted on organisms ranging from bacteria to seals. In summer months, visitors experience an ocean life touch tank and Seal Facility.

THE ROOMS
9 Bonaventure Ave., St. John's (Fort Townsend), 709-757-8000; www.therooms.ca
Visit the new home housing the combined collections of the Provincial Archives of Newfoundland and Labrador, the Provincial Museum of Newfoundland and Labrador, and the Art Gallery of Newfoundland and Labrador. Sixteen galleries and exhibit halls, 180-seat multimedia theater and studio, restaurant, gift shop.

SIGNAL HILL NATIONAL HISTORIC SITE
Signal Hill Road, St. John's, 709-772-5367; www.pc.gc.ca
This site marks the spot where Marconi received the first transatlantic wireless signal in 1901. During the summer, watch cadets perform 19th-century British military drills.

ST. JOHN'S WATERFRONT
Harbor Drive, St. John's
To get a real sense of St. John's, a walk along the waterfront is a must. The harbor, located in historic downtown, has provided shelter to explorers, merchants, soldiers, pirates and mariners of all kinds over the last 500 years. Historic buildings, coves, plaques and parks along the route help depict the history of St. John's.

NEWFOUNDLAND AND LABRADOR

★
★
★
★
★

NOVA SCOTIA

NOVA SCOTIA HAS BEEN DESCRIBED AS A 'MUST-SEE' DESTINATION, AND CAPE BRETON HAS been lauded as the world's most scenic island. All this is thanks to the surprising contradictions of this compact land: a slick and sophisticated urban scene populated with down-to-earth friendly folk; sumptuous accommodations with a rustic twist; and Zen-like Oceanside relaxation alongside the kind of raucous parties and festivals epic to the most seasoned of sailors.

In Nova Scotia, a rich and diverse past is not just showcased at museums and heritage sites. It still lives and breathes in communities throughout the province—with ancient forts, cannons, saltbox houses and fishing villages standing unchanged. Cape Breton Island, in particular, offers a chance to truly explore this province's vivid Celtic culture and history. Here is where they say "ciad mile failte," which means "a hundred thousand welcomes." Throughout each of Nova Scotia's scenic highways, a cosmopolitan experience—from art galleries, live theatre, shopping, spas and major sports events—is presented against a setting of colorful history and rich tradition.

Historic waterfronts are home to great restaurants, live music and popular festivals that use the harbor as a backdrop, including the International Buskers Festival, the Riverfront Music Jubilee and the Tall Ships Challenge. Spend the day shopping at a stylish boutique in Wolfville or Truro. Find the perfect souvenir to remember your trip with a stop at one of the many historic markets or quaint gift shops in the busy shopping districts in Yarmouth Sydney. Spring Garden Road in Halifax, one of the country's oldest retail thoroughfares, is where you'll find the season's must-haves.

Visit the rugged Atlantic Coast and the rich Annapolis Valley, which rolls down to the Bay of Fundy where the world's highest tides rise and fall. Follow the Northumberland Shore where you'll find the warmest waters north of Virginia and long, stretches of beach. Witness the Highlands of Cape Breton rising above the sea. And follow the south shore from Halifax, a chain of seaside villages peppered with hidden coves, beaches, antique stores, crafts and bistros, anchored by Lunenburg, home of the famed Bluenose schooner and UNESCO World Heritage Site. Two beautiful national parks (Kejimkujik National Park and National Historic Site of Canada and the Cape Breton Highlands National Park) and over a hundred provincial parks add to the bounty.

FUN FACTS Marconi sent the first wireless (radio) message across the Atlantic Ocean, from Table Head, Cape Breton Island in 1902.

Information: www.novascotia.com

ANTIGONISH

This harbor town, the commercial and cultural home base for northeast Nova Scotia, was settled by Highland Scottish immigrants and American Revolutionary War soldiers and their families. Antigonish is home to the oldest continuously run Highland

Games in North America. Located just west of the Canso Causeway, the gateway to Cape Breton and its highlands, the town is surrounded by scenic rivers and hills.
Information: www.townofantigonish.ca/main.html

WHAT TO SEE AND DO
SHERBROOKE VILLAGE
42 Main St., Antigonish, 902-522-2400, 1-888-743-7845; www.museum.gov.ns.ca
Restored 1860s village reflects the area's former status as a prosperous river port. Historic buildings of that era are being restored and refurnished, including family homes, a general store, drugstore, courthouse, jail and post office; demonstrations of blacksmith forging, water-powered sawmill operation; horse-drawn wagon rides. Visitors can watch or try spinning, weaving and quilting. Restaurant. June-mid-October, daily.

ST. NINIAN'S CATHEDRAL
Antigonish, 902-863-2338; www.antigonishdiocese.com
Built in 1847 in Roman Basilica style of blue limestone and granite from local quarries. Interior decorated by Ozias LeDuc, Paris-trained Quebec artist. Gaelic words, Tigh Dhe (House of God), appear inside and out, representing the large Scottish population in the diocese who are served by the cathedral.

SPECIAL EVENT
HIGHLAND GAMES
Main Street and Columbus Field, Antigonish; www.antigonishhighlandgames.com
This Scottish festival comprises the longest running Highland Games in North America. Events include pipe band concerts, Highland dancing, traditional athletic events and a massed pipe band tattoo. Mid-July.

HOTELS
★★BEST WESTERN CLAYMORE INN
Church St., Antigonish, 902-863-1050; www.claymoreinn.com
75 rooms. Restaurant, bar. $

★★MARITIME INN
158 Main St., Antigonish, 902-863-4001, 877-768-3969; www.maritimeinns.com
32 rooms. Restaurant, bar. Pets accepted, fee. High-speed Internet access. $

RESTAURANT
★★LOBSTER TREAT
241 Post Road, Antigonish, 902-863-5465
Seafood menu. Closed January-April. $$

BADDECK
This tranquil, scenic village, situated midway between Canso Causeway and Sydney, is a good headquarters community for viewing the many sights on the Cabot Trail and around the Bras d'Or lakes. Fishing, hiking, swimming and picnicking are among favorite pastimes along the beautiful shoreline.
Information: www.baddeck.com

WHAT TO SEE AND DO

ALEXANDER GRAHAM BELL NATIONAL HISTORIC PARK

559 Chebucto St., Baddeck, 902-295-2069; www.capebretonisland.com

Three exhibition halls dealing with Bell's numerous fields of experimentation. Includes displays on his work with the hearing impaired, telephones, medicine, marine engineering and aerodynamics.

CAPE BRETON'S CELTIC MUSIC INTERPRETIVE CENTRE

Judique, 902-787-2708; www.celticmusicsite.com

Learn about the heritage and tradition of local music through photos, vintage recordings, interviews with musicians, live performances and various exhibits. Guided tours. July-August, Monday-Friday; other times by appointment.

CAPE BRETON CENTRE FOR CRAFT & DESIGN

322 Charlotte St., Sydney, 902-539-7491; www.capebretoncraft.com

Items of Scottish and Nova Scotian origins. Examples of handwoven blankets, ties, shopping bags, kilts, skirts.

CAPE BRETON HIGHLANDS NATIONAL PARK

16648 Cabot Trail, 57 miles north on Cabot Trail, Cheticamp,
902-224-2306, 888-773-8888; www.pc.gc.ca

The famous Cabot Trail, a modern 184-mile (294-kilometer) paved highway loop beginning at Baddeck, is among the most scenic drives in North America. It runs through this national park, offering visitors spectacular vistas, beaches and trails. The hiking trail system is large and diverse, providing access to the area's remote interior as well as allowing you to explore its rugged coastline. Beaches and campgrounds are plentiful and golf is also popular, with the Highlands Golf Links in Ingonish being one of the best 18-hole courses in Canada.

FORTRESS OF LOUISBOURG NATIONAL HISTORIC SITE

22 miles (35 kilometers) south of Sydney via Highway 22; www.fortress.uccb.ns.ca

This 11,860-acre (4,800-hectare) park includes the massive Fortress erected by the French between 1720 and 1745 to defend their possessions in the new world. It is the largest reconstructed 18th-century French fortified town in North America. Explore the governor's apartment, soldiers' barracks, the chapel, various guardhouses, the Dauphin Demi-Bastion, the King's storehouse, the engineer's house, several private dwellings and storehouses and the royal bakery. Sample 18th-century food amongst costumed guides who interpret the town as it was in 1744. June-September, daily; May and October, limited tours.

GAELIC COLLEGE

51779 Cabot Trail, St. Ann's, 902-295-3411; www.gaeliccollege.edu

The only institution of its kind in North America dedicated to preservation of Gaelic traditions; special summer and winter programs.

NOVA SCOTIA

★
★
★
★

GLENORA DISTILLERY

Route 19, Glenville, 902-258-2662, 800-839-0491; www.glenoradistillery.com

The only distillery in North America to produce single malt whisky. Museum, pub, restaurant, inn, gift shop. Distillery tours (May-October), Daily 9 a.m.-5 p.m. daily.

GREAT HALL OF THE CLANS

51779 Cabot Trail, St. Ann's, 902-295-3411; www.gaeliccollege.edu

Colorful historic display of Scot-origin clans, tartans and migrations. Genealogical and audiovisual section; life and times of Highland pioneers, relics of Cape Breton giant Angus MacAskill.

HOTELS

★★★AUBERGE GISELE'S INN

387 Shore Road, Baddeck, 902-295-2849, 800-304-0466; www.giseles.com

Overlooking the Bras d'Or Lakes, the inn is close to the Bell Bay Golf Course, Highland Links and Uisge Ban Falls Park. The inn offers bike rentals as well as sailing tours of the lake. Enjoy international cuisine at the award-winning restaurant or a cocktail in the lounge. 75 rooms. Closed mid-October-mid-May. Restaurant, bar. Wireless Internet access in all rooms. $

★★INVERARY RESORT

Highway 205, Baddeck, 902-295-3500, 800-565-5660; www.capebretonresorts.com

124 rooms. Restaurant, beach. Exercise room. Pool. Tennis. $$

★★★KELTIC LODGE RESORT AND SPA

Middle Head Peninsula, Ingonish Beach, 902-285-2880, 800-565-0444;
www.signatureresorts.com

Perched high on a cliff overlooking the Atlantic Ocean, this resort provides a choice of rooms in the main lodge, inn or cottages. A top golf course sits next door, and guests can also enjoy kayaking, hiking, whale-watching, beaches and complimentary bicycles. The Aveda concept spa offers massages and facials. 104 rooms. Closed late October-mid-May. Two restaurants, bar. Beach. Exercise room. Pool. $$$

★★SILVER DART LODGE

257 Shore Road, Baddeck, 902-295-2340, 888-662-7484; www.silverdart.com

88 rooms. Closed mid-October-April. Restaurant, bar. Pool. Tennis, Fitness center. $

RESTAURANT

★★GRUBSTAKE

7499 Main St., Louisbourg, 902-733-2308; grubstake.ca

Steak menu. Closed October-mid-June. $$$

DIGBY

Best known for its delicious scallops and picturesque harbor, this summer resort has many historic landmarks that date back to its founding in 1783 by Sir Robert Digby and 1,500 Loyalists from New England and New York. This Annapolis Basin town is the ideal headquarters for adventures down the Digby Neck peninsula, whose Bay of

Fundy shores measure the highest tides in the world. Off Digby Neck are Long Island and Brier Island, reachable by ferry—both are popular sites for rock collecting, whale watching and bird watching. Swim along sandy beaches and hike shoreline trails past lighthouses and wildflower-filled forests. A 35-mile (11-kilometer) drive to the northeast leads to Annapolis Royal and Port Royal, the first permanent European settlements in North America. Marking this is the restored fur trading fort, the Habitation of Port Royal, built by Samuel de Champlain. With high, imposing cliffs, gently rolling farmland and quiet woodland settings, this seacoast drive creates a study in contrasts.
Information: www.townofdigby.ns.ca

WHAT TO SEE AND DO

FORT ANNE NATIONAL HISTORIC SITE
St. George and Prince Albert streets, 902-532-2397; www.pc.gc.ca
Built between 1702 and 1708 in one of the central areas of conflict between the English and French for control of North America. Of the original site, only the 18th-century earthworks and a gunpowder magazine remain. Museum in restored officers' quarters. On the grounds is Canada's oldest English graveyard, dating from 1720.

POINT PRIM LIGHTHOUSE
Lighthouse and Bayview roads, Digby, 888-463-4429
Rocky promontory with a view of the Bay of Fundy.

PORT ROYAL NATIONAL HISTORIC SITE
53 Historic Lane, Annapolis Royal, 902-532-2898; www.pc.gc.ca
Reconstructed 17th-century fur trading post built by Sieur de Monts. Costumed interpreters deliver talks on the history of the settlement. Mid-May-mid-October, daily.

TRINITY CHURCH
109 Queen St., Digby, 902-245-6744; www.unityserve.org/trinity
The only church in Canada built by shipwrights; the church cemetery is famous for inscriptions by pioneer settlers. Open Monday-Friday; Sunday services.

SPECIAL EVENT

SCALLOP DAYS
Water Street, Digby, 902-245-4531; www.digbyscallopdays.com
Scallop-shucking contests; parade, pet show, entertainment; sporting, fishing, water events. Second week in August.

HOTELS

★★ADMIRAL DIGBY INN
441 Shore Road, Digby, 902-245-2531, 800-465-6262; www.digbyns.com
46 rooms. Closed mid-October-mid-May. Complimentary continental breakfast. Restaurant, bar. Pets accepted, fee. Pool. $

★★COASTAL INN KINGFISHER
111 Warwick Street, Digby, 902-245-4747; www.coastalinns.com
36 rooms. Restaurant. Business center. High-speed internet access. $

NOVA SCOTIA

★
★
★
★
☆

★★DIGBY PINES GOLF RESORT & SPA

103 Shore Road, Digby, 902-245-2511, 800-667-4637; www.signatureresorts.com

Built in 1929, this resort is located in a magnificent setting on a terraced hillside, overlooking the Annapolis Basin. The public rooms are spacious, with many of the original furnishings still in use. Guest rooms reflect the period as well. The property is located approximately one mile from the Saint John's ferry terminal. 147 rooms. Closed mid-October-mid-May. Complimentary full breakfast. Four restaurants, two bars. Pool. Golf. Tennis. **$$**

RESTAURANT

★★FUNDY RESTAURANT

34 Water St., Digby, 902-245-4950; www.fundyrestaurant.com

Seafood menu. Outdoor seating. Dinner. **$$**

GRAND PRÉ

Grand-Pré is a heartland of Acadian culture in Canada—a rich tapestry of history in a pastoral setting of rolling hills, charming villages and vineyards. Founded by Acadian settlers who remained there until their expulsion sbegan in 1755 (immortalized by Henry Wadsworth Longfellow with his epic poem, "Evangeline"), the village of Grand Pré has provided a home for immigrant farmers and artisans for more than 300 years. One of Nova Scotia's best-known wineries, Domaine de Grand Pré, is an evocative culinary destination. Grand-Pré is also Canada's first designated Historic Rural District.

Information: www.valleyweb.com/grandpre

NOVA SCOTIA

WHAT TO SEE AND DO

ACADIAN MEMORIAL CHURCH

1 Annapolis Valley RR, Grand Pré, 902-490-5946;
www.acadian-home.org/grand-pre-church

Display commemorating Acadian settlement and expulsion. Old Acadian Forge; bust of Longfellow Evangeline statue; formal landscaped gardens with original French willows. Guides available.

GRAND PRÉ NATIONAL HISTORIC SITE

Grand Pré, 902-542-3631; www.pc.gc.ca

Grand Pre commemorates the Acadian settlement from 1682 through1755 and the Deportation of the Acadians, which began in 1755 and continued until 1762. Interpretive presentations and multimedia exhibits, mid-May-mid-October. Grounds and gardens open daily.

HOTELS

★★★BLOMIDON INN

195 Main St., Wolfville, 902-542-2291, 800-565-2291; www.blomidon.ns.ca

This inn, overlooking the Bay of Fundy, was built as a sea captain's mansion. The inn includes 4 acres (1.6 hectares) of Victorian gardens, and quaint rooms decorated with antiques. 29 rooms. Closed 10 days in December. Complimentary continental breakfast. Restaurant. Tennis. High-speed Internet access. Pets not accepted. **$$**

★★OLD ORCHARD INN

Highway 101, exit 11, Wolfville, 902-542-5751, 800-561-8090; www.oldorchardinn.com

105 rooms. Restaurant, bar, children's activity center. Pets accepted, fee. Pool. Tennis. High-speed Internet access. $$

★★★TATTINGSTONE INN

620 Main St., Wolfville, 902-542-7696, 800-565-7696; www.tattingstone.ns.ca

This inn is located in the center of Wolfville. Victorian and Georgian period antiques fill the comfortable and inviting rooms. Meals incorporate the locally grown produce. 10 rooms. Complimentary full breakfast. Restaurant. Pool. Tennis. $

SPECIALITY LODGING

VICTORIA'S HISTORIC INN

600 Main St., Wolfville, 902-542-5744, 800-556-5744; www.victoriashistoricinn.com

15 rooms. Complimentary full breakfast. $

HALIFAX AND DARTMOUTH

The capital of Nova Scotia, and the largest city in the Atlantic Provinces, offers a delightful combination of old and new. Founded in 1749 as England's stronghold in the North Atlantic, it is a bustling commercial, scientific and educational center. Centrally situated in the province, Halifax is perfectly suited as the starting point for the Evangeline and Glooscap Trails, the Lighthouse Route and the Marine Drive with their scenic and historic sights. With the world's second-largest natural harbor and an array of historical sites, fishing villages, beaches and pubs within its municipal borders, this city promises some of the most diverse explorations of any urban center in Canada.

Information: www.halifaxinfo.com

WHAT TO SEE AND DO

ART GALLERY OF NOVA SCOTIA

1723 Hollis St., Halifax, 902-424-7542; www.agns.gov.ns.ca

More than 2,000 works are on permanent display, including folk art; changing exhibits. Open daily.

BLACK CULTURAL CENTRE

1149 Main St., Dartmouth, Route 7 at Cherrybrook Road,
902-434-6223, 800-465-0767; www.bccns.com

History and culture of Africans in Nova Scotia, which was the destination for many on the Underground Railroad that led escaped slaves from American plantations. The area, not coincidentally, was also home to the first free black community in North America. Library, exhibit rooms, auditorium.

HALIFAX CITADEL NATIONAL HISTORIC PARK

5425 Sackville and Brunswick Streets, Halifax, 902-426-5080; www.pc.gc.ca

The most visited historic site in Canada. Star-shaped hilltop fort built between 1828 and 1856. Restored signal masts, library, barrack rooms, powder magazine, expense magazine, defense casement and garrison cell. Exhibits on communications, the four Citadels and engineering and construction. Army Museum; orientation center. Coffee

★
★
★
★
☆

bar serving typical 19th-century soldiers' food; sales outlet; guided tours, military displays by uniformed students, bagpipe music, changing of the guard.

HARBOUR HOPPER TOURS
1751 Lower Water St., Halifax, 902-490-8687; www.harbourhopper.com
Narrated tours in amphibious vehicles styled after World War II landing craft. May-late October, daily.

HISTORIC PROPERTIES (PRIVATEERS WHARF)
1869-1870 Upper Water St., Halifax, 902-422-3077; www.historicproperties.ca
Variety of clothing, specialty shops, restaurants and pubs housed in several restored 18th-century buildings along the waterfront.

MARITIME MUSEUM OF THE ATLANTIC
1675 Lower Water St., Halifax, 902-424-7490; www.museum.gov.ns.ca/mma
The museum contains 1,675 exhibits showcasing more than 24,000 artifacts that tell the nautical history of Nova Scotia, including an informative exhibit on the *Titanic*. November-April, closed Monday.

MURPHY'S ON THE WATER
1751 Lower Water St., Halifax, 902-420-1015; www.murphysonthewater.com
Three harbor tour boats. Live narration and historical commentary; two-hour tour. May-mid-October, daily.

NEPTUNE THEATRE
1593 Argyle St., Halifax, 902-429-7070; www.neptunetheatre.com
Home of the internationally recognized theater company; presents five main stage plays per season. Small, intimate theater with excellent acoustics. Reservations advised.

NOVA SCOTIA MUSEUM OF NATURAL HISTORY
1747 Summer St., Halifax, 902-424-7353; www.museum.gov.ns.ca/mnh
Permanent exhibits on man and his environment in Nova Scotia; changing exhibits.

★
★
★
★

PIER 21
1055 Marginal Road, Halifax, 902-425-7770; www.pier21.ns.ca
Pier 21 is Canada's Ellis Island. Between 1928 and 1971, more than 1 million immigrants and wartime evacuees took their first steps on Canadian soil here. Now a National Historic Site, the pier features traveling exhibits, live performances, the Wall of Ships, Immigrant Testimonial Stations and the Wall of Honor.

POINT PLEASANT PARK
5718 Point Pleasant Drive, Halifax, 902-421-6519; www.pointpleasantpark.ca
Visit ruins of several historic forts in the heart of the city. Nature trail, monuments, public beach, picnic areas; cross-country skiing.

PRINCE OF WALES TOWER NATIONAL HISTORIC PARK

S. Tower Road, Point Pleasant Park, Halifax, 902-426-5080; www.pc.gc.ca

Known locally as Martello Tower, this fort was built in the late 1790s to protect British batteries and is said to be first tower of its type in North America. Exhibits portray tower's history, architectural features and significance as a defensive structure. July-early September, 10 a.m.-6 p.m.

PROVINCE HOUSE

1726 Hollis St., Halifax, 902-424-4661; www.gov.ns.ca/legislature

Oldest provincial Parliament building in Canada; office of Premier; legislative library. Guided tours.

PUBLIC ARCHIVES OF NOVA SCOTIA

6016 University Ave., Halifax, 902-424-6060; www.gov.ns.ca/nsarm

Provincial government records, private manuscripts, maps, photos, genealogies, film and sound archives; library, Daily.

PUBLIC GARDENS

5711 Sackville St., Halifax, 902-421-6550; www.halifaxpublicgardens.ca

A more than 16-acre (7-hectare) formal Victorian garden begun by the Nova Scotia Horticultural Society in 1836, with trees, flower beds, fountains; bandstand; duck ponds; concession. The gardens were designated a National Historic Site in 1984. April-November. Pets not allowed; no bikes in the garden; no jogging.

QUAKER WHALER'S HOUSE

57 Ochterloney St., Dartmouth, 902-464-2253;
www.dartmouthheritagemuseum.ns.ca

Originally the home of William Ray, the house is considered one of the oldest domestic structures in the metro area. William Ray was a cooper (barrel maker) who came to Dartmouth as part of a community of Quakers who established a whale fishing industry of Dartmouth. Quaker House is restored and furnished to reflect its era of 1785. Guides provide tours. Herb garden open to visitors. June-September.

SHEARWATER AVIATION MUSEUM

13 Bonaventure Ave., Dartmouth, Shearwater Airport, 902-460-1083;
www.shearwateraviationmuseum.ns.ca

Extensive collection of aircraft and exhibits on the history of Canadian Maritime Military Aviation. Art gallery; photo collection. Daily 10 a.m.-5 p.m.; December-March by appointment only. Closed Monday.

ST. GEORGE'S ROUND CHURCH

2222 Brunswick St., Halifax, 902-423-1059; www.roundchurch.ca

Byzantine-style church built in 1801 at the direction of Edward, Duke of Kent, father of Queen Victoria. Nearby is St. Patrick's Roman Catholic Church, a Victorian Gothic building. On Barrington Street is St. Paul's Church, the first church in Halifax and oldest Protestant church in Canada. "Explosion window" on Argyle Street side; during a 1917 explosion that destroyed a large portion of the city, the third window of the upper gallery shattered, leaving the silhouette of a human head. Tours June-September, daily.

YORK REDOUBT NATIONAL HISTORIC SITE

Purcell's Cove Road, Halifax, 6 miles (9.7 kilometers) southwest of Halifax,
902-426-5080; www.pc.gc.ca

A 215-year-old fortification on a high bluff overlooking the harbor entrance. Features muzzle-loading guns, photo display, picnic facilities, information service. Grounds open daily. Mid-June-Labour Day, daily.

SPECIAL EVENTS

ATLANTIC JAZZ FESTIVAL

Spring Garden Road and Queen, Halifax, 902-492-2225; www.jazzeast.com

JazzEast's mandate runs from the promotion and presentation of soft-seat concerts and bar gigs to planning educational workshops (such as the renowned Creative Music Workshop). It features amateur musicians and established local artists and also attracts world-famous performers. July.

DARTMOUTH NATAL DAY

Lake Banook, Dartmouth, 902-490-6773; www.natalday.org

Parade, sports events, rowing and paddling regattas, entertainment, fireworks. First Monday in August.

HALIFAX HIGHLAND GAMES & SCOTTISH FESTIVAL

Wanderer's Grounds base of Citadel Hill, Sackville Street and Bell Road, Halifax,
902-876-0189; www.halifaxhighlandgames.com

The games are the centerpiece of five days celebrating Scottish culture, including competitions in piping, drumming, pipe bands and heavyweight events. Theme concessions, food vendors and beer tent with Celtic music onsite. July.

INTERNATIONAL BUSKERFEST

Halifax, 902-429-3910; www.buskers.ca

Street performers from all over the world come to Halifax for this 10-day event along the waterfront, put on by the Atlantic Busker Festival Society. August.

MULTICULTURAL FESTIVAL

Alderney Landing, Alderney Drive and Ochterloney St., Dartmouth,
902-423-6534, 800-565-0000; www.multifest.ca

The festival celebrates Nova Scotia's diversity through performances, workshops, food vendors and visual displays. The three-day event takes place on the Dartmouth waterfront. Mid-June.

NOVA SCOTIA INTERNATIONAL AIR SHOW

Shearwater Airport Hines Road and Pleasant Street (Highway 322),
Shearwater, 902-465-2725; www.nsairshow.ca

One of the premier air spectaculars in North America. September.

NOVA SCOTIA INTERNATIONAL TATTOO

Halifax Metro Centre, 1800 Argyle St., Halifax, 902-451-1221; www.nstattoo.ca

The world's largest indoor variety show, with more than 2,000 Canadian and international performers. The 10-day event features military bands, pipes and drums, choirs, gymnasts, dancers and military displays and competitions. Late June-early July.

HOTELS

★★BLUE NOSE INN & SUITES

636 Bedford Highway, Halifax, 902-443-3171; www.bluenoseinnandsuites.com

51 rooms. Restaurant. Free high-speed Internet access. Pets not accepted. Pool. **$**

★★CAMBRIDGE SUITES HOTEL

1583 Brunswick St., Halifax, 902-420-0555, 800-565-1263;
www.cambridgesuiteshotel.com

200 rooms, all suites. Complimentary continental breakfast. Restaurant, bar, Fitness center. Wireless Internet access. **$$**

★★★CITADEL HALIFAX HOTEL

1960 Brunswick St., Halifax, 902-422-1391, 800-565-7162; www.citadelhalifax.com

This comfortable hotel offers a convenient location for both business and leisure travelers. It is adjacent to the Citadel Hill National Historic Site and close to the World Trade and Convention Centre. 267 rooms. Restaurant, bar. Pets accepted, fee. Exercise room. Pool. Business center. **$**

★★★DELTA BARRINGTON

1875 Barrington St., Halifax, 902-429-7410, 888-890-3222; www.deltahotels.com

Connected by the Downtown Link—an enclosed, above ground pedestrian walkway—to two shopping centers, this downtown hotel is also a block from the waterfront. Comfortable guest rooms feature Nova Scotia country pine furniture and pillow-top mattresses. An enclosed central courtyard provides a view of greenery to inner rooms and corridors. 200 rooms. Restaurant, bar. Pets accepted, fee. Exercise room. Pool. **$$**

★★★DELTA HALIFAX

1990 Barrington St., Halifax, 902-425-6700, 888-890-3222; www.deltahotels.com

Located in the heart of downtown, this hotel is adjacent to the Scotia Square Shopping Centre and connected to the pedway. Guest rooms are comfortable and include luxury bath ameneties. 296 rooms. Restaurant, bar. Pets accepted, fee. Exercise room. Pool. Business center. **$$**

★★★HALIFAX MARRIOTT HARBOURFRONT

1919 Upper Water St., Halifax, 902-421-1700; www.marriott.com

This hotel is the home of the only Halifax casino and is located in the heart of downtown. Rooms feature updated linens and pillowtop mattresses, plus large workspaces. 352 rooms. Two restaurants, bar. Pets accepted, fee. Exercise room. Pool. Business center. Fitness center. **$$**

★★HOLIDAY INN HALIFAX-HARBORVIEW

101 Wyse Road, Dartmouth, 902-463-1100, 888-434-0440; www.holiday-inn.com

196 rooms. Restaurant, bar. Pets accepted, fee. Pool. Business center. High-speed Internet access. Fitness center. **$$**

113

NOVA SCOTIA

★
★
★
★
★

★★HOLIDAY INN SELECT HALIFAX CENTRE

1980 Robie St., Halifax, 902-423-1161, 888-810-7288; www.holiday-inn.com

232 rooms. Restaurant, bar. Pets accepted, fee. Pool. Business center. High-speed Internet access. $$

★★★THE LORD NELSON HOTEL & SUITES

1515 S. Park St., Halifax, 902-423-6331, 800-565-2020; www.lordnelsonhotel.com

Conveniently located in downtown Halifax, the Lord Nelson is across the street from the Victorian-style Halifax Public Gardens, a block south of Citadel Hill and close to Dalhousie University. 260 rooms. Restaurant, bar. Pets accepted, fee. Wireless Internet access. Fitness center. $$$

★★★OAK ISLAND RESORT AND SPA

36 Treasure Drive, Western Shore, 902-627-2600, 800-565-5075;
www.oakislandinn.com

This oceanfront resort approximately one hour's drive from Halifax overlooks Mahone Bay and its many islands, including the famous Oak Island, rumored to be the hiding place of Captain Kidd's buried treasure. 105 rooms. Restaurant, bar. Pets accepted, fee. Pool. Tennis. Business center. $$

★★PARK PLACE HOTEL & CONFERENCE CENTER RAMADA PLAZA

240 Brownlow Ave., Dartmouth, 902-468-8888, 800-561-3733; www.ramadans.com

178 rooms, Restaurant, bar. Pets accepted, fee. Pool. Business center. Wireless Internet access. $$

★
★
★
★
★

★★PRINCE GEORGE HOTEL

1725 Market St., Halifax, 902-425-1986, 800-565-1567; www.princegeorgehotel.com

This downtown hotel has classically decorated guest rooms with mahogany furnishings and comfortable beds. A covered walkway connects the hotel to the World Trade and Convention Centre, the Halifax Metro Centre, and the Halifax Casino. 203 rooms. Two restaurants, bar. Pets accepted, fee. Pool. Business center. Fitness center. $$

★★★THE WESTIN NOVA SCOTIAN

1181 Hollis St., Halifax, 902-421-1000, 888-679-3784; www.westin.ns.ca

This historic brick hotel, originally built as a Canadian National Railway hotel, is located just above the Halifax Harbor Waterfront. The hotel includes an Aveda concept spa, a lighted waterfront tennis court and conference and banquet facilities. The lobby is richly traditional in design and furnishings, and guest rooms are well stocked with amenities. 310 rooms. Restaurant, bar, children's activity center. Pool. Business center. $$

SPECIALITY LODGINGS

DAUPHINEE INN

167 Shore Club Road, Hubbards, 902-857-1790, 800-567-1790;
www.dauphineeinn.com

Six rooms. Closed November-April. Complimentary continental breakfast. Restaurant. $

WAVERLEY INN

1266 Barrington St., Halifax, 902-423-9346, 800-565-9346; www.waverleyinn.com
34 rooms. Wireless Internet access. Complimentary continental breakfast. **$**

RESTAURANTS
★★ROCCO'S

313 Prince Albert Road, Dartmouth, 902-461-0211; www.roccosrestaurant.ca
Italian menu. Breakfast, lunch, dinner. **$$**

★★★SALTY'S ON THE WATERFRONT

1869 Upper Water St., Halifax, 902-423-6818; www.saltys.ca
A blue-and-white-striped awning welcomes you to this casual seafood restaurant at the end of the Privateers, a 19th-century wharf, overlooking the Halifax Harbor in the Historic Properties area of downtown. Sample fresh lobsters or grilled swordfish sourced in local waters. Seafood menu. Outdoor seating. Lunch, dinner. **$$$**

★★SOU'WESTER

178 Peggy's Cove Road, Peggy's Cove, 902-823-2561; www.peggys-cove.com
Seafood menu. **$$**

TOWN OF LUNENBURG

Lunenburg, a UNESCO World Heritage Site founded in 1753 by German, Swiss and Montbeliardian Protestants under British patronage, is a mecca of architectural delights and rich marine history. Many of the homes and buildings date back to the mid-1700s. Lunenburg is also the home of Canada's only tall ship, the *Bluenose II*, a replica of the legendary racing champion on the Canadian 10-cent coin. In 1992, the Government of Canada designated "Old Town" Lunenburg as a National Historic District. In 1995, the World Heritage Committee, under the auspices of UNESCO, recognized Lunenburg's cultural and natural heritage by adding it to their World Heritage List. Despite all this recognition, the town offers up a working, authentic heritage as opposed to a canned tourist experience—and some of the best fishcakes and sauerkraut in the country.
Information: www.town.lunenburg.ns.ca

WHAT TO SEE AND DO
BLUENOSE II

Lunenburg waterfront, 800-565-0000; 902-634-4794; www.bluenose2.ns.ca
Bluenose Preservation Trust. An exact replica of the famed racing schooner depicted on the Canadian dime; public cruises tour Nova Scotia's waters.

FISHERIES MUSEUM OF THE ATLANTIC

68 Bluenose Ave., Lunenburg, 902-634-4794, 1-866-579-4909;
www.museum.gov.ns.ca/fma
Learn about offshore and inshore fisheries through exhibits, films and artifacts. Boat shop, model schooner. May-October, daily 9:30 a.m.-5:30 p.m.; off-season, Monday-Friday 8:30 a.m.-4:30 p.m.

SPECIALITY LODGINGS

1775 SOLOMON HOUSE B&B

69 Townsend St., Lunenburg, 902-634-3477; www.bbcanada.com

Three rooms. Inquire before bringing children. Full breakfast. Pets not accepted. **$$**

BOSCAWEN INN

150 Cumberland St., Lunenburg, 902-634-3325, 800-354-5009; www.boscawen.ca

33 rooms. Full breakfast. Pets accepted, fee. **$$**

KAULBACH HOUSE

75 Pelham St., Lunenburg, 902-634-8818, 800-568-8818; www.kaulbachhouse.com

Three rooms. Inquire before bringing children. Full breakfast. Wireless Internet access. **$$**

LUNENBURG ARMS HOTEL

94 Pelham St., Lunenburg, 902-640-4040, 800-679-4950; www.lunenburgarms.com

26 rooms. Restaurant, bar. Spa. Pets accepted. **$$**

RESTAURANTS

★THE GRAND BANKER SEAFOOD BAR & GRILL

82 Montague St., Lunenburg, 902-634-3300; www.grandbanker.com

Seafood. Lunch, dinner, brunch. Children's menu. **$$**

★THE KNOT PUB

4 Dufferin St., Lunenburg, 902-634-3334

Seafood menu. Dinner. **$**

★★MAGNOLIA'S GRILL

128 Montague St., Lunenburg, 902-634-3287

Seafood menu. Dinner. Closed winter. **$**

★THE OLD FISH FACTORY

68 Bluenose Drive, Lunenburg, 902-634-3333, 800-533-9336; www.oldfishfactory.com

Seafood menu. Lunch, dinner. **$$**

TRURO

Truro, once known as the hub of Nova Scotia for its location at the junction between the Canadian National Railway (running between Halifax and Montreal) and the Cape Breton and Central Nova Scotia Railway (running between Truro and Sydney), is one of those towns that's on the way to everywhere—or at least a stopping point from Halifax to everywhere. But Truro has a unique appeal of its own, with a charming heritage main street and a surprising number of attractions and dining establishments for a small town. When the town lost many trees after an outbreak of Dutch Elm disease, locals created unique wooden sculptures from the stumps of lost trees throughout downtown.

Information: www.town.truro.ns.ca

WHAT TO SEE AND DO
COLCHESTER HISTORICAL SOCIETY MUSEUM
29 Young St., Truro, 902-895-6284; www.genealogynet.com/colchester
Exhibits depict human and natural history of the county; changing exhibits. Archives, genealogy library.

LITTLE WHITE SCHOOLHOUSE MUSEUM
Nova Scotia Community College, 20 Arthur St., Truro,
902-895-5170; www.lwsm.ednet.ns.ca
One-room schoolhouse built in 1871, furnished with desks, artifacts and textbooks from 1867-1952. June-August, daily; rest of year, by appointment.

TIDAL BORE
Highway 102 and Tidal Bore Road, Truro, 902-895-9241; www.tidalboreinn.com
A wave of water rushes backward up the Salmon River before high tide. Bores range in height from a ripple to several feet. A timetable can be obtained from the Chamber of Commerce.

VICTORIA PARK
Brunswick St. and Park Road, Truro, 902-893-6078; www.town.truro.ns.ca
A 1,000-acre protected forest which contains hiking trails, an outdoor pool, a playground, tennis courts, picnic grounds and a baseball field, as well as Lepper Brook, which has two waterfalls that may be seen from several walking trails.

SPECIAL EVENT
INTERNATIONAL TULIP FESTIVAL
577 Prince St., Truro, 902-895-9258; www.tulipfestival.ca
More than 250,000 tulips planted in flower gardens throughout the city. Picnics, art displays, entertainment. Late May.

HOTELS
★★BEST WESTERN GLENGARRY
150 Willow St., Truro, 902-893-4311, 800-567-4276; www.bestwestern.com
90 rooms. Restaurant, bar. Pool. High-speed Internet access. Pets not accepted. $

★WILLOW BEND MOTEL
277 Willow St., Truro, 902-895-5325, 800-594-5569; www.willowbendmotel.com
28 rooms. Complimentary continental breakfast. Pool. $

YARMOUTH
This historic seaport is the largest town southwest of Halifax and the gateway to Nova Scotia from New England. During the 1800s, this was one of the major shipbuilding ports in the world. Travel north on the Evangeline Trail, which passes through French Acadian settlements, fishing centers and rich orchards and farmlands. Going south, follow the Lighthouse Route, which parallels the Atlantic coastline and passes near many picturesque lighthouses, beaches and fishing ports.
Information: www.aboutyarmouth.com

WHAT TO SEE AND DO

CAPE FORCHU LIGHTHOUSE
Cape Forchu Island, 7 miles (11 kilometers) southwest of Yarmouth, linked
by causeway to the mainland, 800-565-0000; www.capeforchulight.com
Entrance to Bay of Fundy and Yarmouth Harbor. Route travels along rocky coastline
and through colorful fishing villages.

THE CAT
58 Water St., Yarmouth, 902-742-6800; www.catferry.com
Advance reservations required. Passenger and car ferry service to Bar Harbor, Maine.
June-October.

FIREFIGHTERS' MUSEUM OF NOVA SCOTIA
451 Main St., Yarmouth, 902-742-5525; www.firefighters.museum.gov.ns.ca
Permanent display of history of firefighting service, including hand pumps, steamers
and horse-drawn apparatus. July-August, Monday-Saturday 9 a.m.-9 p.m., Sunday
10 a.m.-5 p.m.; June and September, Monday-Saturday 9 a.m.-5 p.m.; October-May,
Monday-Friday 9 a.m.-4 p.m., Saturday 1-4 p.m.

YARMOUTH ARTS REGIONAL CENTRE
76 Parade St., Yarmouth, 902-742-8150; www.yarcplayhouse.com
Center for visual and performing arts for southwestern Nova Scotia. Summer theater,
drama, musical comedy, concerts, art shows, courses, workshops and seminars.

NOVA SCOTIA

YARMOUTH COUNTY MUSEUM AND ARCHIVES
22 Collins St., Yarmouth, 902-742-5539; www.yarmouthcountymuseum.ednet.ns.ca
Displays detail the history of the county, with an emphasis on the Victorian period.
Features marine exhibits, period rooms, blacksmith shop and a stagecoach. Of special
interest is a runic stone found near Yarmouth Harbor in 1812, bearing a clear inscrip-
tion alleged to be left by Leif Ericson on a voyage in 1007; Yarmouth Lighthouse
lens.

SPECIAL EVENTS

SEAFEST
Waterfront Water and Lovitt streets, Yarmouth, 902-742-7585;
www.playarmouthevents.com
Sporting events, entertainment, cultural productions, parade, Queen's Pageant. Dory
races, Fish feast. Mid-July.

★
★
★
★
☆

WESTERN NOVA SCOTIA EXHIBITION
Western Nova Scotia Exhibition Grounds, Cottage Lane and Forest Street,
Yarmouth, 902-742-8222. www.yarmouthexhibition.com
Equestrian events, agricultural displays, craft demonstrations and exhibits, midway
and entertainment. Early August.

HOTELS

★BEST WESTERN MERMAID

545 Main St., Yarmouth, 902-742-7821, 800-772-2774; www.bestwestern.com

45 rooms, Restaurant, bar. Pool. High-speed Internet access. Pets accepted. **$**

★★★THE MANOR INN

417 Main St., Route 1, Hebron, 902-742-2487, 800-626-6746; www.manorinn.com

This resort on the shores of Doctors Lake was once the summer cottage of Commodore H. H. Raymond, an American shipping magnate. The house is now a country inn with an extensive roster of activities, including fishing, bicycle rentals and boating. The guest rooms in the main house are Victorian and the adjacent two-story coach house offers several rooms. 53 rooms. Closed mid-October-late May. Complimentary continental breakfast. Restaurant, bar. Pool. Tennis. **$**

★★RODD COLONY HARBOR INN

6 Forest St., Yarmouth, 902-742-9194, 800-565-7633; www.rodd-hotels.ca

65 rooms. Restaurant, bar. Pets accepted, fee. Free wireless Internet access. Fitness center. **$**

★★RODD GRAND YARMOUTH

417 Main St., Yarmouth, 902-742-2446, 800-565-7633; www.rodd-hotels.ca

This hotel is located in the downtown core of Yarmouth. Many of the guest rooms have full views of the waterfront, with traditional décor. 138 rooms. Restaurant, bar. Pets accepted. Pool. Business center. Free wireless Internet access. Fitness center **$**

RESTAURANTS

★★AUSTRIAN INN

Highway 1, Yarmouth, 902-742-6202.

German menu. Closed mid-December-March. **$$**

★★LOTUS GARDEN

67 Starrs Road, Yarmouth, 902-742-1688; www.lotusgarden.ca

Chinese menu. Lunch, dinner, brunch. Bar. Children's menu. **$$**

★PRINCE ARTHUR STEAK AND SEAFOOD HOUSE

73 Starrs Road, Yarmouth, 902-742-1129

Seafood, steak menu. Lunch, dinner, Sunday brunch. Bar. Children's menu. **$$**

NOVA SCOTIA

★
★
★
★
★

ONTARIO

metropolitan hub and its surrounding province justify its ego. A colorful and endless mishmash of wilderness adventure, diverse cultures, urbane cosmopolitanism and rustic rural scenery, the province of Ontario has it all.

Ontario can be divided into north and south—the far northern wilderness dominated by lakes, forests and logging camps, while the southern is an agricultural, industrial and commercial hive inhabited by 90 percent of the population.

Toronto, the provincial capital, and Ottawa, the nation's capital, offer tourists a wide spectrum of vibrant and world-class theater, restaurants, galleries, museums and recreational facilities. The Stratford Festival in Stratford, the Shaw Festival in Niagara-on-the-Lake and Upper Canada Village in Morrisburg are not to be missed, and the same goes for the spectacular Niagara Falls. Ontario's many recreational areas, such as Algonquin and Quetico provincial parks and St. Lawrence Islands National Park, offer a bounty of camping, hiking and all varieties of outdoor adventure. To the north lie Sudbury and Sault Ste. Marie; to the northwest, Thunder Bay, Fort Frances and Kenora, with canoeing, fishing and hunting. Perhaps more appealing than any one attraction is the vast, unspoiled nature of the province itself. More than 400,000 lakes and magnificent forests form a huge vacationland just a few miles from the U.S. border stretching all the way to Hudson Bay.

Provincial Capital: Toronto www.ontariotravel.net

120

ONTARIO

★
★
★
★
★

BRANTFORD

Brantford offers world-class gardens, museums and cultural attractions, scenic trails and paddling—all just an hour's drive from Toronto. Home to the Alexander Graham Bell Homestead National Historic Site, it was here that the great inventor conceived his idea for the telephone. Brantford is also the hometown of hockey legend Wayne Gretzky—and for the ultimate dose of Canada's national sport and spirit, view memorabilia from the career of The Great One alongside other local sports legends at the Gretzky Sports Hall of Recognition.

Information: www.visitbrantford.ca

WHAT TO SEE AND DO
BRANT COUNTY MUSEUM
57 Charlotte St., Brantford, 519-752-2483; www.brantmuseum.ca

This small museum boasts an impressive collection of Native American artifacts, and the life histories of Captain Joseph Brant and Pauline Johnson. There are also displays of pioneer life in Brant County, including Brant Square and Brant Corners, where former businesses are depicted. Wednesday-Friday 10 a.m.-4 p.m., Saturday-Sunday 1-4 p.m., (July and August only).

GLENHYRST ART GALLERY OF BRANT

20 Ava Road, Brantford, 519-756-5932; www.glenhyrst.ca

The gallery at this 16-acre estate contains changing exhibits of paintings, sculpture, photography and crafts from both local and international artists. Don't skip the beautiful grounds and nature trails surrounding the estate. Tuesday-Friday 10 a.m.-5 p.m., Saturday-Sunday 1-5 p.m.; closed Monday.

HER MAJESTY'S ROYAL CHAPEL OF THE MOHAWKS

301 Mohawk St., Brantford, 519-756-0240; www.mohawkchapel.ca

The first Protestant church in Ontario, the Mohawk Chapel is the only Royal Native Chapel in the world belonging to Six Nations people. Daily 10 a.m.-5 p.m.

MYRTLEVILLE HOUSE MUSEUM

34 Myrtleville Drive, Brantford, 519-752-3216

This Georgian house is one of the oldest in Brant County with original furniture of the Good family, who lived here for more than 150 years. Picnicking. Mid-April-mid-September.

SANDERSON CENTRE FOR THE PERFORMING ARTS

88 Dalhousie St., Brantford, 519-758-8090, 800-265-0710;
www.sandersoncentre.on.ca

This 1919 vaudeville house has been restored and transformed to a theater featuring music, dance and dramatic performances.

WOODLAND CULTURAL CENTRE

184 Mohawk St., Brantford, 519-759-2650; www.woodland-centre.on.ca

Preserves and promotes the culture and heritage of the First Nations of the eastern woodland area. There are education, research and museum programs, art shows and annual festivals.

SPECIAL EVENTS

INTERNATIONAL VILLAGES FESTIVAL

320 N. Park, Brantford, 519-756-8767; www.brantfordvillages.ca

Ethnic villages celebrate their heritage with ethnic folk dancing, pageantry and food. Early July.

RIVERFEST

Lions Park Arena, 12 Edge St., Brantford, 519-751-9900

This three-day festival celebrates the Grand River with entertainment, fireworks and crafts. Last weekend in May.

SIX NATIONS FALL FAIR & POWWOW

Ohsweken Fairgrounds, Fourth Line and Chiesswood, Brantford, 519-445-0783

Native dances, authentic craft and art exhibits. Weekend after Labor Day.

ONTARIO

★
★
★
★
★

SIX NATIONS NATIVE PAGEANT

Seneca and Sour Springs roads, Brantford, 519-445-4528;
www.sixnationspageant.com

This pagent takes place at the Forest Theatre at Six Nations reserve, where Six Nations people reenact their history and culture. First three weekends in August.

HOTELS
★★BEST WESTERN BRANT PARK INN AND CONFERENCE CENTRE

19 Holiday Drive, Brantford, 519-753-8561, 877-341-1234; www.bestwestern.com
158 rooms. Restaurant, bar. Children's activity center. Pool. Wireless Internet access. $

★★★HOLIDAY INN BRANTFORD

664 Colborne St. E., Brantford, 519-758-9999, 800-465-4329
The rooms at this Holiday Inn are spacious. Enjoy free hot breakfasts that are certainly above average and high-speed Internet access. 98 rooms. Restaurant, bar. Pool. High-speed Internet access. $

RESTAURANT
★★★OLDE SCHOOL RESTAURANT

Paris Road West at 687 Powerline Road W., Brantford, 519-753-3131, 888-448-3131;
www.theoldeschoolrestaurant.ca

This steak and seafood restaurant, located in a relatively rural area, is housed in a 1850s schoolhouse with a bell tower and beautifully landscaped grounds. Before or after dinner, stop by the piano lounge offered six nights a week. Steak, seafood menu. Lunch. $$$

GANANOQUE

Nestled in the heart of the Thousand Islands, Gananoque is homebase for endless boating, sailing, canoeing, kayaking, jet skiing, scuba diving, water taxis and charters. St. Lawrence Islands National Park made up of nearly two-dozen beautiful islands, features nature trails, parks, beaches and island camping. Visitors can enjoy unique exhibits at the Historic Thousand Islands Village, a heritage center located on the waterfront. The Thousand Islands Playhouse is one of the region's most acclaimed professional theaters, featuring stage productions from May until October.

Information: www.1000islandsgananoque.com

WHAT TO SEE AND DO
1000 ISLANDS CAMPING RESORT

1000 Islands Parkway, Gananoque, 613-659-3058;
www.1000islandsinfo.com/camping.htm

Beautiful campground area with a pool. Tent and trailer sites are available, as well as a playground, nature trails, miniature golf.

1000 ISLANDS SKYDECK

Hill Island, Lansdowne, 613-659-2335; www.1000islandsskydeck.com
The 400-foot tower offers views of the 1000 Islands and the St. Lawrence River. Visitors ride an elevator that takes 40 seconds to reach the first of three observation decks.

Mid-April-late October, daily 8:30 a.m.-dusk; spring, fall, 9 a.m.-6 p.m.; summer, 9 a.m.-8 p.m.

GANANOQUE BOAT LINE

6, Water St., Gananoque, 613-382-2144; www.ganboatline.com

Get out on the open water with a three-hour tour through the 1000 Islands with a stop at Boldt Castle. Mid-May-mid-October, one-hour trips. July-August.

GANANOQUE HISTORICAL MUSEUM

10 King St. E., Gananoque, 613-382-4024

This former Victoria Hotel from 1863 allows you to explore how life was back then, with access to the parlor, dining room, bedroom, and kitchen all furnished in the Victorian style. Military and indigenous artifacts; china, glass, 19th- and 20th-century costumes. June-October, daily.

ST. LAWRENCE ISLANDS NATIONAL PARK

2 County Road 5, 14 miles (30 kilometers) East of Gananoque, Mallorytown, 613-923-5261, 800-839-8221; www.pc.gc.ca

Established in 1904, this park lies on a 50-mile stretch of the St. Lawrence River between Kingston and Brockville. It consists of 20 island areas and a mainland headquarters at Mallorytown Landing. The park offers boat launching facilities, beaches, natural and historic interpretive programs, island camping, picnicking, hiking and boating. A visitor reception center and the remains of an 1817 British gunboat are at Mallorytown Landing and open mid-May to mid-October. The islands can be accessed by water taxi or by rental boats at numerous marinas along both the Canadian and American sides. Monday-Friday 8 a.m.-4:30 p.m.

HOTELS

★★★GANANOQUE INN

550 Stone St. S., Gananoque, 613-382-2165, 800-465-3101; www.gananoqueinn.com

This historic inn is located on the banks of the St. Lawrence River in the heart of the Thousand Islands. Many of the rooms have fireplace and Jacuzzis, and all are heavy on personalized charm and coziness. 57 rooms. Restaurant, bar. Spa. High-speed Internet access. $

★★QUALITY INN

650 King St. E., Gananoque, 613-382-1453, 800-228-5151; www.qualityinn.com

54 rooms. Restaurant. Pool. $

★★RAMADA PROVINCIAL INN

846 King St. E. Highway 2, Gananoque, 613-382-2038, 800-272-6232; www.ramada.com

77 rooms. Closed November-March. Restaurant, bar. Pool. Tennis. High-speed Internet access. $

★★★TRINITY HOUSE

90 Stone St. S., Gananoque, 613-382-8383, 800-265-4871; www.trinityinn.com

In the heart of the famous Thousand Islands, this fully restored 1859 home has antiques mixed together with modern amenities. Guests can wander through

Victorian perennial gardens with herbs and flowers used by the chef in preparing the evening meals. Eight rooms. Complimentary continental breakfast. Restaurant, bar. Spa. **$**

RESTAURANT

★★GOLDEN APPLE

45 King St. W., Gananoque, 613-382-3300
Seafood menu. Closed January-March. Outdoor seating. **$$$**

HAMILTON

Hamilton, linked to Toronto by the majestic Skyway Bridge, is a vibrant community with excellent dining, galleries and shopping. Emerging artists make their home downtown, a bustling engine of creative energy with a thriving gallery scene. Browse for antiques and collectibles, or wander through cobbled streets for a club scene that swings till the wee hours. The waterfront is a mecca for hikers, boarders and water sports enthusiasts, while buyers flock to the cornucopia of ethnic food stores and shops on Ottawa Street. Circling the cosmopolitan pleasures of the city is the splendor of the Royal Botanical Gardens, the famous Bruce Trail and an abundance of conservation areas, water parks and walking paths.
Information: www.hamiltonundiscovered.com

WHAT TO SEE AND DO

AFRICAN LION SAFARI

1386 Cooper Road, Flamborough, 519-623-2620, 800-461-9453; www.lionsafari.com
Drive-through this active wildlife park and spy exotic animals and bird shows, as well as training demonstrations. Check Web site for details.

ART GALLERY OF HAMILTON

123 King St. W., Hamilton, 905-527-6610; www.artgalleryofhamilton.on.ca
This gallery boasts a collection of more than 8,000 sculptures and photographs covering several centuries by American, Canadian, British and European artists. Exhibits change frequently and include both international and artists. Tuesday-Wednesday noon-7 p.m., Thursday-Friday noon-9 p.m., Saturday-Sunday noon-5 p.m.

BATTLEFIELD HOUSE AND MONUMENT

77 King St., Stoney Creek, 905-662-8458; www.battlefieldhouse.ca
Devoted to the Battle of Stoney Creek, this 1795 settler's home and monument honors one of the most significant encounters of the War of 1812. Some rooms furnished as a farm home of the 1830s. Guides in period costumes. June 15-Labor Day Tuesday-Sunday 11 a.m.-4 p.m.; Labor Day-June 14, Tuesday-Sunday 1-4 p.m.; closed Christmas Day, Boxing Day and New Year's Day.

CANADIAN FOOTBALL HALL OF FAME AND MUSEUM

58 Jackson St. W., Hamilton, 905-528-7566; www.cfhof.ca
Sports fans will rejoice once inside this national shrine to Canadian sports, tracing 120 years of football's history.

★
★
★
★
★

CHILDREN'S MUSEUM

1072 Main St. E., Hamilton, 905-546-4848; www.myhamilton.ca

Participatory learning center where children ages 2 to 13 can expand sensory awareness of the world. Hands-on exhibits will keep kids occupied for hours. April-September, Tuesday-Saturday 9:30 a.m.-3:30 p.m.; October-March, Wednesday-Saturday 9:30 a.m.-3:30 p.m., Sunday 11 a.m.-4 p.m.; closed holidays.

DUNDURN CASTLE

610 York Blvd., Hamilton, 905-546-2872; www.hamilton.ca

Home of Sir Allan Napier MacNab, Prime Minister of the United Provinces of Canada from 1854-1856, this 35-room mansion has been restored to its former splendor. Exhibits and programs run all year. Canada Day-Labor Day, daily 10 a.m.-4 p.m., Labor Day-Canada Day, Tuesday-Sunday noon-4 p.m.

FLAMBORO DOWNS

967 Highway 5 W., Flamborough, 905-627-3561; www.flamborodowns.com

Harness racing draws crowds here year-round, with a grandstand that seats 3,000, restaurants and lounges. The Confederation Cup race for the top three-year-old pacers in North America is held here every August. Wednesday-Friday, Sunday-Monday 6 p.m.

HAMILTON MILITARY MUSEUM

Dundurn Park, 610 York Blvd., Hamilton, 905-546-4974

This small museum displays military paraphernalia from the 1800s including Canadian uniforms, equipment and antique weapons.

HAMILTON'S FARMERS MARKET

55 York Blvd., Hamilton, 905-546-2096; www.hamilton.ca

Fresh produce, flowers, meat, poultry, fish, cheese and baked goods are brought from all over the Niagara garden belt. Tuesday, Thursday 7 a.m.-6 p.m., Friday 8 a.m.-6 p.m., Saturday 6 a.m.-6 p.m.; closed on Monday, Wednesday, Sunday and all statutory holidays.

MCMASTER MUSEUM OF ART

Alvin A. Lee Building, McMaster University, 1280 Main St. W., Hamilton, 905-525-9140; www.mcmaster.ca/museum

On McMaster University campus 27,328 students. Houses the university's collection of 6,000 works of art, changing public programs and the Herman H. Levy Collection of Impressionist and Post-Impressionist paintings. Tuesday-Wednesday, Friday 11 a.m.-5 p.m., Thursday 11 a.m.-7 p.m., Saturday noon-5 p.m.; closed Sunday-Monday, statutory holidays and the week between Christmas and New Year's Day.

MUSEUM OF STEAM AND TECHNOLOGY

900 Woodward Ave., Hamilton, 905-546-4797; www.hamilton.ca

An 1859 pumping station contains unique examples of 19th-century steam technology; gallery features permanent and temporary exhibits on modern technology; also special events. June-Labor Day, Tuesday-Sunday 11 a.m.-11 p.m., Labor Day-May, Tuesday-Sunday noon-4 p.m.; closed Christmas Day, Boxing Day and New Year's Day.

ONTARIO WORKERS ART & HERITAGE CENTRE

51 Stuart St., Hamilton, 905-522-3003; www.wahc-museum.ca

This is Canada's only museum dedicated to preserving the legacy of labor and working people. The space includes a public resource center, café, reading room and gift shop. Tuesday-Saturday 10 a.m.-4 p.m.; closed Sunday-Monday.

ROYAL BOTANICAL GARDENS

680 Plains Road W., Hamilton, at Highways 2, 6 and 403, 905-527-1158; www.rbg.ca

Colorful gardens, natural areas and a wildlife sanctuary comprise Hamilton's many gardens, including a rock garden with seasonal displays, laking garden with herbaceous perennialsm, an arboretum containing world-famous lilacs in late May, a rose garden, a teaching garden, along with woodland, scented and medicinal gardens. At Cootes Paradise Sanctuary, trails wind around more than 1,200 acres of water, marsh and wooded ravines.

WHITEHERN HISTORIC HOUSE & GARDEN

41 Jackson St. W., Hamilton, 905-546-2018; www.hamilton.ca

Former home of the McQuesten family, this 19th-century Georgian mansion remains furnished with original family possessions. The landscaped gardens are worth a stroll. June 15-Labor Day, Tuesday-Sunday 11 a.m.-4 p.m.; Labor Day-June 14, Tuesday-Sunday 1-4 p.m.; closed holidays.

SPECIAL EVENTS

★
★
★
★
★

AROUND THE BAY ROAD RACE

The Around the Bay Road Race Inc., 1439 Upper Ottawa St., Hamilton, 905-624-0046; www.aroundthebayroadrace.com

Join in Canada's oldest footrace, dating back to 1894. Just dress accordingly—it's often chilly and wet. Late March.

FESTITALIA

1 Summers Lane, Hamilton, 905-546-5300

This is a testament to all things Italian: Opera, concerts, bicycle races, fashion shows and ethnic foods. Mid-September.

FESTIVAL OF FRIENDS

Main Street and Gage Avenue, Hamilton, 905-525-6644; www.creativearts.on.ca

A perfecting outing for the kids, this festival is packed with musicians, artists, craftsmen, puppets, dancer, mimes and theater preformances. Second weekend in August.

HOTELS

★★ADMIRAL INN

149 Dundurn St. N., Hamilton, 905-529-2311, 866-236-4662; www.admiralinn.com

60 rooms. Restaurant. Pets accepted, fee. High-speed Internet access. **$**

★★★SHERATON HAMILTON HOTEL
116 King St. W., Hamilton, 905-529-5515, 888-627-8161; www.sheraton.com
Located in downtown Hamilton, this contemporary hotel has direct access to a shopping mall, the Convention Centre and Hamilton Place Concert Hall. Business travelers will appreciate the fitness room, business center and the wireless Internet access. 301 rooms. Wireless Internet access. Restaurant, bar. Pets accepted, fee. Pool. Business center. $$

RESTAURANTS
★★★ANCASTER OLD MILL INN
548 Old Dundas Road, Ancaster, 905-648-1827; www.ancasteroldmill.com
Originally this building was a gristmill, built in 1792. Today it's a great spot to grab consistently good American fare with many organic options and farm fresh ingredients. American menu. Outdoor seating. Lunch, Dinner, Sunday brunch. $$$

★★SHAKESPEARE'S DINING LOUNGE
181 Main St. E., Hamilton, 905-528-0689; www.shakespeares.ca
Seafood, steak menu. Reservations recommended. Lunch, dinner. $$$

KINGSTON
Nestled where the Rideau Canal and the St. Lawrence River meet Lake Ontario, Kingston is a freshwater sailor's dream, a city that exquisitely blends history and modern sophistication. Stroll through the bustling downtown and its boutiques and bistros, through its meandering waterfront with heritage-filled neighborhoods and breathtaking parklands.
Information: www.kingstoncanada.com

ONTARIO

★
★
★
★
★

WHAT TO SEE AND DO
AGNES ETHERINGTON ART CENTRE
University Avenue and Queen's Crescent, Kingston, 613-533-2190; www.aeac.ca
This family-friendly art center hosts ever-changing exhibitions of contemporary and historical art. Tuesday-Friday 10 a.m.-4:30 p.m., Saturday-Sunday 1-5 p.m.

BELLEVUE HOUSE NATIONAL HISTORIC SITE
35 Centre St., Kingston, 613-545-8666; www.pc.gc.ca
This Italianate villa from 1840 was home of Sir John A. Macdonald, the first prime minister of Canada and is replete with restored and furnished period pieces, Multimedia displays and video presentation at the visitor center. April-May, 10 a.m.-5 p.m., June-Labor Day, 9 a.m.-6 p.m. Labor Day-October, 10 a.m.-5 p.m.

CANADIAN EMPRESS
253 Ontario St., departs from the front of City Hall, Kingston,
613-549-8091, 800-267-7868
This replica of a traditional steamship cruises the St. Lawrence and Ottawa rivers on six different routes; trips span four or five nights, some reaching Montréal and Québec City. Ages 12 and up. Mid-May-November.

CONFEDERATION TOUR TROLLEY

209 Ontario St., (Leaves from Confederation Park, Kingston,) 613-548-4453, 888-548-4555

The Confederation Tour Trolley has been entertaining visitors and Kingston residents since 1967. It runs 50 minutes and covers 10 miles of Kingston. Mid-May-June, 10 a.m.-5 p.m. Labor Day-Thanksgiving, 10 a.m.-2 p.m.

CORRECTIONAL SERVICE OF CANADA MUSEUM

555 King St. W., Kingston, 613-530-3122;
www.csc-scc.gc.ca/text/organi/org05-3-e.shtml

The museum displays a variety of artifacts and documents related to the early history of Canadian penitentiaries. It includes displays of contraband weapons and escape devices.

FORT FREDERICK & COLLEGE MUSEUM

Kingston Martello Tower, 613-541-6000; www.rmc.ca

Exhibits depict the history of the college and the earlier Royal Dockyard circa 1789-1853, with a Douglas Collection of small arms and weapons that once belonged to General Porfirio Diaz, president of Mexico from 1886-1912. Late June-Labor Day, daily.

FORT HENRY

1 Fort Henry Drive, Kingston, East at the junction of Highways 2 and 15,
613-542-7388, 800-437-2233; www.forthenry.com

One of Ontario's most spectacular historic sites, the present fortification was built in the 1830s and restored during the 1930s. Guided tour; 19th-century British infantry and artillery drills; military pageantry; exhibits of military arms, uniforms, equipment; garrison life activities. Mid-May-early October, daily 10 a.m.-5 p.m.

GRAND THEATRE

218 Princess St., Kingston, 613-530-2050; www.whatsonkingston.com/thegrand

This century-old, renovated theater hosts live theater, dance, symphonic and children's performances by professional companies and local groups. There is also a nice summer theater program. Monday-Saturday 10:30 a.m.-5:30 p.m.

INTERNATIONAL ICE HOCKEY FEDERATION MUSEUM

277 York St., Kingston, 613-544-2355; www.ihhof.com

Hockey is a big deal in Canada, and this museum proves it with displays tracing the history of hockey from its beginning in Kingston in 1885 to the present. Monday-Saturday 10 a.m.-4 p.m., Sunday noon-4 p.m.

ISLAND QUEEN

6 Princess St., (departs from Kingston Harbor) Kingston, 613-549-5544;
www.1000islandscruises.on.ca

The IslandQueen is a triple decked paddlewheeler in the Mississippi River boat style that caters to island tours, weddings, receptions and corporate events. The oak panels and antique tin on the interior make her appear all the more historic. May-October, daily.

MACLACHLAN WOODWORKING MUSEUM

2993 Highway 2 E., Kingston, 613-542-0543; www.cityofkingston.ca

"Wood in the service of humanity" is the theme of this circa 1850 museum. It highlights the life of the pioneer farmer in both the field and the kitchen, as well as workshops of a cooper, blacksmith, cabinetmaker.

MARINE MUSEUM OF THE GREAT LAKES AT KINGSTON

55 Ontario St., Kingston, 613-542-2261; www.marmuseum.ca

Ships have been built in Kingston since 1678. This museum explores the tales, adventures and enterprise of Inland Seas history. Ship building gallery, 1889 engine room, with dry dock engines and pumps; artifacts; changing exhibits. Library and archives. The Museum Ship Alexander Henry, a 3,000-ton icebreaker, is open for tours and bed and breakfast accommodations.

MURNEY TOWER MUSEUM

King and Barrie streets, Kingston, 613-544-9925; www.kingstonhistoricalsociety.ca

Built in 1846, the Murney Redoubt was positioned on the shores of Lake Ontario as part of the defences of Kingston. Forty years later, it was no longer deemed necessary and fell into disrepair. In the early 1920s, the Kingston Historical Society took over and turned the structure into a museum that exhibits the area's military and social history. Mid-May-Labor Day 10 a.m.-5 p.m.

SPECIAL EVENT
PITTSBURGH SHEEPDOG TRIALS

Grass Creek Park, 2993 Highway 2 E., Kingston, 888-855-4555

Includes sheep-shearing demonstrations and a variety of sheepdog-related activities. Early August.

HOTELS
★★BEST WESTERN FIRESIDE INN

1217 Princess St., Kingston, 613-549-2211; www.bestwestern.com

77 rooms. Restaurant, bar. Pool. High-speed Internet access. $

★FIRST CANADA INN

1 First Canada Court, Kingston, 613-541-1111, 800-267-7899;
www.first-canada-inns.com

74 rooms. Complimentary continental breakfast. Wireless Internet access. Pets accepted, fee. $

★★★ISAIAH TUBBS RESORT & CONFERENCE CENTRE

RR 1, West Lake Road, Picton, 613-393-2090; www.isaiahtubbs.com

This resort is located on the shores of West Lake and is open year-round. Adjacent to Sandbanks Provincial Park, it's ideal for families or business travelers seeking a little outdoor R&R. 70 rooms. Restaurant, bar. Children's activity center. Pool. Tennis. $$

ONTARIO

★★★MERRILL

343 Main St. E., Picton, 613-476-7451; www.merrillinn.com

This Victorian house was built in 1878 for Edwards Merrill, one of Canada's top barristers. Guest rooms are all decorated with period antiques, and the inn-keepers will make you feel like family. 13 rooms. Complimentary continental breakfast. Restaurant. $$

★SEVEN OAKES

2331 Princess St. Highway 2, Kingston, 613-546-3655; www.7oakesmotel.com

44 rooms. Pets accepted, fee. Pool. Tennis. High-speed Internet access. $

★★TRAVELODGE

2360 Princess St., Kingston, 613-546-4233; www.travelodge.com

66 rooms. Restaurant, bar. Pool. High-speed Internet access. $

SPECIALTY LODGINGS

GREEN ACRES INN

2480 Princess St. Highway 2, Kingston, 613-546-1796,
800-267-7889; www.greenacresinn.com

31 rooms. Complimentary continental breakfast. Pool. $

HOCHELAGA INN

24 S. Sydenham St., Kingston, 613-549-5534, 877-933-9433;
www.hochelagainn.com

23 rooms. Complimentary continental breakfast. $

ROSEMOUNT INN

46 Sydenham St. S., Kingston, 613-531-8844, 888-871-8844;
www.rosemountinn.com

11 rooms. Closed mid-December-early January. Wireless Internet access. Children over 13 years only. Complimentary full breakfast. $

RESTAURANT

★★AUNT LUCY'S

1399 Princess St., Kingston, 613-542-2729;
www.auntlucysdinnerhouse.com

Seafood, steak menu. Lunch, dinner, Sunday brunch. $$

KITCHENER-WATERLOO

The twin cities of Kitchener-Waterloo were settled in the early 1800s by Mennonites, Amish and Germans whose cultural heritage is still widely celebrated. Not far to the north in Elmira is the heart of Ontario's Pennsylvania German country, with a Maple Sugar Festival and tours of Mennonite country. A vigorous spirit of youth and industry pervades both cities, which sparkle with a dynamic nightlife, fabulous restaurants, world-class cultural facilities, over 200 kilometers of community trails and lovely golf courses.

Information: www.kwtourism.ca

WHAT TO SEE AND DO

BINGEMAN PARK

425 Bingemans Centre Drive, Kitchener, 519-744-1555; www.bingemans.com

Recreation center on the banks of the Grand River includes a swimming pool, wave pool, water sliding, bumper boats, go-cart track, arcade, roller skating, miniature golf, golf driving range, batting cages, cross-country skiing, picnicking, restaurant, playground and camping facilities.

DOON HERITAGE CROSSROADS

10 Huron Road, Homer Watson Boulevard, Kitchener, 519-748-1914; www.region.waterloo.on.ca

Get a sense of life as it was in an early 20th-century village, with a museum, grocery store, post office/tailor shop, blacksmith, church, two farms and several houses. May-late December.

FARMERS MARKET

300 King St. E., Kitchener, 519-741-2287; www.kitchenermarket.ca

More than 100 vendors sell fresh produce, meat, cheese and handicrafts. Mennonite specialties are featured. Saturday 7 a.m.-2 p.m.

GLOCKENSPIEL

King and Benton streets, Hamilton

Canada's first glockenspiel tells the fairy tale of Snow White. Twenty-three bells form the carillon. Performance lasts 15 minutes. Four times daily.

JOSEPH SCHNEIDER HAUS

466 Queen St. S., Kitchener-Waterloo, 519-742-7752; www.region.waterloo.on.ca/jsh

The Joseph Schneider Haus Museum and Gallery is a community museum in downtown Kitchener that includes a Georgian-style frame farmhouse. Adjacent Heritage Galleries includes Germanic folk art and exhibits change every three months. Museum July-September, Monday-Saturday 10 a.m.-5 p.m., Sunday 1-5 p.m., September 2-December 24; also by appointment Wednesday-Saturday 10 a.m.-5 p.m., Sunday 1-5 p.m.

LAUREL CREEK CONSERVATION AREA

Northwest Corner of Waterloo, bounded by Westmount Road, Conservation Drive and Beaver Creek Road, 519-884-6620; www.city.waterloo.on.ca

Approximately 750 acres of multipurpose area, perfect for swimming boating, hiking, camping, picnicking, bird-watching and relaxing on the beach. May-mid-October.

MUSEUM & ARCHIVE OF GAMES

B.C. Matthews Hall, 200 University Ave. W., Waterloo, 519-888-4567; www.gamesmuseum.uwaterloo.ca

On the University of Waterloo campus, this collection includes more than 3,500 games. Many hands-on exhibits range from Inuit bone games to computer games. Exhibits change every four months. Archive contains documents pertaining to games and game-playing.

ONTARIO

★
★
★
★
☆

PIONEER MEMORIAL TOWER

Pioneer Tower Road and Lookout Lane, Kitchener-Waterloo, 519-571-5684;
www.kwtourism.ca

This tower stands as a tribute to industrious spirit of pioneers who first settled Waterloo County. Cemetery on grounds includes the graves of several original founders. It offers excellent view of Grand River. May-October.

WATERLOO PARK

100 Westmount Road N., Waterloo, 519-725-0511; www.city.waterloo.on.ca

Log schoolhouse built in 1820 is surrounded by picnic area and lake; playground. Small zoo and band concerts in summer. Sunday.

WATERLOO-ST. JACOBS RAILWAY

10 Father David Bauer Drive, Kitchener-Waterloo, 519-746-1950;
www.steam-train.org

Streamliner tourist train rolls into the heart of Mennonite farm country. Stops on the 90-minute (round-trip) ride allow exploration of the quaint village of St. Jacobs and the St. Jacobs Farmers Market. May-October, daily; November-April, weekends.

WOODSIDE NATIONAL HISTORIC SITE

528 Wellington St. N., Kitchener, 519-742-5273; www.pc.gc.ca

As the boyhood home of William Lyon Mackenzie King, Canada's tenth prime minister, this 1890s Victorian acts as an interpretive center for theater and displays on King's early life and career. Monday-Sunday 1-5 p.m.

132

ONTARIO

★
★
★
★
☆

SPECIAL EVENTS

ALE TRAIL

Guelph Visitor and Convention Services, 55 Wyndham St. N., Guelph,
800-334-4519; www.visitguelphwellington.ca

Showcases region's brewing industry and allows visitors to experience the craft of brewing at six different area breweries. Mid-June.

KITCHENER-WATERLOO MULTICULTURAL FESTIVAL

102 King St. W., Kitchener-Waterloo, 519-745-2531;
www.kwmc.on.ca/html/festival.html

Festival will celebrate the festival that Echo readers voted one of the best in the community. Late June.

WATERLOO BUSKER CARNIVAL

100 Regina St. S., Kitchener-Waterloo, 519-747-8769;
www.waterloo-buskers.com

Unique, long-standing and innovative the Waterloo Busker Carnival is a volunteer driven International Street Performers Festival. Late August.

WATERLOO COUNTY QUILT FESTIVAL

519-699-5628, 800-265-3353; www.waterlooquiltfestival.com

Quilt exhibits, displays, workshops and demonstrations. Nine days in mid-May.

WELLESLEY APPLE BUTTER & CHEESE FESTIVAL

519-656-2400; www.wellesleyabcfestival.ca

Pancake breakfast, farmers market, free tours of farms, cider mill; horseshoe tournament, quilt auction, smorgasbord dinner, model boat regatta, antique cars and tractors. Last Saturday in September.

HOTELS

★BEST WESTERN CAMBRIDGE HOTEL

730 Hespeler Road, Cambridge, 519-623-4600; www.bestwestern.com

116 rooms. Complimentary continental breakfast. Pool. Spa. High-speed Internet access. $

★★ELORA MILL

77 Mill St. W., Elora, 519-846-9118, 866-713-5672; www.eloramill.com

32 rooms. Complimentary continental breakfast. Restaurant, bar. $$

★★HOLIDAY INN

30 Fairway Road S., Kitchener, 519-893-1211; www.holiday-inn.com/kitcheneron

183 rooms. Restaurant, bar. Fitness center. Spa. High-speed Internet access. Pets accepted, fee. Pool. $

★★★LANGDON HALL COUNTRY HOUSE HOTEL & SPA

1 Langdon Drive, Cambridge, 519-740-2100; www.langdonhall.ca

One would not guess that Langdon Hall Country House is a hotel as you approach the red brick mansion with graceful tall white columns that face a vast, manicured lawn. Tucked away in seclusion, the Langdon is an ideal retreat from the hustle and bustle of the city. Country-style décor and antique charm awaits visitors, who will appreciate the variety of room styles, from the Stable Terrace to the Rose Suite. The house, formerly Eugene Langdon Wilks' vacation home more than 100 years ago, was designed in the classic American Federal Revival style, much of which is maintained today. The hotel is complete with wedding services, a spa and high-end restaurant, but the best feature is its 200-acre "backyard," home to the Cloister Garden, Maple Lane and the Woodland Walk. 52 rooms. High-speed Internet access. Restaurant, bar. Fitness center, business center. Spa. $$$

★★WALPER TERRACE HOTEL

1 King St. W., Kitchener, 519-745-4321, 800-265-8749; www.walper.com

79 rooms. Complimentary continental breakfast. Restaurant, bar. $

★★★WATERLOO INN

475 King St. N., Waterloo, 519-884-0220, 800-361-4708; www.waterlooinn.com

This hotel is close to the famous St. Jacob's Farmers Market, the Elora Gorge and the Stratford Festival. The rooms are charming and comfortable, with personal touches throughout. 155 rooms. Restaurant, bar. Wireless Internet access. Pets accepted, fee. Fitness center. Pool. $

ONTARIO

★
★
★
★
★

RESTAURANTS

★★BENJAMIN'S

1430 King N., St. Jacobs, 519-664-3731; www.stjacobs.com/benjamins

Contemporary menu. Reservation recommended. $$$

★★★CHARCOAL STEAK HOUSE

2980 King St. E., Kitchener, 519-893-6570; www.charcoalsteakhouse.ca

Consistently delicious steaks and a relaxing, serene atmosphere have made the Charcoal Steak House a Kitchener favorite for more than 50 years. The menu, which highlights Canadian AAA steaks and fresh seafood, offers choices for all. A number of cocktails choices are offered in addition to an award-winning wine list. Steak menu. Lunch, dinner, Sunday brunch. Reservations recommended. $$$

★★★★THE DINING ROOM AT LANGDON HALL

1 Langdon Drive, Cambridge, 519-740-2100; www.langdonhall.ca

Executive chef Jonathan Gushue heads this extraordinary award-winning restaurant. The Dining Room's true star is its dinner menu, but it is also open for breakfast, brunch and lunch. For dinner, try the robust herb-basted rainbow trout or the dry-aged Aberdine beef tenderloin. If you're really looking for an unforgettable dining experience, Gushue also prepares a $95 tasting menu with wine pairings, featuring poached Arctic char with local morels and a crispy St. Jacobs pig cheek, followed by delightful strawberry compote with lime sorbet. American-French menu. Breakfast, lunch, dinner, Sunday brunch. Formal attire for dinner. Reservation recommended. $$$$

★★WATERLOT

17 Huron St., New Hamburg, 519-662-2020; www.waterlot.com

French menu. Lunch, dinner, Sunday brunch. $$$

SPA

★★★THE SPA AT LANGDON HALL

1 Langdon Drive, Cambridge, 519-624-3220; www.langdonhall.ca/spa.htm

Along with the traditional body and facial treatments, the Spa at Langdon Hall offers hydrotherapy sessions, which include destressing, detoxifying or a remineralizing bath. The private baths are powerful, with 100 jets that promise to relax the tightest knots. A detoxifying seaweed wrap will leave you feeling rejuvenated, but it is the Vichy Aroma Rain Body Therapy—a sea salt and jojoba body scrub under rainfall—that will leave you wallowing in utter relaxation.

LONDON

London is a busy, modern city with a charming small-town atmosphere. Located on the Thames River, its street names echo "the other" London, as does the contrast of Victorian architecture and contemporary skyscrapers.

Near to the downtown core are historic sites, theaters, provincial parks and some of the best freshwater beaches in the world. Every summer evening, the lights dim and the curtain rises on stages throughout the area for the famous Stratford Festival, London's entertainment flagship.

Information: www.londontourism.ca

WHAT TO SEE AND DO

DOUBLE-DECKER BUS TOURS

300 Dufferin Ave., London, 519-661-5000, 800-265-2602;
www.doubledeckertours.com

Two-hour guided tour aboard authentic double-decker English bus with stops at Storybook Gardens in Springbank Park and the Regional Art Museum. Tours depart from City Hall, Wellington Street and Dufferin Avenue. July-Labor Day, daily. Reservations suggested.

ELDON HOUSE

481 Ridout St. N., London, 519-661-5169; www.museumlondon.ca/EldonHouse

As the oldest house in town, built in 1834, it was occupied by the same family until it was donated to the city. Furnished much as it was in the 19th century with many antiques from abroad. Be sure to visit the spacious grounds, lawns, brick paths, gardens and conservatory-greenhouse. Check Web site for hours.

FANSHAWE PIONEER VILLAGE

2609 Fanshawe Park Road E., east end of Fanshawe Park Road, London,
519-457-1296; www.fanshawepioneervillage.ca

Living history museum of 24 buildings moved to this site to display artifacts and recreate the life of a typical 19th-century crossroads community in southwestern Ontario. There are log cabins, barns and a stable; blacksmith, weaver, harness, gun, woodworking and barber shops; general store, church, fire hall, school and sawmill; costumed interpreters. Also at Fanshawe Conservation Area is Ontario's largest flood control structure; swimming, sailing, fishing, camping, various sports activities and nature trails. Victoria Day Weekend-Thanksgiving: Tuesday-Sunday 10 a.m.-4:30 p.m.

GRAND THEATRE

471 Richmond St., London, 519-672-8800, 800-265-1593; www.grandtheatre.com

Contemporary façade houses a 1901 theater, built by Colonel Whitney of Detroit and Ambrose Small of Toronto. The interior has been restored to include proscenium arch, murals and cast plasterwork. October-May.

GUY LOMBARDO MUSIC CENTRE

205 Wonderland Road S., London, 519-473-9003;
www.guylombardomusic.com/museum.html

Institution housing artifacts belonging to London-born musician. Exhibits on other big-band era greats as well.

LONDON MUSEUM OF ARCHAEOLOGY

1600 Attawandaron Road, London, 519-473-1360; www.uwo.ca/museum

This museum traces prehistory of southwestern Ontario with more than 40,000 artifacts showing how indigenous people lived thousands of years before Columbus was born. There are archeological and ethnographic exhibits from southwestern Ontario, as well as a gallery, theater and native gift shop. May-August, 10 a.m.-4:30 p.m.; September-December, 10 a.m.-4:30 p.m.; closed Monday-Tuesday; January-April, Saturday-Sunday 1-4 p.m.

ONTARIO

LONDON REGIONAL CHILDREN'S MUSEUM

21 Wharncliffe Road S., London, 519-434-5726; www.londonchildrensmuseum.ca

Hands-on galleries allow children to explore, touch and discover. Artifacts to touch, costumes to put on and crafts to construct make this a perfect day-time activity for kids.

ROYAL CANADIAN REGIMENT MUSEUM

650 Elizabeth St., London, Wolseley Hall, Canadian Forces Base, 519-660-5102; www.thercr.ca

Displays include artifacts, battle scenes from 1883-present, weapons and uniforms. Tuesday-Friday 10 a.m.-4 p.m., Saturday-Sunday noon-4 p.m.; closed Monday, holidays.

SKA NAH DOHT INDIAN VILLAGE

Longwoods Road Conservation Area, 20 miles (32 kilometers) west via Highway 2 in the London, 519-264-2420; www.lowerthames-conservation.on.ca/SkaNahDoht.htm

Recreated Iroquoian village depicting native culture in southwest Ontario 800-1,000 years ago. Guided tours, slide shows, displays; nature trails, picnicking, group camping.

STORYBOOK GARDENS

1958 Storybook Lane, Springbank Park, London, 519-661-5770; www.storybook.london.ca

Family-oriented theme park, children's playworld and zoo, eight acres within London's largest park of 281 acres. Early May-mid-October: daily.

SPECIAL EVENTS

HOME COUNTY FOLK FESTIVAL

Victoria Park, Charles and Water streets, London, 519-432-4310; www.homecounty.ca

Three-day outdoor music fest. Mid-July.

LONDON FRINGE THEATRE FESTIVAL

476 Richmond St., London, 519-433-3332; www.londonfringe.ca

Citywide theatrical event. Mid-August.

★
★★
★★
★
SUNFEST

Victoria Park, Charles and Water streets, London, 519-663-9170, 800-265-2502

Features 25 music and dance ensembles from around the world, plus 70 food and craft vendors. Early July.

WESTERN FAIR

Western Fairgrounds, 900 King St., London, 519-438-7203; www.westernfair.com

Entertainment and educational extravaganza; horse shows, musicians, exhibits, livestock shows. Ten days in early September.

HOTELS

★★DELTA LONDON ARMORIES HOTEL

325 Dundas St., London, 519-679-6111, 800-668-9999; www.deltahotels.com

246 rooms. Restaurant, bar. Children's activity center. Pets accepted, fee. Pool. Business center. $

★★★HILTON LONDON ONTARIO

300 King St., London, 519-439-1661; www.hiltonlondon.com

An attached heated walkway makes access to the convention center easy from this hotel and the indoor pool provides a great break to the winter doldrums. The rooms are updated and spacious. 322 rooms. Restaurants, bar. Wireless Internet access. Fitness center. Pool. Pet accepted. Business center. $$

★RAMADA INN

817 Exeter Road, London, 519-681-4900, 800-303-3733;
www.ramadainnlondon.com

124 rooms. Restaurant, bar. Business center. High-speed Internet access. Fitness room. Pool. $

RESTAURANT
★★MICHAEL'S ON THE THAMES

1 York St., London, 519-672-0111; www.michaelsonthethames.com

French, Italian menu. Reservations recommended. $$$

NIAGARA FALLS

To more than 12 million annual visitors, Niagara is magic—either for the spectacle of Niagara Falls or for the bounty of ripening grapes and the taste of heavenly fresh fruit. In particular, the Canadian side of Niagara Falls offers viewpoints different from, and in many ways superior to, those on the American side. With over 40 world-class golf courses, over 70 award-winning wineries and over 200 kilometers of spectacular cycling and hiking trails, the greater Niagara region offers more than one of the world's most incredible views.

Information: www.tourismniagara.com

WHAT TO SEE AND DO
CANADA ONE FACTORY OUTLETS

7500 Lundy's Lane, Niagara Falls, 905-356-8989, 866-284-5781;
www.canadaoneoutlets.com

This outlet sells many nationally recognized brands of merchandise. Stores here include The Body Shop, Club Monaco, Guess, Tommy Hilfiger and Reebok.

GUINNESS WORLD OF RECORDS MUSEUM

4943 Clifton Hill, Niagara Falls, 905-356-2299, 866-656-0310;
www.guinnessniagarafalls.com

Based on the popular book of records, hundreds of original exhibits, artifacts, and laser video galleries are on display, as well as recreations of many of the world's greatest accomplishments. Daily.

IMAX THEATRE NIAGARA FALLS

6170 Fallsview Blvd., Niagara Falls, 905-358-3611, 866-405-4629;
www.imaxniagara.com

This six-story-high movie screen shows *Niagara: Miracles, Myths and Magic*, a film highlighting the Falls. Daredevil Adventure has displays, exhibits and some of the actual barrels used to traverse the Falls throughout history.

★
★
★
★

JOURNEY BEHIND THE FALLS

6650 Niagara Parkway, Queen Victoria Park, Niagara Falls, 905-354-1551;
www.niagaraparks.com

Elevator descends to a point about 25 feet above the river, offering an excellent view of the Falls from below and behind; waterproof garments are supplied. Open year-round at 9 a.m.; closed Christmas.

LOUIS TUSSAUD'S WAXWORKS

4960 Clifton Hill, Niagara Falls, 905-356-2238; www.ripleysniagara.com

Louis Tussaud's Waxworks is a collection of instantly recognizable, true-to-life wax figures crafted by recognized wax artists from around the world. Life-size, historically-costumed wax figures of the past and present are on display. If you're looking for a scare, head into the Chamber of Horrors.

LUNDY'S LANE HISTORICAL MUSEUM

5810 Ferry St., Niagara Falls, 905-358-5082; www.lundyslanemuseum.com

The Lundy's Lane Historical Museum was established in 1961 on the site of the Battle of Lundy's Lane in 1814. The museum interprets the early settlement and tourism of Niagara Falls, including 1812 war militaria, a Victorian parlor, an early kitchen, toys, dolls and photographs.

MARINELAND

7657 Portage Road, Niagara Falls, 905-356-8250; www.marinelandcanada.com

Killer whales, dolphins and sea lions perform for your viewing pleasure. After the show, visit wildlife displays with deer, bears, buffalo and elk, thrill rides, including one of the world's largest steel roller coasters. There are restaurants and picnic areas for when you get hungry.

MINOLTA TOWER CENTRE

6732 Fallsview Blvd., Niagara Falls, 905-356-1501; www.niagaratower.com

This awesome 325-foot tower offers a magnificent 360-degree view of the Falls and surrounding areas. Eight levels at top; specially designed glass for ideal photography; Minolta exhibit floor; Waltzing Waters water and light spectacle; gift shops; incline railway to Falls; Top of the Rainbow dining rooms overlooking Falls reservations suggested.

NIAGARA FALLS AVIARY

5651 River Road, Niagara Falls, 905-356-8888, 866-994-0090;
www.niagarafallsaviary.com

Wander through this 15,000-square-foot 1,394-square-meter conservatory amidst lush foliage. The environment simulates a tropical rainforest in which free-flying birds soar overhead. Guided and self-guided tours; café, restaurant.

NIAGARA FALLS MUSEUM

5651 River Road, Niagara Falls, 416-596-1396; www.niagaramuseum.com

One of North America's oldest museums, founded in 1827, it contains 26 galleries of rare, worldwide artifacts, including Niagara's Original Daredevil Hall of Fame, Egyptian mummy collection and dinosaur exhibit.

NIAGARA PARKS BOTANICAL GARDENS

2565 Niagara Parkway, Niagara Falls, 905-356-8554, 877-642-7275;
www.niagaraparks.com
Nearly 100 acres of horticultural exhibits. Nature shop.

NIAGARA PARKS BUTTERFLY CONSERVATORY

2405 Niagara Parkway, Niagara Falls, 905-358-0025, 877-642-7275
Approximately 2,000 butterflies make their home in this 11,000-square-foot, climate-controlled conservatory filled with exotic greenery and flowing water. Nearly 50 species of butterflies can be viewed from a 600-foot 180-meter network of walking paths. Outdoor butterfly garden. Gift shop.

NIAGARA SPANISH AERO CAR

Niagara Falls, 3½ miles north on Niagara Parkway, 905-354-5711;
www.niagaraparks.com
The 1,800-foot cables support a car that crosses the whirlpool and rapids of the Niagara River. Five-minute trip each way. Mid-April-mid-October, daily.

OLD FORT ERIE

350 Lake Shore Road, Fort Erie, 905-871-0540
Site of some of the fiercest fighting of the War of 1812; restored to the period. Guided tours of the Glengarry Light Infantry by interpreters dressed in uniform. May-November, daily 10 a.m.-6 p.m.

SKYLON TOWER

139

5200 Robinson St., Niagara Falls, 905-356-2651, 866-434-4202; www.skylon.com
Stands 775 feet above the base of the Falls. Three-level dome contains an indoor/outdoor observation deck and revolving and stationary dining rooms served by three external, glass-enclosed Yellow Bug elevators. Specialty shops at base of tower.

SPECIAL EVENT
WINTER FESTIVAL OF LIGHTS

Queen Victoria Park, Murray Street and River Road, Niagara Falls,
800-563-2557; www.wfol.com
Celebrate the start of the winter season with parades, fireworks, light displays and Disney shows. Late November-late January.

HOTELS
★★ASTON MICHAEL'S INN BY THE FALLS

5599 River Road, Niagara Falls, 905-354-2727, 800-263-9390; www.michaelsinn.com
130 rooms. Restaurant, bar. Pool. Wireless Internet access. **$**

★★BEST WESTERN CAIRN CROFT HOTEL

6400 Lundy's Lane, Niagara Falls, 905-356-1161, 800-263-2551;
www.bestwestern.com
166 rooms. Restaurant, bar. Pool. High-speed Internet access. Spa. **$**

ONTARIO

★
★
★
★
★

★★★DOUBLETREE RESORT LODGE & SPA FALLSVIEW NIAGARA FALLS

6039 Fallsview Blvd., Niagara Falls, 905-358-3817, 800-222-8733;
www.niagarafallsdoubletree.com

Cathedral ceilings with wood beams, slate floors and freshly baked chocolate chip cookies welcome guests. The property is within walking distance to area attractions. The spacious guest rooms offer panoramic views of the upper Niagara River. Art lovers can check out the in-house gallery, Ochre Art Gallery. For pure relaxation, the Five Lakes AVEDA Day Spa is the place to go for relaxation. Buchanans Chophouse is the perfect spot to unwind. 224 rooms. Restaurant, two bars, children's activity center, spa. Pool. Business center. Fitness center. Wireless Internet access. **$$**

★★EMBASSY SUITES HOTEL NIAGARA FALLS/FALLSVIEW

6700 Fallsview Blvd., Niagara Falls, 905-356-3600, 800-420-6980;
www.embassysuitesniagara.com

512 rooms, all suites. Complimentary full breakfast. Restaurant, bar. Pool. Wireless Internet access. **$**

★★★HILTON NIAGARA FALLS

6361 Fallsview Blvd., Niagara Falls, 905-354-7887, 888-370-0325;
www.hiltonniagarafalls.com

Located in the heart of the bustling Niagara Falls tourist area, this hotel is near all the area attractions. The dramatic lobby features lots of pale ochre marble and blond wood. Many of the elegant guest rooms offer outstanding views. 516 rooms. Restaurant, two bars. Pool. Business center. **$$**

★★★MARRIOTT NIAGARA FALLS FALLSVIEW

6740 Fallsview Blvd., Niagara Falls, 905-357-7300, 888-501-8916;
www.niagarafallsmarriott.com

Directly across from Horseshoe Falls, this is a prime Niagara Falls location. Area attractions, restaurants and shops are nearby. The interior of this elegant hotel has a light, sunny feel. The Falls can be viewed from many of the guest rooms as well as right in the lobby. 432 rooms. Restaurant, bar. Pool. Business center. Wireless Internet access. **$$**

★OAKES HOTEL OVERLOOKING THE FALLS

6546 Fallsview Blvd., Niagara Falls, 905-356-4514, 877-843-6253;
www.niagarahospitalityhotels.com

256 rooms. Pool. **$**

★★OLD STONE INN

5425 Robinson St., Niagara Falls, 905-357-1234, 800-263-6208;
www.oldstoneinn.on.ca

114 rooms. Restaurant, bar. Pool. **$**

★★★RENAISSANCE FALLSVIEW HOTEL

6455 Fallsview Blvd., Niagara Falls, 905-357-5200, 888-238-9176;
www.renaissancefallsview.com

This hotel is very close to Niagara Falls and the Queen Victoria Park. The rooftop dining room provides views of the falls. 262 rooms. Two restaurants, bar. Pool. Business center. $$

★★★SHERATON FALLSVIEW HOTEL AND CONFERENCE CENTRE

6755 Fallsview Blvd., Niagara Falls, 905-374-1077, 800-618-9059; www.fallsview.com

Guests can walk to the Falls and numerous area attractions, restaurants and shops. The large two-story lobby has a curved staircase with comfortable, casual seating. Guest rooms are attractive and feature deep blue bed coverings, luxurious linens and comfortable mattresses. 402 rooms. Three restaurants, two bars. Pets accepted, fee. Pool. Business center. $$

SPECIALTY LODGINGS

BEDHAM HALL

4835 River Road, Niagara Falls, 905-374-8515; www.bedhamhall.com

Four rooms, all suites. Continental breakfast. $$

CHESTNUT INN

4983 River Road, Niagara Falls, 905-374-7623; www.chestnutinnbb.com

Four rooms. Complimentary full breakfast. $$

EASTWOOD LODGE

141

5359 River Road, Niagara Falls, 905-354-8686, 877-354-8688; www.theeastwood.com

Six rooms. Complimentary full breakfast. Wireless Internet access. $

RESTAURANTS

★★BUCHANAN'S CHOPHOUSE

6039 Fallsview Blvd., Niagara Falls, 905-353-4111; www.niagarafallsdoubletree.com

Steak menu. Breakfast, lunch, dinner. Reservations recommended. Outdoor seating. $$

ONTARIO

★★CAPRI

5438 Ferry St., Niagara Falls, 905-354-7519

Italian menu. Reservations recommended. $$

★★MILLERY

5425 Robinson St., Niagara Falls, 905-357-1234, 800-263-6208;
www.oldstoneinn.on.ca

American menu. Lunch, dinner. Reservations recommended. $$

★★QUEENSTON HEIGHTS

14184 Niagara Parkway., Niagara Falls, 905-262-4274, 877-642-7275;
www.niagaraparks.com/dining/queenstonres.php

American menu. Lunch, dinner. Reservations recommended. Outdoor seating. $$

6342 Niagara Parkway, Niagara Falls, 905-356-2217; www.niagaraparks.com
American menu. Closed mid-October-mid-May. Outdoor seating. **$$$**

NIAGARA-ON-THE-LAKE

Often called the loveliest in Ontario, this picturesque town has a long and distinguished history that parallels the growth of the province, which was once a busy shipping, shipbuilding and active commercial center. The beautiful old homes lining the tree-shaded streets testify to the area's prosperity, and the town's attractions include theater, historic sites, beautiful gardens and Queen Street's shops, hotels and restaurants. Delightful in any season, this is one of the best-preserved and prettiest remnants of the Georgian era.

Information: www.niagara-on-the-lake.com

WHAT TO SEE AND DO
BROCK'S MONUMENT

14184 Niagara River Parkway, Niagara, 905-468-4257
This monument emcompassess a massive, 185-foot memorial to Sir Isaac Brock, who was felled by a sharpshooter while leading his troops against American forces at the Battle of Queenston Heights in October 1812. A Narrow, winding staircase leads to tiny observation deck inside the monument. Other memorial plaques in park; walking tour of important points on the Queenston Heights Battlefield begins at Brock Monument; Brock and his aide-de-camp, Lieutenant-Colonel Macdonell, are buried here. Mid-May-Labor Day: daily.

142

FORT GEORGE NATIONAL HISTORIC SITE

26 Queen St., Niagara-on-the-Lake, Niagara Parkway, 905-468-4257; www.pc.gc.ca
Once the principal British post on the frontier, this fort saw much action during the War of 1812. Eleven restored, refurnished buildings and massive ramparts. April-October, daily 10 a.m.-5 p.m.; rest of year, by appointment.

LAURA SECORD HOMESTEAD

29 Queenston St., Queenston, 905-371-0254; www.niagaraparks.com
Restored home of Canadian heroine is furnished with early Upper Canada furniture. After overhearing the plans of Americans billeted in her home, Laura Secord made an exhausting and difficult 19-mile 30-kilometer walk to warn British troops, which resulted in a victory over the Americans at Beaverdams in 1813.

MCFARLAND HOUSE

15927 Niagara Parkway, Niagara-on-the-Lake, 905-356-2241
Georgian brick home used as a hospital in the War of 1812; furnished in the Loyalist tradition, 1835-1845. July-Labor Day, daily; mid-May-June and Labor Day-September, Saturday-Sunday.

NIAGARA APOTHECARY

5 Queen St., Niagara-on-the-Lake, 905-468-3845; www.niagaraapothecary.ca
Restoration of a pharmacy that operated on the premises from 1866-1964. Has a large golden mortar and pestle over door; original walnut and butternut fixtures, apothecary

ONTARIO

★
★
★
★
☆

glass and interesting remedies of the past. May-Labor Day, daily. Check Web site for
additional schedules.

NIAGARA HISTORICAL SOCIETY MUSEUM

43 Castlereagh St., Niagara-on-the-Lake, 905-468-3912;
www.niagarahistorical.museum

Opened in 1907, this is the earliest museum building in Ontario. Items from the time
of the United Empire Loyalists, War of 1812, early Upper Canada and the Victorian
era. May-October daily 10 a.m.-5 p.m.; November-April daily 1-5 p.m.; rest of year,
weekends or by appointment.

ST. MARK'S ANGLICAN CHURCH

47 Byron St., Niagara-on-the-Lake, 905-468-3123; www.stmarks1792.com

Original church damaged by fire after being used as a hospital and barracks during
the War of 1812. Rebuilt in 1822 and enlarged in 1843. Unusual three-layer stained-
glass window. Churchyard dates from earliest British settlement. July-August, daily;
rest of year, by appointment.

ST. VINCENT DE PAUL ROMAN CATHOLIC CHURCH

73 Picton St., Niagara-on-the-Lake, 905-468-1383

First Roman Catholic parish in Upper Canada and an excellent example of Gothic
Revival architecture; enlarged in 1965; older part largely preserved.

SPECIAL EVENT

SHAW FESTIVAL

Queen's Parade and Wellington Street, Niagara-on-the-Lake,
905-468-2153, 800-657-1106; www.shawfest.com

Shaw Festival Theatre, specializing in the works of George Bernard Shaw and his con-
temporaries, presents 10 plays each year in repertory. Housed in three theaters, including the Court House Theatre. Staged by internationally acclaimed ensemble company.
Also lunchtime theater featuring one-act plays by Shaw. Mid-April-October.

ONTARIO

HOTELS

★★★GATE HOUSE HOTEL

142 Queen St., Niagara-on-the-Lake, 905-468-3263; www.gatehouse-niagara.com

This property has a contemporary Italian design and is located within walking distance of shops, historic sites and the three theaters of the Shaw Festival. The rooms
are small, but quaint and cozy. 10 rooms. Closed January-mid-March. Complimen-
tary continental breakfast. Restaurant, bar. Pets accepted, fee. **$$**

★★★OBAN INN

160 Front St., Niagara-on-the-Lake, 905-468-2165, 888-669-5566; www.obaninn.ca

Once the home of a Scottish ship captain, it is now a modern hotel in a wonder-
fully quaint, historic property. The grounds, which overlook Lake Ontario, feature
charming English-style gardens. Individually decorated guest rooms have four-poster
beds and antique furnishings with nice touches like complimentary turndown service.
Take advantage of the complimentary in-town shuttle service when going sightseeing.
26 rooms. Complimentary full breakfast. Restaurant, bar. Pets accepted. Spa. **$$**

★★★PILLAR AND POST

48 John St., Niagara-on-the-Lake, 905-468-2123, 888-669-5566; www.vintageinns.com
This unique inn is located in a restored turn-of-the-century fruit canning factory. The lobby is full of plants and antique furniture. Don't miss a visit to the 100 Fountain Spa. 122 rooms. Restaurant, bar, spa. Pets accepted, fee. Pool. Business center. **$$**

★★★PRINCE OF WALES

6 Picton St., Niagara-on-the-Lake, 905-468-3246, 888-669-5566;
www.vintageinns.com
This historic treasure dates to 1864. Its unique character and formal charm make it one of Canada's most beloved hotels. A cozy day spa celebrates the English countryside in its treatment rooms and afternoon tea is a daily ritual. There is sophisticated dining at Escabeche restaurant, where a modern French menu tempts and delights. 112 rooms. Restaurant, bar. Spa. Fitness center. Pool. Business center. Pets accepted. **$$$**

★★★QUEEN'S LANDING

155 Byron St., Niagara-on-the-Lake, 905-468-2195, 888-669-5566;
www.vintageinns.com
Built with Victorian charm, this inn overlooks the Niagara River, opposite historic Fort Niagara. The Georgian-style theme carries from the lobby to the guest rooms with plush furnishings and wood detailing. The Tiara Restaurant offers peerless views of Niagara-on-the-Lake Harbour. 142 rooms. Restaurant, bar. Spa. Fitness center. Pool. **$$$**

★★★WHITE OAKS CONFERENCE RESORT AND SPA

253 Taylor Road SS4, Niagara-on-the-Lake, 905-688-2550, 800-263-5766;
www.whiteoaksresort.com
This large, modern resort has relaxation and comfort in mind. This is reflected in the guest room amenities such as Frette robes, nightly turndown service and pillow topped mattresses. The attitude is carried over to the full-service spa and LIV, the resort's concept restaurant. 220 rooms. Restaurant, bar. Spa. Pool. Golf. Tennis. Fitness center. Business center. **$$**

SPECIALTY LODGING

MOFFAT INN

60 Picton St., Niagara-on-the-Lake, 905-468-4116; www.moffatinn.com
22 rooms. Restaurant. Wireless Internet access. Bar. **$**

RESTAURANTS

★★BUTTERY THEATRE

19 Queen St., Niagara-on-the-Lake, 905-468-2564; www.thebutteryrestaurant.com
American menu. Lunch, dinner. Dinner theater. Outdoor seating. **$$**

★★★CARRIAGES

48 John St., Niagara-on-the-Lake, 905-468-2123, 888-669-5566; www.vintageinns.com
This cozy, candlelit dining room of the Pillar and Post hotel features exposed beams and a working brick oven. The rack of Australian lamb is superb, as are many of the seafood options, including Marrakech salmon. American menu. Breakfast, lunch, dinner, Sunday brunch. Reservations recommended. Valet parking. Outdoor seating. **$$$**

★★★ESCABÉCHE

6 Picton St., Niagara-on-the-Lake, 905-468-3246, 888-669-5566;
www.vintageinns.com

The formal dining room of the Prince of Wales hotel makes the Victorian experience truly memorable. Enjoy afternoon tea or a long, elaborate dinner. The wine list is equally impressive if you're in the mood to imbibe. International menu. Breakfast, lunch, dinner. Reservations recommended. Valet parking. **$$$**

FANS COURT

135 Queen St., Niagara-on-the-Lake, 905-468-4511

Chinese menu. Closed Monday; also January. Reservations recommended. Outdoor seating. **$$**

OTTAWA

With its parks full of flowers and its universities, museums and diplomatic embassies, Ottawa is one of Canada's most beautiful cities. Ottawa is a city of waterways: the majestic Ottawa River, the fast-flowing Gatineau, the placid Rideau. But no waterway has defined Ottawa like the Rideau Canal, which is a playground for skaters in winter and for boaters in summer. The oldest continuously operated canal in North America, it celebrated its 175th anniversary in 2007. Filled with festivals, buskers, theater, music and dance, Ottawa also prides itself on a superb collection of museums—such as the Canadian Museum of Contemporary Photography, the Canadian Museum of Civilization and Ottawa's rowdy, lumberjack past as captured by the Bytown Museum. For everyone, the nation's capital showcases Canada's art, music, people and politics with grace and verve—in both English and French.

Information: www.ottawatourism.ca

WHAT TO SEE AND DO

BEAVERTAILS

This popular Canadian pastry resembles the tail of a beaver and comes with a variety of sweet and salty toppings. The original kiosk serving this pastry is still operating in the ByWard Market district at the corner of George and William streets. The pastry is based on an ancient North American Voyageur recipe and is a descendant of the quick bread the Voyageurs baked.

BYTOWN MUSEUM

540 Wellington St., 613-234-4570; www.bytownmuseum.com

Located in the heart of downtown, the museum occupies Ottawa's oldest stone building. Artifacts, documents and pictures relating to Colonel By, Bytown and the history and social life of the region. Tours by appointment. April-May 16, Thursday-Monday 10 a.m.-2 p.m.; May 17-October 12, daily 10 a.m.-5 p.m.; October 13-November, Thursday-Monday 10 a.m.-2 p.m., December-March, Monday-Friday by appointment only.

ONTARIO

★
★
★
★
★

BYWARD MARKET

55 ByWard Market Square, Ottawa, Bounded by Dalhousie and Sussex Drive,
George and Clarence streets, 613-562-3325; www.byward-market.com
Traditional farmers market; building houses boutiques and art galleries; outdoor cafés. Exterior market: daily; interior market: April-December, daily, rest of year, Tuesday-Sunday.

CANADIAN MUSEUM OF NATURE

Metcalf and McLeod streets, Ottawa, 613-566-4700, 800-263-4433; www.nature.ca
Exhibits and displays focus on nature and the environment. Topics include dinosaurs, insects, gems and minerals, birds and mammals of Canada and the evolution of the planet. Winter, Tuesday-Sunday 9 a.m.-5 p.m., Thursday until 8 p.m.; summer, daily 9 a.m.-6 p.m., Wednesday-Thursday until 8 p.m.

CANADIAN PARLIAMENT BUILDINGS

Wellington Street on Parliament Hill, Ottawa, 613-996-0896; www.parl.gc.ca
Neo-Gothic architecture dominates this part of the city. House of Commons and Senate meet here; visitors may request free tickets to both chambers when Parliament is in session. Guided tour includes House of Commons, Senate Chamber, Parliamentary Library. Also here are the Centennial Flame, lit in 1967 as a symbol of Canada's 100th birthday, and Memorial Chapel, dedicated to Canadian servicemen who lost their lives in the Boer War, WWI, WWII and the Korean War. Observation Deck atop the Peace Tower.

146

ONTARIO

★
★
★
★
★

CENTRAL EXPERIMENTAL FARM

88 Prince of Wales Drive, Ottawa, 613-991-3044
Approximately 1,200 acres of field crops, ornamental gardens, arboretum; showcase herds of beef and dairy cattle, sheep, swine, horses. Tropical greenhouse, agricultural museum, clydesdale horse-drawn wagon or sleigh rides.

CURRENCY MUSEUM

245 Sparks St., Ottawa, 613-782-8914; www.currencymuseum.ca
Artifacts, maps and exhibits tell the story of money and its use throughout the world. May-October, Monday-Saturday 10:30 a.m.-5 p.m., Sunday 1-5 p.m.; October 2-April, Tuesday-Saturday 10:30 a.m.-5 p.m., Sunday 1-5 p.m.

HOUSE NATIONAL HISTORIC SITE OF CANADA

335 Laurier Ave. E., Ottawa, 613-992-8142; www.parkscanada.gc.ca/laurierhouse
Former residence of two prime ministers: Sir Wilfrid Laurier and W. L. Mackenzie King. Recreated study of Prime Minister Lester B. Pearson. Books, furnishings and memorabilia. Daily 9 a.m.-5 p.m.

MUSEUM OF CANADIAN SCOUTING

1345 Base Line Road, Ottawa, 613-224-5131; www.scouts.ca
Depicts the history of Canadian Scouting; exhibits on the life of Lord R.S.S. Baden-Powell, founder of the Boy Scouts; pertinent documents, photographs and artifacts.

NATIONAL ARTS CENTRE

53 Elgin St., Ottawa, 613-947-7000; www.NAC-CNA.ca

Center for performing arts; houses a concert hall and two theaters for music, dance, variety and drama; home of the National Arts Centre Orchestra; more than 800 performances each year; canal-side café. Landscaped terraces with panoramic view of Ottawa.

NATIONAL AVIATION MUSEUM

11 Aviation Parkway, Rockcliffe Airport, Ottawa, 613-990-1985, 800-463-2038; www.aviation.technomuses.ca

More than 100 historic aircraft, 49 of which one on display in the Walkway of Time. Displays demonstrate the development of aircraft in peace and war, emphasizing Canadian aviation.

NATIONAL GALLERY OF CANADA

380 Sussex Drive, Ottawa, 613-990-1985, 800-319-2787; www.national.gallery.ca

Permanent exhibits include European paintings from the 14th century to the present; Canadian art from the 17th century to the present; contemporary and decorative arts, prints, drawings, photos and Inuit art; video and film. Reconstructed 19th-century Rideau convent chapel with Neo-Gothic fan-vaulted ceiling, only known example of its kind in North America. Changing exhibits fee, gallery talks, films; restaurants, bookstore. May-September, daily 10 a.m.-5 p.m., Thursday to 8 p.m.; October-April, Tuesday-Sunday 10 a.m.-5 p.m., Thursday to 8 p.m.

NATIONAL MUSEUM OF SCIENCE AND TECHNOLOGY

1867 St. Laurent Blvd., Ottawa, 613-991-3044; www.sciencetech.technomuses.ca

More than 400 exhibits with many do-it-yourself experiments; Canada's role in science and technology shown through displays on Canada in space, transportation, agriculture, computers, communications, physics and astronomy. Unusual open restoration bay allows viewing of various stages of artifact repair and refurbishment. Labor Day-April, Tuesday-Sunday 9 a.m.-5 p.m.; May-Labor Day, Monday-Sunday 9 a.m.-5 p.m.

PAUL'S BOAT LINES, LTD

Suffux and Rideau streets, Ottawa, 613-225-6781; www.paulsboatcruises.com

Rideau Canal sightseeing cruises depart from Conference Centre mid-May-mid-October, daily. Ottawa River sightseeing cruises depart from foot of Rideau Canal Locks mid-May-mid-October, daily.

RIDEAU CANAL

34A Beckwith St. S., runs 125 miles between Kingston and Ottawa, Ottawa, 613-992-8142, 800-230-0016; www.pc.gc.ca

Constructed under the direction of Lieutenant-Colonel John By of the Royal Engineers between 1826 and 1832 as a safe supply route to Upper Canada. The purpose was to bypass the St. Lawrence River in case of an American attack. There are 24 lock stations where visitors can picnic, watch boats pass through the hand-operated locks and see wooden lock gates, cut stone walls and many historic structures. In summer there are interpretive programs and exhibits at various locations. Areas of special interest include Kingston Mills Locks, Jones Falls Locks off Highway 15,

Smith Falls Museum off Highway 15, Merrickville Locks on Highway 43 and Ottawa Locks. Boating is popular (mid-May-mid-October), and ice skating is possible mid-December-late February.

ROYAL CANADIAN MINT
320 Sussex Drive, Ottawa, 613-993-8990, 800-276-7714; www.rcmint.ca
See how Canadian coins are produced, as well as expansive collections of coins and medals. Guided tours and film; detailed process of minting coins and printing bank notes is shown.

VICTORIA MEMORIAL MUSEUM BUILDING
240 McLeod St., Ottawa, 613-566-4700; www.nature.ca
Castle-like structure houses museum that interrelates man and his natural environment. Houses the Canadian Museum of Nature. Natural history exhibits from dinosaurs to present day plants and animals. Outstanding collection of minerals and gems.

SPECIAL EVENTS
CANADA DAY
90 Wellington St., Ottawa, 613-239-5000, 800-465-1867;
www.canadascapital.gc.ca
Celebration of Canada's birthday with many events throughout the city, including canoe and sailing regattas, concerts, music and dance, arts and craft demonstrations, children's entertainment and fireworks. July 1.

CANADIAN TULIP FESTIVAL
Canadian Tulip Festival, 130 Albert St., Ottawa, 613-567-5757; www.tulipfestival.ca
Part of a two-week celebration, culminated by the blooming of more than 3 million tulips presented to Ottawa by Queen Juliana of the Netherlands after she sought refuge here during WWII. Tours of flower beds; craft market and demonstrations, kite flying, boat parade. May.

OTTAWA INTERNATIONAL JAZZ FESTIVAL
61A Yorks St., Ottawa, 613-241-2633, 888-226-4495; www.ottawajazzfestival.com
Jazz artists from around the world perform at this week-long celebration. Ten days in mid-July.

WINTERLUDE
90 Wellington St., Ottawa, 613-239-5000; www.canadascapital.gc.ca
Extravaganza devoted to outdoor concerts, fireworks, skating contests, dances, music and ice sculptures. Three weekends in February.

HOTELS
★★ALBERT AT BAY SUITE HOTEL
435 Albert St., Ottawa, 613-238-8858, 800-267-6644; www.albertatbay.com
197 rooms, all suites. Two restaurants, one bar. $

★★BEST WESTERN HOTEL JACQUES CARTIER

131 Laurier St., Hull, 819-770-8550; www.bestwestern.com

144 rooms. Restaurant, bar. Fitness center. High-speed Internet access. Pool. **$**

★BEST WESTERN VICTORIA PARK SUITES

377 O'Connor St., Ottawa, 613-567-7275, 800-465-7275; www.victoriapark.com

123 rooms. Complimentary continental breakfast. **$**

★★DELTA OTTAWA HOTEL & SUITES

361 Queen St., Ottawa, 613-238-6000, 888-890-3222; www.deltahotels.com

328 rooms. Two restaurants, one bar. Children's activity center. Pets accepted, fee. Pool. Business center. **$**

★★★THE FAIRMONT CHATEAU LAURIER

1 Rideau St., Ottawa, 613-241-1414, 800-441-1414; www.fairmont.com

This impressive castle enchants visitors with its setting overlooking Parliament Hill, the Rideau Canal and the Ottawa River. It is conveniently located in the city center. Enjoy elegant dining at Wilfrid's, while Zoe's Lounge is a more casual alternative. Guest services include a full-service fitness club with a stunning Art Deco pool. 429 rooms. Restaurant, bar. Spa. Pets accepted, fee. Pool. Business center. **$$**

★★★THE FAIRMONT LE CHATEAU MONTEBELLO

392 rue Notre Dame, Montebello, 819-423-6341, 800-441-1414; www.fairmont.com

Stretched out along the banks of the Ottawa River, this log cabin-style lodge charms with spectacular scenery. From hiking, biking and boating, the recreational pursuits offered here are endless. Sybaritic-minded visitors enjoy the pampering treatments at the spa, while gastronomes savor the cuisine at the resort's dining rooms. 210 rooms. Restaurant, bar. High-speed Internet access, children's activity center. Pets accepted, fee. Pool. Golf. Tennis. Spa. Business center. **$$**

★★★GASTHAUS SWITZERLAND INN

89 Daly Ave., Ottawa, 613-237-0335; www.ottawainn.com

This charming inn is located in a restored 1872 house. Enjoy traditional Swiss hospitality during a visit to Canada's capital. Though some of the rooms are small, they all offer personalized touches and comfortable beds. 22 rooms. High-speed Internet access. Children over 12 years only. Complimentary full breakfast. Restaurant. **$**

★★★HILTON LAC-LEAMY

3 Blvd. Du Casino, Hull, 819-790-6444; www.hiltonlacleamy.com

Located on the shore of Lake Leamy and Des Carrieres Lake, connected to a casino, close to Gatineau's shopping district and right outside of an all-season walking/biking trail, this hotel has something for everyone. Various dining options abound with the French-style bistro, Le Cellier, or a fine dining experience at Le Baccara. The rooms are what you would expect from a Hilton: comfortable and well-appointed. 349 rooms. Restaurant, bar. Wireless Internet access. Pool. Business center. **$$**

★
★
★
★
★

★★LORD ELGIN HOTEL

100 Elgin St., Ottawa, 613-235-3333, 888-268-1113; www.lordelginhotel.ca

359 rooms. Spa. Restaurant, two bars. Pets accepted, fee. Pool. **$**

★★★MARRIOTT OTTAWA

100 Kent St., Ottawa, 613-238-1122, 800-853-8463; www.ottawamarriott.com

Located in the heart of downtown, the hotel is close to local attractions such as Canada's Parliament Buildings, the Rideau Canal, the Ottawa Congress Centre and the National Gallery of Canada. Enjoy a panoramic view of the city with your meal at the Merlot Rooftop Grill, a revolving restaurant. 480 rooms. Two restaurants, one bar. High-speed Internet access. Children's activity center. Pets accepted, fee. Pool. Business center. **$**

★★★MINTO PLACE SUITE HOTEL

185 Lyon St. N., Ottawa, 613-232-2200, 800-267-3377; www.mintosuitehotel.com

The conveniences of this city hotel are enjoyed both onsite and off in Canada's capital city. Outside its doors, explore Parliament Hill, Casino Lac-Leamy and the Historic Byward Market. Inside, guests dine, shop, bank and pamper themselves. The rooms are updated with modern amenities. 417 rooms, all suites. Pool. Fitness center. Two restaurants, two bars. **$$$**

★★★THE WESTIN OTTAWA

11 Colonel By Drive, Ottawa, 613-560-7000, 800-937-8461; www.westin.com

Located only blocks from Parliament Hill and the historic Byward Market, this hotel is connected to the Rideau Center Shopping Complex and the Ottawa Congress Center. Guest rooms are decorated in neutral tones and many rooms have soaking tubs. 487 rooms. Three restaurants, one bar. Spa. Pets accepted, fee. Pool. Business center. **$$**

RESTAURANTS

★★★DOMUS CAFÉ

87 Murray St., Ottawa, 613-241-6007; www.domuscafe.ca

For years, this was a simple café adjacent to the cooking store of the same name. It was recently bought by chef John Taylor. The café offers innovative combinations of local and international flavors. French bistro menu. Lunch, dinner. Bar. Reservations recommended. **$$$**

★★LA GONDOLA

188 Bank St., Ottawa, 613-235-3733

Italian menu. Reservations recommended. Outdoor seating. **$$**

★★THE MILL

555 Ottawa River Parkway, Ottawa, 613-237-1311; www.the-mill.ca

Steak menu. Reservations recommended. Outdoor seating. **$$$**

ST. CATHARINES

St. Catharines, "the Garden City of Canada," is located in the heart of the wine country and the Niagara fruit belt, which produces half of the province's output of fresh fruit. Originally a Loyalist settlement, it was also a depot of the Underground

Railroad, which smuggled American slaves from southern plantations to freedom in Canada. Located on the Welland Ship Canal in North America, St. Catharines was also the home of the first electric streetcar system in North America and is highlighted by a plethora of boats, beaches, world-class rowing, tree-lined streets and gardens and diverse festivals.

Information: www.stcatharines.ca/tourism/index.asp

WHAT TO SEE AND DO

FARMERS MARKET

50 Church St., St. Catharines, 905-688-5601; stcatharines.ca

Large variety of fruit and vegetables from fruit belt farms of the surrounding area. Tuesday, Thursday, Saturday.

HAPPY ROLPH BIRD SANCTUARY & CHILDREN'S FARM

Reed Road, St. Catharines, 905-937-7210; www.stcatharines.ca

Feeding station for native fowl and farm animals; three ponds; nature trail, picnicking, playground. Victoria Day-Thanksgiving.

MORNINGSTAR MILL

2710 DeCew Road, St. Catharines, at De Cew Falls,
905-688-6050; www.morningstarmill.ca

Water powered, fine old mill containing rollers and millstones for grinding flour and feed. Picnic area. Victoria Day-Thanksgiving.

RODMAN HALL ARTS CENTRE

109 St. Paul Crescent, St. Catharines, 905-684-2925; www.brocku.ca/rodmanhall

Art exhibitions, films, concerts, children's theater. Tuesday-Sunday; closed holidays.

ST. CATHARINES MUSEUM

1932 Government Road, St. Catharines, 905-984-8880;
www.stcatharineslock3museum.ca

Illustrates development, construction and significance of Welland Canal; working scale model lock; displays on history of St. Catharines. Exhibitions on loan from major museums. Daily 9 a.m.-5 p.m.

WELLAND CANAL VIEWING COMPLEX AT LOCK III

1932 Government Road, St. Catharines, 905-688-5601; www.stcatharines.ca

Unique view of lock operations from an elevated platform. Ships from more than 50 countries can be seen as they pass through the canal. Arrival times are posted.

SPECIAL EVENTS

FOLK ARTS FESTIVAL

85 Church St., St. Catharines, 905-685-6589; www.folk-arts.ca

Folk Art Multicultural Centre. Open houses at ethnic clubs, concerts, ethnic dancing and singing. Art and craft exhibits; big parade. Two weeks in late May.

151

ONTARIO

★
★
★
★
★

NIAGARA GRAPE AND WINE FESTIVAL

8 Church St., St. Catharines, 905-688-2570; www.niagaragrapeandwinefestival.com

Wine and cheese parties, athletic events, grape stomping, arts and crafts, ethnic concerts and parade with bands and floats to honor ripening of the grapes. Grand Parade last Saturday of festival. Ten days in late September.

NIAGARA SYMPHONY ASSOCIATION

73 Ontario St., St. Catharines, 905-687-4993; www.niagarasymphony.org

Professional symphony orchestra; amateur chorus; sumer music camp. September-May.

ROYAL CANADIAN HENLEY REGATTA

Henley Rowing Course, 61 Main, St. Catharines, 905-935-9771; www.henleyregatta.ca

Champion rowers from all parts of the world. Second in size only to the famous English regatta. Several nation- and continent-wide regattas take place on this world-famous course. April-October.

SALMON DERBY

Lighthouse and Lake Shore roads, St. Catharines, 905-935-6700

Open season on Lake Ontario for coho and chinook salmon; rainbow, brown and lake trout. Prizes for all categories. Mid-April-mid-May.

HOTELS

★★FOUR POINTS BY SHERATON

3530 Schmon Parkway, Thorold, 905-984-8484, 877-848-3782;
www.starwoodhotels.com

129 rooms. Restaurant, bar. High-speed Internet access. Pets accepted, fee. Pool. Business center. $

★★HOLIDAY INN

2 N. Service Road, St. Catharines, 905-934-8000, 877-688-2324;
www.stcatharines.holiday-inn.com

141 rooms. Wireless Internet access. Fitness center. Restaurant, bar. Pets accepted, fee. Pool. $

★★QUALITY INN

325 Ontario St., St. Catharines, 905-688-2324; www.qualityparkway.com

125 rooms. Restaurant, bar. Pets accepted, fee. Pool. $

STRATFORD

The names Stratford and Avon River can conjure up only one name—Shakespeare. And that is exactly what you will find in this lovely city. World-renowned, this festival of fine theater takes place here every year. For a relatively small town, Stratford offers up a wonderful variety of shows, concerts, plays, art galleries and spas—ideal for a weekend escape, and sealed with plentiful gardens and a Victorian city core.

Information: www.welcometostratford.com

★
★
★
★
★

WHAT TO SEE AND DO

CONFEDERATION PARK

52 Romeo St. N., Stratford, 519-273-3352; www.welcometostratford.com

Features rock hill, waterfall, fountain, Japanese garden and commemorative court.

GALLERY OF STRATFORD

54 Romeo St. N., Stratford, 519-271-5271; www.gallerystratford.on.ca

Public gallery in parkland setting; historical and contemporary works. Guided tours on request. Tuesday-Sunday 10 a.m.-5 p.m.

SHAKESPEAREAN GARDENS

Huron St., Stratford, 519-271-5140; www.welcometostratford.com

Fragrant herbs, shrubs and flowering plants common to William Shakespeare's time.

SPECIAL EVENT

STRATFORD FESTIVAL

55 Queen St., Stratford, 519-273-1600, 800-567-1600; www.stratford-festival.on.ca

Contemporary, classical and Shakespearean dramas and modern musicals. Performances at Festival, Avon and Tom Patterson theaters. May-November, matinees and evenings.

HOTELS

★★FESTIVAL INN

1144 Ontario St., Stratford, 519-273-1150, 800-463-3581; www.festivalinnstratford.com

182 rooms. Restaurant, bar. Pool. $

★★★QUEEN'S INN

161 Ontario St., Stratford, 519-271-1400; www.queensinnstratford.ca

This lovely Victorian inn is located on the main street of downtown, close to a variety of shops and restaurants. It features uniquely decorated rooms that give the guest a home-away-from-home feel. 32 rooms. Two restaurants. Wireless Internet access. Pets accepted, fee. $

★STRATFORD SUBURBAN

2808 Ontario St. E., Stratford, 519-271-9650; www.suburbanmotel.com

25 rooms. Wireless Internet access. Pool. Tennis. $

★★★TOUCHSTONE MANOR

325 St. David St., Stratford, 519-273-5820; www.touchstone-manor.com

This 1938 inn is located in a quiet, residential neighborhood within walking distance of downtown and about a 1/2 hour walk to the Shakespeare Festival area. The rooms boast period antiques and personalized detailing. Four rooms. Closed late December-late January. Children over 12 years only. Complimentary full breakfast. $$$

ONTARIO

★
★
★
★
★

★★VICTORIAN INN

10 Romeo St. N., Stratford, 519-271-4650, 800-741-2135;
www.victorian-inn.on.ca
115 rooms. Restaurant. Pets accepted. Pool. Fitness center. $

RESTAURANTS

★★★CHURCH RESTAURANT AND THE BELFRY

70 Brunswick St., Stratford, 519-273-3424; www.churchrestaurant.com
Housed in a 19th-century Gothic church, it features painted walls, wooden arches and stained-glass windows, and showcases opulent French meals. The restaurant is located behind several of the festival theaters. For three weeks in summer, it offers cabaret performances. French menu. Dinner. Reservations recommended. $$$

★★KEYSTONE ALLEY CAFE

34 Brunswick St., Stratford, 519-271-5645; www.keystonealley.com
American menu. Lunch, dinner. Closed Sunday-Monday; two weeks in March. Reservations recommended. Outdoor seating. $$$

★HOUSE OF GENE

108 Downie St., Stratford, 519-271-3080
Chinese menu. $$

★MADELYN'S DINER

377 Huron St., Stratford, 519-273-5296; www.madelynsdiner.com
American dinner. $$

★★OLD PRUNE

151 Albert St., Stratford, 519-271-5052; www.oldprune.on.ca
Continental menu. Lunch, dinner. Closed Monday; November-mid-April. $$$

★★★RUNDLE'S

9 Cobourg St., Stratford, 519-271-6442; www.rundlesrestaurant.com
Located on the river at ground zero for the Stratford Festival, this longtime favorite affords the most elegant dining in the area. Like the environment, the chef's food is simple, elegant and thoroughly enjoyable. American menu. Lunch, dinner. Outdoor seating. $$$$

THUNDER BAY

Thanks to its prime location on Lake Superior, Thunder Bay is a major grain shipping port with a colorful history tied to the fur trade of the early 19th century. The town's Fort William, inland headquarters for the trade, relives the glory of Canada's wilder days. History aside, Thunder Bay offers skiing, parks and a home base for explorations around Lake Superior.
Information: www.visitthunderbay.com

WHAT TO SEE AND DO

AMETHYST MINE PANORAMA

400 Victoria Ave., Thunder Bay, 807-622-6908; www.amethystmine.com

Open-pit quarry adjacent to Elbow Lake. The quarrying operation, geological faults, Canadian Pre-Cambrian shield and sample gem pockets are readily visible. Gem picking. Daily.

CENTENNIAL PARK

Centennial Park Road and Hudson Avenue, Thunder Bay, near Boulevard Lake, 807-683-6511

Summer features include a reconstructed 1910 logging camp; logging camp museum. Playground. Cross-country skiing; sleigh rides in winter.

INTERNATIONAL FRIENDSHIP GARDENS

2000 Victoria Ave., Thunder Bay, 807-625-3166; www.thunderbay.ca

This park is composed of individual gardens designed and constructed by various ethnic groups including Slovakian, Polish, German, Italian, Finnish, Danish, Ukrainian, Hungarian and Chinese.

KAKABEKA FALLS PROVINCIAL PARK

Thunder Bay, 20 miles/32 kilometers west via Highway 11/17, 807-473-9231; www.ontarioparks.com

A spectacular waterfall on the historic Kaministiquia River, formerly a voyageur route from Montréal to the West. The 128-foot falls can be seen from highway pull-offs. The flow of water is best in spring and on weekends; the flow is reduced during the week. There's a sandy beach in the park, plus hiking trails, areas for camping, a playground and a visitor service center.

OLD FORT WILLIAM

1 King Road, Thunder Bay, Off Highway 61 S, 807-577-8461; www.thunderbay.ca

Authentic reconstruction of the original Fort William as it was from 1803 to 1821. Visitors experience the adventure of the Norwesters convergence for the Rendezvous re-creation staged 10 days in mid-July. Costumed staff populate 42 buildings on the site, featuring tradesmen's shops, farm, apothecary, fur stores, warehouses, Great Hall, voyageur encampment, indigenous encampment; historic restaurant.

QUETICO PROVINCIAL PARK

Thunder Bay, 27 miles west on Highway 11/17, 218-387-2075; www.ontarioparks.com

Quetico is a wilderness park composed largely of rugged landscape. There are no roads in the park, but its vast network of connecting waterways allows for some of the best canoeing in North America. Fishing and swimming are the primary activities in the park. Appropriate fishing licenses are required. Car camping is permitted at 107 sites in two areas of the Dawson Trail Campgrounds. Permits can be obtained at park ranger stations. Picnic facilities, trails and a large assortment of pictographs may be enjoyed. In winter, vacationers can ice fish and cross-country ski, although there are no maintained facilities. Victoria Day-Thanksgiving: daily.

155

ONTARIO

★
★
★
★

THUNDER BAY ART GALLERY

1080 Keewatin St., Thunder Bay, 807-577-6427; www.theag.ca

Changing exhibitions from major national and international museums; regional art; contemporary native art. Tours, films, lectures, concerts.

HOTELS

★COMFORT INN

660 W. Arthur St., Thunder Bay, 807-475-3155; www.comfortinn.com

80 rooms. Pets accepted, fee. $

★★GOLDEN TULIP VALHALLA INN THUNDER BAY

1 Valhalla Inn Road, Thunder Bay, 807-577-1121, 800-964-1121; www.valhallainn.com

267 rooms. High-speed Internet access. Restaurant, bar. Pets accepted, fee. Pool. $$

★★PRINCE ARTHUR

17 N. Cumberland, Thunder Bay, 807-345-5411; www.princearthur.on.ca

121 rooms. Restaurant, bar. Pets accepted, fee. Pool. $

★★VICTORIA INN

555 W. Arthur St., Thunder Bay, 807-577-8481, 800-387-3331; www.tbaytel.net/vicinn

182 rooms. Restaurant, bar. Pets accepted, fee. Pool. $

RESTAURANT

★★THE KEG

735 Hewitson St., Thunder Bay, 807-623-1960; www.kegsteakhouse.com

Seafood, steak menu. Lunch, dinner. Bar. $$$

TORONTO

Toronto is one of Canada's leading industrial, commercial and cultural centers. Having earned its name from the native word for "meeting place," Toronto is an awesome cosmopolitan city—the United Nations recently deemed it the world's most ethnically diverse city. A performing arts powerhouse, the city presents everything from Broadway musicals to standup comedy and opera to dance. Good shopping can be found throughout the city, but Torontonians are most proud of their Underground City, a series of subterranean malls linking more than 300 shops and restaurants in the downtown area. For professional sports fans, Toronto offers the Maple Leafs (hockey), Blue Jays (baseball), Raptors (basketball) and Argonauts (football). A visit to the harbor front, a boat tour to the islands, or enjoying an evening on the town should round out your stay.

Information: www.torontotourism.com

WHAT TO SEE AND DO

ALLAN GARDENS

19 Horticultural Ave., Toronto, 416-392-7288; www.toronto.ca

Indoor/outdoor botanical displays, wading pool, picnicking, concerts. Daily 10 a.m.-5 p.m.

BATA SHOE MUSEUM

327 Bloor St. W., Toronto, 416-979-7799; www.batashoemuseum.ca

When Mrs. Sonja Bata's passion for collecting historical shoes began to surpass her personal storage space, the Bata family established The Bata Shoe Museum Foundation. Architect Raymond Moriyama's award-winning five-story, 3,900-square-foot building now holds more than 10,000 shoes, artfully arranged in four galleries to celebrate the style and function of footwear throughout 4,500 years of history. One permanent exhibition, "All About Shoes," showcases a collection of 20th-century celebrity shoes; artifacts on exhibit range from Chinese bound-foot shoes and ancient Egyptian sandals to chestnut-crushing clogs and Elton John's platforms. Monday-Saturday 10 a.m.-5 p.m., Sunday noon-5 p.m.

BLACK CREEK PIONEER VILLAGE

1000 Murray Ross Parkway, Downsview, 416-736-1733; www.blackcreek.ca

Step back in time with a visit to this village. Workers wearing period costumes welcome you into 35 authentically restored homes, workshops, public buildings and farms and demonstrate skills such as open-hearth cooking, breadmaking, looming, milling, blacksmithing, sewing and printing.

BLOOR/YORKVILLE AREA

Bounded by Bloor Street West, Avenue Road, Davenport Road and Yonge Street, Toronto, 416-928-3553; www.bloor-yorkville.com

The Bloor/Yorkville area is one of Toronto's most elegant shopping and dining sections, with nightclubs, music, designer couture boutiques and first-rate art galleries. The area itself is fun to walk around, with a cluster of courtyards and alleyways. There's also a contemporary park in the heart of the neighborhood with a huge piece of granite called The Rock. It was brought here from the Canadian Shield, a U-shaped region of ancient rock covering about half of Canada. Monday-Friday 8:30 a.m.-5 p.m.

CANADA'S SPORTS HALL OF FAME

115 Princes' Blvd., Toronto, 416-260-6789; www.cshof.ca

Erected to honor the country's greatest athletes in all major sports, Canada's Sports Hall of Fame features exhibit galleries, a theater, library, archives and kiosks that show videos of Canada's greatest moments in sports. Don't miss the Heritage Gallery lower level, which contains artifacts showcasing the development of 125 years of sport. Also stop in at the 50-seat Red Foster Theatre, which projects films clips that highlight Canadian sports, such as The Terry Fox Story.

CANADIAN TROPHY FISHING

143 Clifton Ave., Downsview, Ontario, 416-540-0839; www.cdntrophyfishing.com

Canadian Trophy Fishing supplies the equipment, facilities, and fishing license for Chinook salmon, coho salmon, Atlantic salmon, rainbow trout, brown trout, lake trout or whitefish. They suggest you bring a large cooler to take home all of your catches, but for an extra fee they will smoke, fillet, freeze and ship. Ice fishing season is January-mid-March.

157

ONTARIO

★
★
★
★

CASA LOMA

1 Austin Terrace, Toronto, 416-923-1171; www.casaloma.org

Grab an audio cassette and a floor plan and take a self-guided tour of this domestic castle, built in 1911 over three years at a cost of $3.5 million. As romantic as he was a shrewd businessman, Sir Henry Pellatt, who founded the Toronto Electric Light Company, had an architect create this medieval castle. Soaring battlements, secret passageways, flowerbeds warmed by steam pipes, secret doors, servants' rooms and an 800-foot tunnel are just some of the treats you'll discover. Daily 9:30 a.m.-5 p.m.

COLBORNE LODGE

Colborne Lodge Drive and The Queensway, Toronto, 416-392-6916;
www.city.toronto.on.ca

The successful 19th-century architect John Howard was just 34 when he completed this magnificent manor, named for the architect's first patron, Upper Canada Lieutenant Governor Sir John Colborne. It stands today as an excellent example of Regency-style architecture, with its stately verandas and lovely placement in a beautiful setting. Check Web site for hours.

CN TOWER

301 Front St. W., Toronto, 416-868-6937; www.cntower.ca

Toronto's CN Tower is the tallest freestanding structure in the world. At 1,815 feet from the ground to the tip of its communications aerial, it towers over the rest of the city. Take the elevator to the top, where on a clear day it's said you can see the spray coming off Niagara Falls 62 miles away. Any level provides spectacular views. Daily 9 a.m-10 p.m., Friday-Saturday to 10:30 p.m.

★
★
★
★
☆

DISCOVERY HARBOUR

93 Jury Drive, Penetanguishene, 705-549-8064; www.discoveryharbour.on.ca

Established in 1817, the site includes a 19th-century military base. Now rebuilt, the site features eight furnished buildings and an orientation center. Replica of 49-foot British naval schooner, H.M.S. Bee; also H.M.S. Tecumseth and Perseverance. Costumed interpreters bring the base to life, circa 1830. Sail training and excursions. May 20-June 27, Monday-Friday 10 a.m.-5 p.m.; June 28-August 31, daily 10 a.m.-5 p.m.

DRAGON CITY SHOPPING MALL

280 Spadina Ave., Toronto, 416-596-8885

Located in the heart of Chinatown, the Dragon City Shopping Mall consists of more than 30 stores and services. Buy Chinese herbs, look at Asian jewelry, browse chic Chinese housewares and gifts, or admire Oriental arts and crafts. Afterwards treat yourself to a meal at Sky Dragon Cuisine in the Dragon City tower, an upscale Chinese restaurant with a beautiful view of the Toronto skyline.

EASY AND THE FIFTH

225 Richmond W., Toronto, 416-979-3000

A dance club for the over 25 crowd, it offers music ranging from tango to Top 40. The dress code is upscale casual, and the atmosphere is loft-apartment-open, with two bars and several specialty bars such as The Green Room, where you can shoot pool, play craps and smoke a cigar to the accompaniment of live jazz. On Thursday from 6-10 p.m., enjoy cocktail hour with a complimentary buffet. Thursday 6 p.m.-2 a.m.; Friday-Saturday from 9 p.m.

EATON CENTRE

220 Yonge St., Toronto, 416-598-8560; www.torontoeatoncentre.com

This 3 million-square-foot building is a masterpiece of architecture and environment. Its glass roof rises 127 feet above the mall's lowest level. The large, open space contains glass-enclosed elevators, dozens of long, graceful escalators and porthole windows. A flock of fiberglass Canadian geese floats through the air. Even if shopping isn't a favorite vacation activity, Eaton Centre is worth a trip.

EDWARDS GARDENS

777 Lawrence Ave. E., Toronto, 416-392-8188;
www.toronto.ca/parks

Civic garden center; rock gardens, pools, pond, rustic bridges.

ELGIN & WINTER GARDEN THEATRE CENTRE

189 Yonge St., Toronto, 416-872-5555; www.heritagefdn.on.ca

The 80-year history of the two theaters speaks more volumes than one of its excellent productions. Built in 1913, each theater was a masterpiece in its own right: The Elgin was ornate, with gold leaf, plaster cherubs and elegant opera boxes; the walls of the Winter Garden were hand-painted to resemble a garden and its ceiling was a mass of beech bows and twinkling lanterns. Through the years, the stages saw the likes of George Burns and Gracie Allen, Edger Bergen and Charlie McCarthy, Milton Berle and Sophie Tucker. The Ontario Heritage Foundation offers year-round guided tours on Thursdays at 5 p.m. and Saturdays at 11 a.m.

GEORGE R. GARDINER MUSEUM OF CERAMIC ART

111 Queen's Park, Toronto, 416-586-8080; www.gardinermuseum.on.ca

One of the world's finest collections of Italian majolica, English Delftware and 18th-century continental porcelain.

GIBSON HOUSE

5172 Yonge St., North York, 416-395-7432; www.toronto.ca

Home of land surveyor and local politician David Gibson; restored and furnished to 1850s style. Costumed interpreters conduct demonstrations.

HARBOURFRONT CENTRE

235 Queens Quay W., Toronto, 416-973-4600; www.harbourfront.on.ca

This 10-acre waterfront community is alive with theater, dance, films, art shows, music, crafts and children's programs. Most events are free. Daily.

HIGH PARK

1873 Bloor St. W. and Keele St., Toronto, 416-392-1111; www.highpark.org

High Park is an urban oasis with expansive fields for sports, picnicking and cycling; a large lake that freezes in the winter; a small zoo, swimming pool, tennis courts and bowling greens.

159

ONTARIO

★
★
★
★

HISTORIC FORT YORK

100 Garrison Road, Toronto, 416-392-6907; www.city.toronto.on.ca

It may not have seen a lot of action—just one battle during the War of 1812—but Fort York's place in Toronto's history is secure. It is the birthplace of modern Toronto, having played a major role in saving York (now Toronto) from being invaded by 1,700 American soldiers. Today's Fort York has Canada's largest collection of original War of 1812 buildings and is a designated National Historic Site.

ICE SKATING AT GRENADIER POND

1873 Bloor St., 416-392-6916; www.toronto.ca/parks

One of the most romantic ice-skating spots you'll find is Grenadier Pond in High Park, one of 25 parks offering free artificial rinks throughout the city. In addition to vendors selling roasted chestnuts, there's a bonfire to keep toasty. Other free ice rinks include Nathan Phillips Square in front of City Hall and an area at Harbor front Centre. Equipment rentals are available on site.

KENSINGTON MARKET

College Street and Spadina Avenue, Toronto

This maze of narrow streets is lined with food shops, vintage clothing stores, restaurants and jewelry vendors. There are bargain hunters haggling, café owners enticing diners and little stores brimming with items from Asia, South America, the Middle East and Europe.

KORTRIGHT CENTRE FOR CONSERVATION

9550 Pine Valley Drive, Woodbridge, 905-832-2289; www.kortright.org

Environmental center with trails, bee house, maple syrup shack, wildlife pond and plantings. Naturalist-guided hikes. Cross-country skiing; picnic area, cafe; indoor exhibits and theater.

LITTLE ITALY

West of Bathurst Street between Euclid Avenue and Shaw Street, Toronto;
www.torontotourism.com

After the British, Italians make up the largest cultural group in Toronto. Though the Italian community moved north as it grew, the atmosphere of Little Italy remains. Restaurants and bars open onto the sidewalks.

MACKENZIE HOUSE

82 Bond St., Toronto, 416-392-6915; www.toronto.ca

Restored 19th-century home of William Lyon Mackenzie, first mayor of Toronto; furnishings and artifacts of the 1850s; 1840s print shop. January-April, Saturday-Sunday noon-5 p.m.; May-Labor Day, Tuesday-Sunday noon-5 p.m. September-December, Tuesday-Friday noon-4 p.m., Saturday-Sunday noon-5 p.m.

MARKET GALLERY

95 Front St. E., Toronto, 416-392-7604; www.stlawrencemarket.com

Exhibition center for Toronto archives; displays on city's historical, social and cultural heritage; art, photographs, maps, documents and artifacts. Wednesday-Saturday, Sunday afternoons.

ONTARIO

★
★
★
★
★

MARTIN GOODMAN TRAIL

Toronto, 416-392-8186; www.city.toronto.on.ca/parks

Leave it to fitness-conscious Toronto not just to have a beautifully maintained waterfront, but to build a trail that takes you from one end to the other. The Martin Goodman Trail is a public jogging, biking, walking and in-line skating path that connects all the elements of the waterfront, traversing 13 miles. It also runs past several spots for bike and skate rentals.

MCMICHAEL CANADIAN ART COLLECTION

10365 Islington Ave., Kleinburg, 905-893-1121; www.mcmichael.com

Works by Canada's most famous artists—the Group of Seven, Tom Thomson, Emily Carr, David Milne, Clarence Gagnon and others. Also Inuit and contemporary indigenous art and sculpture. Constructed from hand-hewn timbers and native stone, the gallery stands on 100 acres on the crest of Humber Valley. Restaurant, book, gift shop.

MEDIEVAL TIMES

Exhibition Place, Dufferin Gate, Toronto, 416-260-1234; www.medievaltimes.com

This 11th-century castle was created to replicate an 11th-century experience, complete with knightly competitions and equestrian displays.

MOUNT PLEASANT CEMETERY

375 Mount Pleasant Road, Toronto, 416-485-9129;
www.mountpleasantgroupofcemeteries.ca

One of the oldest cemeteries in North America, the Mount Pleasant Cemetery is the final resting place of many well-known Canadians, including Sir Frederic Banting and Charles Best, the discoverers of insulin; renowned classical pianist Glenn Gould and Prime Minister William Lyon Mackenzie King, who led Canada through World War II. The grounds hold rare plants and shrubs as well as a Memorial Peony Garden. Its many paths are used frequently by walkers and cyclists and who want a few quiet moments.

ONTARIO PARLIAMENT BUILDINGS

Queen's Park, 111 Wellesley St. West, Toronto, 416-325-7500;
www.parliamenthill.gc.ca

Guided tours of the Legislature Building and walking tour of grounds. Gardens; art collection; historic displays.

ONTARIO PLACE

955 Lakeshore Blvd. W., Toronto, 416-314-9900; www.ontarioplace.com

This is a 96-acre cultural, recreational and entertainment complex on three artificial islands in Lake Ontario. It includes an outdoor amphitheater for concerts, two pavilions with multimedia presentations, Cinesphere theater with IMAX films year-round; three villages of snack bars, restaurants and pubs; miniature golf; lagoons, canals, two marinas; 370-foot water slide, showboat, pedal and bumper boats; Wilderness Adventure Ride. Mid-May-early September.

ONTARIO SCIENCE CENTRE

770 Don Mills Road, Toronto, 416-696-1000; www.ontariosciencecentre.ca

Ten huge exhibition halls in three linked pavilions are filled with exhibits on space and technology. Stand at the edge of a black hole, watch bees making honey, test your reflexes, heart rate or grip strength, use pedal power to light lights or raise a balloon, hold hands with a robot, or land a spaceship on the moon. Throughout the museum there are slide shows and films that demonstrate various aspects of science and two Omnimax theaters show larger-than-life films. Daily 10 a.m.-5 p.m.

PARACHUTE SCHOOL OF TORONTO

Baldwin Airport, 5714 Smith Blvd., 800-361-5867; www.parachuteschool.com
For the ultimate in memorable vacation experiences, morning instruction is followed by an afternoon jump.

PARAMOUNT CANADA'S WONDERLAND

9580 Jane St., Vaughan, 905-832-8131; www.canadaswonderland.com
This 300-acre theme park is situated 30 minutes outside Toronto and features more than 140 attractions including a 20-acre water park, live shows and more than 50 rides. Specialties among the rides are the park's roller coasters, from creaky old-fashioned wooden ones to "The Fly," a roller coaster designed to make every seat feel as if it's the front car.

PIER: TORONTO'S WATERFRONT MUSEUM

245 Queen's Quay W., Toronto
Original 1930s pier building on Toronto's celebrated waterfront includes two floors of hands-on interactive displays, rare historical artifacts, re-creations of marine history stories, art gallery, boat-building center, narrated walking excursions, children's programs. March-October, daily.

QUEEN STREET WEST

From University Avenue to Bathurst Street, Toronto
Come to Queen West for vintage clothing stores, trendy home furnishings, hip styles that used to be original grunge and street vendor bohemia, as well as the handiwork of many up-and-coming fashion designers. In between the boutiques are antique stores, used bookstores and terrific bistros and cafés.

★
★
★
★
★

RIVOLI

334 Queen St. West, Toronto, 416-596-1908; www.rivoli.ca
This offbeat, artsy performance club was opened in 1982 on the site of Toronto's 1920s Rivoli Vaudeville Theatre. The focus is on eclectic and cutting-edge music and performances and includes everything from grunge and rock to poetry readings and comedy. The Indigo Girls, Tory Amos and Michelle Shocked all made their Toronto debuts here. Don't forget to check out the 5,000-square-foot pool hall with 13 vintage tables, including a 1870s Brunswick Aviator and a 1960s futuristic AMF seen in the Elvis movie "Viva Las Vegas."

ROGERS CENTRE

1 Blue Jays Way, Toronto, 416-341-2770; www.rogerscentre.com
Home of Toronto Blue Jays MLB and Argonauts CFL.

ROYAL ONTARIO MUSEUM

100 Queen's Park, Toronto, 416-586-5549; www.rom.on.ca

When the Royal Ontario Museum opened its doors to the public in 1914, its mission was to inspire wonder and build understanding of human cultures and the natural world. And its collections in archaeology, geology, genealogy, paleontology and sociology have moved in that direction ever since. One of the most-visited galleries is the Nubia Gallery, built in 1998 after a ROM team discovered a new archaeological culture in the Upper Nubia region of Northern Sudan, unearthing the remains of a settlement dating to 1000-800 B.C. The discovery has been officially recognized by UNESCO as "Canada's contribution to the United Nations' Decade for Cultural Development."

SECOND CITY

51 Mercer St., Toronto, 416-343-0011; www.secondcity.com

The Toronto branch of the famous Improv Club has turned out its own respectable list of veterans. Among those who have trained here are Gilda Radner, Mike Meyers, Martin Short, Ryan Stiles and dozens of others.

SONY CENTRE FOR THE PERFORMING ARTS

1 Front St. E., Toronto, 416-393-7469; www.sonycentre.ca

Stage presentations of Broadway musicals, dramas and concerts by international artists. Home of the Canadian Opera Company and National Ballet of Canada. Pre-performance dining.

SPADINA HISTORIC HOUSE AND GARDEN

285 Spadina Road., Toronto, 416-392-6910; www.toronto.ca/culture

163

Built for financier James Austin and his family, this 50-room house has been restored to its 1866 Victorian glory and is open to those who want to see how the upper crust spent quiet evenings at home. It's filled with the family's art, artifacts and furniture and until 1982 it was filled with the family itself; that's when the last generation of Austins left and the house was turned over to public ownership. Docents tend to the glorious gardens and orchard, which are open to the public in the summer.

ST. LAWRENCE CENTRE FOR THE ARTS

27 Front St. E., Toronto, 416-366-7723; www.stlc.com

Performing arts complex features theater, music, dance, films and other public events.

ST. LAWRENCE MARKET

92 Front St. E., Toronto, 416-329-7120; www.stlawrencemarket.com

In 1803, Governor Peter Hunt designated an area of land to be market block. Today, the St. Lawrence Market provides a good snippet of the way Toronto used to be, with enough of the character of the original architecture to make you feel as though the old city were alive and well. The market itself, Toronto's largest indoor market, sells 14 different categories of foods, which include incredibly fresh seafood, poultry, meat, organic produce, baked goods, gourmet teas and coffees, plus fruits and flowers.

ONTARIO

STE.-MARIE AMONG THE HURONS

East of Midland on Highway 12

Reconstruction of 17th-century Jesuit mission that was Ontario's first European community. Twenty-two furnished buildings include native dwellings, workshops, barn, church, cookhouse, hospital. Candlelight tours, canoe excursions. Café features period-inspired meals and snacks. Orientation center, interpretive museum. World-famous Martyrs' Shrine site of papal visit is located across the highway. Other area highlights include pioneer museum, replica indigenous village, Wye Marsh Wildlife Centre.

TASTE OF THE WORLD NEIGHBORHOOD BICYCLE TOURS AND WALKS

Station P Toronto, 416-923-6813; www.torontowalksbikes.com

Equal parts fact and food, the tour walks visitors through a forgotten hanging square, a hidden gallery and a lost pillory site. The eats include East Indian treats with new twists, decadent offerings with Belgian chocolate, sandwich samples at Carousel Bakery and a spread at St. Urbain Bagel. On Sunday, a different tour focuses on the contributions of 200 years of immigrant activity in the Kensington market, exploring Jewish and East Indian snacks, Lebanese treats and, of course, chocolate truffles. The tour company suggests a light breakfast with the St. Lawrence Tour and no breakfast with the Kensington tour. Daily 9:30 a.m.-1 p.m.

TORONTO BLUE JAYS MLB.

Rogers Centre, 1 Blue Jays Way, Toronto, 416-341-1000; www.bluejays.mlb.com

Professional baseball team.

164

TORONTO ISLAND PARK

9 Queens Quay, Toronto, South across Inner Harbor, 416-392-8186;
www.toronto.ca/parks/island

Just seven minutes by ferry from Toronto lie 14 beautiful islands ripe for exploration. Centre Island is the busiest, and home to Centreville, an old-fashioned amusement park with an authentic 1890s carousel, flume ride, turn-of-the-century village complete with a Main Street, tiny shops, firehouse and even a small, working farm. Alternately, all the islands are great for renting bikes and exploring the 612 acres of shaded paths.

TORONTO MAPLE LEAFS NHL.

Air Canada Centre, 40 Bay St., Toronto, 416-815-5700; www.mapleleafs.com

Professional hockey team.

TORONTO MUSIC GARDEN

475 Queen's Quay W., Toronto, 416-973-3000; www.city.toronto.on.ca

In the mid-1990s, internationally renowned cellist Yo-Yo Ma worked with several other artists to produce a six-part film series inspired by the work of Johann Sebastian Bach's "Suites for Unaccompanied Cello." The first film was entitled The Music Garden and used nature to interpret the music of Bach's first suite. Toronto was approached to create an actual garden based on The Music Garden and the result—Toronto Music Garden—now graces the waterfront, a symphony of swirls and curves and wandering trails. In the summertime, free concerts are given. Tours are offered, with a guide or self-guided with a hand-held audiotape.

ONTARIO

TORONTO RAPTORS NBA.

Air Canada Centre, 40 Bay St., Ste. 400, Toronto, 416-366-3865; www.raptors.com
Professional basketball team.

TORONTO STOCK EXCHANGE

130 King St. W., Toronto, 416-947-4676; www.tsx.com
The Stock Market Place visitor center has multimedia displays, interactive games and archival exhibits to aid visitors in understanding the market.

TORONTO SYMPHONY

212 King Street W., Toronto, 416-598-3375; www.tso.ca
Classical, pops and children's programs; Great Performers series. Wheelchair seating, audio enhancement for the hearing impaired.

TORONTO TOURS LTD.

60 Harbour St., Toronto, 416-869-1372; www.torontotours.com
Four different boat tours of Toronto Harbor.

TORONTO ZOO

361A Old Finch Ave., Scarborough, 416-392-5929; www.torontozoo.com
There are more than 5,000 animals representing over 450 species at the Toronto Zoo. Well-designed and laid out, four large tropical indoor pavilions and several smaller indoor viewing areas, plus numerous outdoor exhibits compose 710 acres of geographic regions, which can be explored on six miles of walking trails. When you're tired of walking, sit down for a refreshment or take a ride on a pony, camel or a safari simulator.

165

ONTARIO

★
★
★
★
★

WADDINGTON MCLEAN & COMPANY

111 Bathurst St., Toronto, 416-504-9100; www.waddingtons.ca
The largest and oldest auction house in Canada, Waddington's professional services have stayed the same for more than 150 years. They do appraisals, consultation and valuation. But the real fun comes every Wednesday, when the Canadian-owned house holds weekly estate/household auctions. Twice a year, in spring and fall, they host a fine art auction with catalogued items up for bid.

WOODBINE RACETRACK

555 Rexdale Blvd., Rexdale, 416-675-7223; www.woodbineentertainment.com
The only track in North America that can offer both standard-bred and thoroughbred racing on the same day, Woodbine is home to Canada's most important race course events. It hosts the $1 million Queens Plate, North America's oldest continuously run stakes race; the $1 million ATTO; the $1.5 million Canadian International; and the $1 million North America Cup for Standard-bred. It also has an outstanding grass course; it was here, in 1973, that Secretariat bid farewell to racing with his win of the grass championship. Woodbine has 1,700 slot machines and many different dining options for those times when you might need intake instead of outgo.

BEACHES INTERNATIONAL JAZZ FESTIVAL

1798 Queen St. E., Toronto, 416-698-2152; www.beachesjazz.com

For four days every summer since 1989, the Beaches community of Toronto has resonated with the sound of world-class jazz at the Beaches International Jazz Festival, a musical wonder that attracts nearly 1 million people to the water's edge. More than 40 bands play nightly, with over 700 musicians casting their spell over a crowd that includes children waving glow sticks, toe-tapping seniors and just about everyone in between. In addition to international artists with a focus on Canadians, the Festival also serves as a springboard for talented amateurs. Mid-late July.

BLOOR YORKVILLE WINE FESTIVAL

Events held throughout the city; 416-928-3553; www.santewinefestival.net

In the late 1990s, three separate organizations, among them the Wine Council of Ontario, began a festival that has grown to include more than 70 wineries from 11 countries. Activities include five days of international wine tasting, dinners, parties and discussions that are held at various restaurants, bars and hotels all over town. There is a strong educational element to the festival, with seminars held throughout the week. If you're truly a wine aficionado you'll definitely want to wait until Saturday, the last day of the festival, which includes eight specially designed wine- and food-related seminars. And if you're a novice, sign up for the Pre-tasting Seminar to learn how to swish, sip and savor like the pros. May.

CANADIAN INTERNATIONAL

166

Woodbine Racetrack, 555 Rexdale Blvd., Rexdale, 416-675-7223, 888-675-7223; www.woodbineentertainment.com

World-class thoroughbreds compete in one of Canada's most important races. Mid-late October.

CANADIAN NATIONAL EXHIBITION

Exhibition Place, Lake Shore Boulevard and Strachan Avenue, Toronto, 416-393-6300; www.theex.com

This gala celebration originated in 1879 as the Toronto Industrial Exhibition for the encouragement of agriculture, industry and the arts, though agricultural events dominated the show. Today sports, industry, labor and the arts are of equal importance to the exhibition. The "Ex," as it is locally known, is so inclusive of the nation's activities that it is a condensed Canada. A special 350-acre (141-hectare) park has been built to accommodate the exhibition. Hundreds of events include animal shows, parades, exhibits, a midway and water and air shows. Virtually every kind of sporting event is represented, from frisbee-throwing to the National Horse Show. Mid-August-Labor Day.

CARIBANA

Exhibition Place, Lake Shore Boulevard and Strachan Avenue, Toronto; www.caribana.com

Caribbean music, grand parade, floating nightclubs, dancing, costumes and food at various locations throughout city. Late July-early August.

ONTARIO

CELEBRATE TORONTO STREET FESTIVAL

Yonge Street, between Lawrence Avenue and Dundas Street, Toronto, 416-395-0490; www.city.toronto.on.ca

Each July, on the first weekend after Canada Day, Toronto's Yonge Street—the longest street in the world—is transformed into more than 500,000 square feet (46,452 square meters) of free entertainment, with something for people of all ages and tastes. Each of five intersections along Yonge Street runs its own distinctive programming mix; one has nothing but family entertainment, another has world music, a third has classic rock and so forth. Jugglers, stilt-walkers and buskers enliven street corners; spectacular thrill shows captivate pedestrians. Call for schedule. Early July.

CHIN INTERNATIONAL PICNIC

Exhibition Place, Lake Shore Boulevard and Strachan Avenue, Toronto, 416-531-9991; www.chinradio.com

Contests, sports, picnicking. First weekend in July.

DESIGNS ON ICE

100 Queen St. W., Toronto, 416-395-0490; www.toronto.ca

This ice sculpture competition gives contestants exactly 48 hours to chisel a block of ice into a winter work of art. Each year brings a different theme. A recent one, for example, was J.R.R. Tolkien's epic *The Lord of the Rings*, which brought forth a wonderland of hobbits, dwarves, trolls, orcs, wizards and elves. The public chooses the winners and the award ceremony is part of a family skating party with live music. The sculptures stay up as long as the weather cooperates. Last weekend in December.

ROYAL AGRICULTURAL WINTER FAIR

Coliseum Building, Exhibition Place, Lake Shore Boulevard and Strachan Avenue, Toronto, 416-263-3400; www.royalfair.org

World's largest indoor agricultural fair exhibits the finest livestock. Food shows. Royal Horse Show features international competitions in several categories. Early November.

SUNDAY SERENADES

5100 Yonge St., Toronto, 416-338-0338; www.city.toronto.on.ca

See if moonlight becomes you and play Fred and Ginger under the stars at Mel Lastman Square. Each Sunday evening in June and July you can Lindy Hop, Big Apple and Swing to live big band and swing music. It's free, easy and lots of fun. Mid-July-mid-August.

TORONTO INTERNATIONAL FILM FESTIVAL

Eaton Centre, 220 Yonge St., Toronto, 416-968-3456; www.tiffg.ca

Celebration of world cinema in downtown theaters; Canadian and foreign films, international moviemakers and stars. Early September.

TORONTO KIDS TUESDAY

100 Queen St. W., Toronto; www.city.toronto.on.ca

For four consecutive Tuesdays in July and August, Nathan Philips Square is turned into a kid's fantasyland. There's entertainment, face painting, coloring, chalk art,

ONTARIO

★
★
★
★
★

make-and-take crafts, make your own t-shirts, build-a-kite; activities depend on who is entertaining and what the theme of the day is. The Stylamanders bring zany choreography and championship yo-yo tricks, which was followed by a high-energy day of play, including interactive games with the Toronto Maple Leafs. July-August.

TORONTO WINE AND CHEESE SHOW

6900 Airport Road, Mississauga, 800-265-3673; www.towineandcheese.com
A mainstay since 1983, the Toronto Wine and Cheese show brings a world of top-tier wines, beers, lagers, ales, single malt whiskies, cheeses and specialty food to town. Learn from famous chefs, sample an exquisite collection of cigars, find out how to buy the perfect bottle of wine and enjoy free seminars by well-known food and wine experts. Ages 19 and up only. Mid-April.

HOTELS

★★★DELTA CHELSEA

33 Gerrard St. W., Toronto, 416-595-1975, 800-243-5732; www.deltachelsea.com
Located in the heart of downtown Toronto, guests are within minutes of the city's best theatre, shopping and attractions. After a long day, unwind in an elegant guest room with choice amenities and deep soaking tubs. 1,590 rooms. Two restaurants, two bars. Pet. Swim. Business center. High-speed Internet access. $$$

★★DELTA TORONTO EAST

2035 Kennedy Road, Scarborough, 416-299-1500, 800-663-3386; www.deltahotels.ca
371 rooms. Restaurant, bar. Children's activity center. High-speed Internet access. Pets accepted, fee. Pool. $$

★★★FAIRMONT ROYAL YORK

100 Front St. W., Toronto, 416-368-2511, 866-540-4489; www.fairmont.com
The Royal York became known as a city within a city, with its 1½ acres of public rooms including a 12,000-book library, a concert hall with a 50-ton pipe organ and 10 ornate passenger elevators. A $100 million project restored the guest rooms and public spaces to their original elegance and added a health club. You're unlikely to live in a mansion this big again, so enjoy yourself. 1,365 rooms. Five restaurants, four bars. Pets accepted. Pool. Business center. High-speed Internet access. Fitness center. $$$

★★★★FOUR SEASONS HOTEL TORONTO

21 Avenue Road, Toronto, 416-964-0411; www.fourseasons.com/toronto
The Four Seasons Hotel Toronto is in a prime location in the upscale neighborhood of Yorkville. Guest rooms feature elegant colonial décor, plush furnishings and charming views of Yorkville, or stunning views of the city's downtown. Not forgotten are business travelers who are pampered with the in-house business center and complimentary limousine service. Guests can relax by the heated indoor and outdoor pool, sauna, whirlpool and fitness center. Dinner should not be missed at the hotel's classic French cuisine restaurant, Truffles. 380 rooms. Pets accepted, some restrictions. Children's amenities. High-speed Internet access. Two restaurants, two bars. Fitness room. Indoor pool, outdoor pool, whirlpool. Business center. $$$$

★★★★THE HAZELTON HOTEL

118 Yorkville Ave., Toronto, 416-963-6300, 866-473-6301; www.thehazeltonhotel.com

Sleek luxury with hints of old Hollywood glam permeates the rooms and suites of the Hazelton hotel. You can almost get lost in the spacious rooms, each with an average of 620 square feet with 9-foot-tall ceilings. The luxe experience extends beyond the rooms and into the Hazleton's signature restaurant, One, led by chef Mark McEwan. The hotel even has its very own built-in screening room, an elegant mini-movie theater that seats 25 on plush, leather seats. 62 rooms, 15 suites. High-speed Internet access. Restaurant, bar. Fitness center, business center. $$$$

★★★HILTON TORONTO

145 Richmond St. W., Toronto, 416-869-3456, 800-445-8667;
www.toronto.hilton.com

Guests will enjoy the location of this hotel in Toronto's financial and entertainment districts. The guest rooms are draped in neutral tones and include work stations for busy business travelers. 600 rooms. Two restaurants, two bars. Pets accepted, fee. Pool. Business center. High-speed Internet access. Fitness room. $$

★HOLIDAY INN EXPRESS

50 Estates Drive, Scarborough, 416-439-9666, 800-465-4329; www.holiday-inn.com

140 rooms. Complimentary continental breakfast. High-speed Internet access. $

★★★HOTEL LE GERMAIN

30 Mercer St., Toronto, 416-345-9500, 866-345-9501; www.germaintoronto.com

Sleek lines, modern architecture and a two-level lobby define this new hotel. Facilities such as a massage room, two rooftop terraces and a library with an open-hearth fireplace enhance guests' stays. Four suites have fireplaces and private terraces. 122 rooms. Complimentary deluxe continental breakfast. High-speed Internet access. Restaurant, bar. Pets accepted, fee. Fitness center. $$

★★★INTERCONTINENTAL HOTEL TORONTO CENTRE

225 Front St. W., Toronto, 416-597-1400, 800-422-7969; www.intercontinental.com

The downtown InterContinental caters to business travelers who need meeting space, business support and proximity to the adjacent Metro Toronto Convention Centre. The hotel is great for leisure travelers too who want to stay close to theater, dining and shopping venues. The rooms are sizeable and pet-friendly, so Fido can come along. 586 rooms. Restaurant, bar. Fitness center. Pool. Business center. High-speed Internet access. Pets accepted. Fitness center. Spa. $$$$

★★★INTERCONTINENTAL TORONTO

220 Bloor St. W., Toronto, 416-960-5200, 888-567-8725; www.intercontinental.com

Located in the exclusive Yorkville neighborhood, this modern hotel has guest rooms designed to be both inviting and efficient. Thoughtful details are offered through out the hotel, such as an international newspaper service. 208 rooms. Restaurant, bar. Pets accepted, fee. Fitness center. Pool. Business center. High-speed Internet access. $$

ONTARIO

★
★
★
★
★

★★★LE ROYAL MERIDIEN KING EDWARD

37 King St. E., Toronto, 416-863-9700, 800-543-4300;
www.lemeridien-kingedward.com

Le Royal Meridien King Edward is the grande dame of Toronto. This historic landmark opened to the public in 1903 and has been hosting the world's elite ever since. Sharing the hotel's affinity for England in its décor, the Cafe Victoria and Consort Bar are essential elements of the superb King Edward experience. 298 rooms. Two restaurants, bar. Pets accepted. Business center. High-speed Internet access. Spa. Fitness center. **$$$**

★★★MARRIOTT BLOOR YORKVILLE

90 Bloor St. E., Toronto, 416-961-8000, 800-859-7180; www.marriott.com

Situated in the fashionable Yorkville neighborhood, this hotel's creative and artistic décor makes it fit right in. Although it's located at perhaps the city's busiest intersection, the hotel feels tucked away and serene. In-room amenities abound and are only enhanced by the attractions of the tourist-friendly neighborhood. 258 rooms. Restaurant, bar. Business center. High-speed Internet access. Fitness center. Pets accepted. **$$$**

★★★MARRIOTT TORONTO AIRPORT

901 Dixon Road, Toronto, 416-674-9400, 800-905-2811; www.marriott.com

Both business and leisure travelers will like this property's proximity to Pearson International Airport and many of the city's other top attractions. The property offers a variety of dining options. Mikada serves traditional Japanese dishes, while the Terrace's menu is Continental. Toucan's Lounge & Patio is a nice place to meet up with friends for a quick drink. 424 rooms. Three restaurants, bar. Pets accepted, fee. Pool. Business center. Fitness center. High-speed Internet access. **$$**

★★★MARRIOTT TORONTO EATON CENTRE

525 Bay St., Toronto, 416-597-9200, 800-905-0667; www.marriotteatoncentre.com

In the financial district and near the theater district, this property attracts all types of visitors with its extensive offerings. There is a top-floor pool overlooking the city. Guest rooms are well lit and include custom duvets and a choice of pillows to fit your preference. 459 rooms. Restaurant, bar. Pool. Business center. High-speed Internet access. Fitness center. **$$**

★★★METROPOLITAN HOTEL TORONTO

108 Chestnut St., Toronto, 416-977-5000, 800-668-6600; www.metropolitan.com

All of Toronto is within easy reach from the Metropolitan Hotel, close proximity to world-renowned shopping, art galleries and museums, the hotel has the services of a large property and the intimacy of a private residence. Fully-staffed fitness and business centers are also on hand to assist all guests. The Lai Wah Heen is a serene setting for its luscious Cantonese cuisine which is considered an excellent example of authentic dim sum. 422 rooms. Pets accepted, some restrictions. Two restaurants, bar. Fitness room. Indoor pool, whirlpool. Business center. High-speed Internet access. **$$$$**

★★★THE MILLCROFT INN & SPA

55 John St., Alton, 519-941-8111, 800-383-3976; www.millcroft.com

This former knitting mill dating back to 1881 is situated on 100 acres on the Credit River and boasts some of the most impressive accommodations in the city. Rooms

★
★
★
★
☆

have personalized touches along with modern-day amenities such as flat-screen TVs and large Jacuzzi tubs. Be sure to visit the award-winning spa for a rejuvenating treatment or a relaxing herbal steam. 52 rooms. Complimentary continental breakfast. Restaurant, bar. Pool. Tennis. **$$**

★★NOVOTEL TORONTO CENTER

45 The Esplanade, Toronto, 416-367-8900; www.novotel.com

The Novotel Toronto Center in downtown Toronto is ideal for business or vacation travel. This three star hotel features an indoor pool, gym, restaurant, free WiFi and meeting facilities. Many attractions are nearby including the Air Canada Centre, Hockey Hall of Fame, Rogers Centre, Harbourfront Centre, Eaton Centre, St. Lawrence Market, Centre Island (ferry docks) and the financial district. Union Station and public transport nearby. 262 rooms. Bar. Pets accepted, fee. **$$**

★★★PANTAGES SUITES HOTEL AND SPA

210 Victoria St., Toronto, 416-362-1777, 866-852-1777; www.pantageshotel.com

Unique amenities and services such as a complimentary meditation channel, yoga mats, 400-thread-count Egyptian cotton linens, 27-inch flatscreen TVs and in-room European kitchens. Guests are close to The Eaton Centre mall and other Toronto attractions and just two minutes from the subway and Toronto's underground walkway. 111 rooms, all suites. Complimentary continental breakfast. Fitness center. Pool. Business center. Wireless Internet access. **$$$**

★★★OLD MILL INN AND SPA

21 Old Mill Road, Toronto, 416-236-2641, 866-653-6455; www.oldmilltoronto.com

This Tudor-style inn and the adjacent meeting and conference facility exude old-world charm. In summer and winter, the setting is spectacular. The inn sits 15 minutes northwest of downtown Toronto in the Humber River Valley, which offers opportunities for hiking, biking and in-line skating. 57 rooms. Complimentary continental breakfast. Two restaurants, bar. Exercise. Business center. High-speed Internet access. **$$$**

★★★★PARK HYATT TORONTO

4 Avenue Road, Toronto, 416-925-1234, 800-977-4197; www.parktoronto.hyatt.com

The Park Hyatt Toronto calls the stylish Yorkville area home. Located at the intersection of Avenue Road and Bloor Street, this hotel has some of the world's leading stores just outside its doors. Public and private spaces have a rich feeling completed with handsome furnishings and a clean, modern look dominates the rooms and suites. The demands of the world dissipate at the Stillwater Spa. International dishes are the specialty at Annona, while the grilled steaks and seafood of Morton's of Chicago are always a treat. 346 rooms. Restaurant, bar. Business center. Fitness center. High-speed Internet access. **$$$**

★★QUALITY SUITES TORONTO AIRPORT

262 Carlingview Drive, Etobicoke, 416-674-8442, 877-755-4900; www.qualityinn.com

253 rooms. Restaurant, bar. Pets accepted, fee. Wireless Internet access. **$**

★★RADISSON HOTEL TORONTO EAST

55 Hallcrown Place, North York, 416-493-7000, 888-201-1718; www.radisson.com

228 rooms. Restaurant, bar. Pool. High-speed Internet access. Fitness center. Pets accepted. Business center. **$**

★★RADISSON PLAZA HOTEL ADMIRAL

249 Queens Quay West, Toronto, 416-203-3333, 888-201-1718; www.radisson.com
157 rooms. Two restaurants, bar. Pool. Business center. High-speed Internet access.
Fitness center. $$

★★RENAISSANCE TORONTO HOTEL DOWNTOWN

1 Blue Jays Way, Toronto, 416-341-7100, 800-237-1512; www.renaissancehotels.com
348 rooms. Restaurant, bar. Business center. Pets accepted. Fitness center. Pool.
High-speed Internet access. $$$

★★★SHERATON CENTRE HOTEL

123 Queen St. W., Toronto, 416-361-1000, 800-325-3535; www.starwoodhotels.com
Though large in size, this hotel specializes in personalized service. Each guest room
has been revamped with upgraded amenities and signature Sheraton Sweet Sleeper
beds. The 2½-acre waterfall garden that runs through the new lobby emphasizes the
urban oasis that is Toronto. 1,377 rooms. Restaurant, bar. Pets accepted, fee. Pool.
Fitness center. Business center. $$

★★★SHERATON GATEWAY HOTEL

Toronto International Airport, Terminal 3, Toronto, 905-672-7000, 800-325-3535;
www.sheraton.com
Pefect for a layover, the hotel is connected to Terminal 3 at Toronto International
Airport. First-class soundproofing ensures a good night's sleep before an early flight.
This glass-walled hotel is thoroughly modern, with every facility for the business
traveler and comfort and convenience for the leisure traveler. 474 rooms. Restaurant,
bar. Airport. Pets accepted, fee. Pool. Business center. High-speed Internet access.
Complimentary breakfast. $$

★★★SOHO METROPOLITAN HOTEL

318 Wellington St. W., Toronto, 416-599-8800; www.metropolitan.com
This boutique hotel earns high marks for its urban chic interiors, stylish food, central
location and smart technology. The accommodations appeal with clean, simple lines
and light wood furnishings. The SoHo Metropolitan's Senses Bakery & Restaurant
offers the contemporary gourmet experience with its artfully designed and creatively
prepared cuisine. 366 rooms. Two restaurants, bar. Pets accepted. Pool. Business cen-
ter. Wireless Internet access. $$$

★★★THE SUTTON PLACE

955 Bay St., Toronto, 416-924-9221; www.suttonplace.com
You get an old Europe feel from the rich surroundings, including mahogany trim in
the meeting rooms and crystal chandeliers. Original art and antiques grace the guest
rooms and suites. Grab a drink before dinner in the elegant lobby bar. 294 rooms.
Restaurant, bar. Spa. Pets accepted, fee. Pool. Business center. Fitness center. $$

★★★ THE WESTIN BRISTOL PLACE TORONTO AIRPORT

950 Dixon Road, Toronto, 416-675-9444, 877-999-3223;
www.starwoodhotels.com/westin
Just five minutes from Pearson International Airport, this is a good choice for those
on a short trip. The indoor pool and state-of-the-art workout facility will get you up

and going in no time, and the proximity to downtown is convenient for those looking to experience the city's nightlife. 287 rooms. Restaurant. Pool. Business center. High-speed Internet access. $$

★★★WESTIN HARBOUR CASTLE

1 Harbour Square, Toronto, 416-869-1600, 800-228-3000;
www.westin.com/harbourcastle

The striking towers of this hotel are among the most recognized landmarks in the city. The glass-walled foyer offers a wide, clear view of Lake Ontario. The hotel is close to a host of tourist attractions, including the Air Canada Centre, the CN Tower, the Eaton Centre and the theater district. 977 rooms. Two restaurants, two bars. Children's activity center. Pets accepted. Pool. Tennis. Business center. Spa. $$$$

★★★THE WESTIN PRINCE TORONTO

900 York Mills Road, Toronto, 416-444-2511, 800-228-3000; www.westin.com

Located in the center of downtown Toronto, this hotel is just minutes from both the Ontario Science Centre and the Ford Centre for the Performing Arts. Activity is paramount here, as the hotel's 15 acres include tennis courts, an outdoor pool and walking trails. Guest rooms offer views of the Toronto skyline and the surrounding greenery. 381 rooms. Restaurant, bar. Fitness center. Pool. Tennis. Business center. High-speed Internet access. $$

★★★WINDSOR ARMS HOTEL

18 St. Thomas St., Toronto, 416-971-9666, 877-999-2767; www.windsorarmshotel.com

The accommodations in this intimate and stylish hotel are sleek, modern and sublime. The Tea Room serves a traditional tea by day and at night is transformed into Toronto's only champagne and caviar bar. Club 22 entertains with piano entertainment and live bands and the Cigar Lounge offers decadent treats. 28 rooms, all suites. Complimentary continental breakfast. Restaurant, bar. Pets accepted. Pool. Spa. $$$

RESTAURANTS

★★★360

301 Front St. W., Toronto, 416-362-5411; www.cntower.ca

As the name suggests, this restaurant completes a 360-degree rotation, offering a breathtaking view from the CN Tower. The scenery inside is attractive as well, with colorful décor and a fresh, seasonal menu. International menu. Reservations recommended. $$$

★★★AUBERGE DU POMMIER

4150 Yonge St., Toronto, 416-222-2220; www.aubergedupommier.com

Located north of the city, this restaurant in an industrial park manages to feel like it is actually in rural France. The attentive service and comfortable décor are pleasing. And the pommes frites are divine. French, American menu. Reservations recommended. Lunch, dinner. $$$

★★BAROOTES

220 King St. W., Toronto, 416-979-7717; www.barootes.com

International menu. Reservations recommended. Lunch, dinner. $$

★★★BIAGIO

155 King St. E., Toronto, 416-366-4040; www.biagioristorante.com.

This modern Italian restaurant is situated in the historic St. Lawrence Hall near the theater district and serves specialties from the north. An ornate ceiling and a lovely patio with a fountain add to the ambience. Italian menu. Outdoor seating. **$$$**

★BUMPKINS

21 Gloucester St., Toronto, 416-922-8655; www.bumpkins.ca

French menu. Reservations recommended. Outdoor seating. Dinner, lunch. **$$**

★★CARMAN'S CLUB

26 Alexander St., Toronto, 416-924-8558; www.carmans.sites.toronto.com

Steak, seafood menu. **$$$**

★★★★CANOE

66 Wellington St. W., Toronto 416-364-0054; www.oliverbonacini.com

Canoe is a stunning venue in which to experience creative, satisfying regional Canadian cuisine. While dazzling ingredients tend to be sourced from wonderful local producers, many organic, the kitchen borrows flavors and techniques from the world at large, including Asia, France and the American South. The end product is inventive food and an equally original room. The five-course tasting menu is a rollercoaster of succulent flavors including tenderloin tartare, broiled Sablefish and carmelized honey crisp apple almond cake. The wine list is equally indulgent. Canadian menu. Reservations recommended. Lunch, dinner. Bar. **$$$**

★★★CENTRO GRILL & WINE BAR

2472 Yonge St., Toronto, 416-483-2211; www.centro.ca

A lot of tastes are rolled into one destination at this contemporary European restaurant with a downstairs sushi and oyster bar. A colorful, New Age-style dining room and a worldly menu means you'll never be bored with novelties like caribou chop with juniper berry oil, Alsatian spatzle and Arctic cloudberry sauce. International menu. Reservations recommended. **$$$**

★★★★CHIADO

864 College St., Toronto, 416-538-1910; www.chiadorestaurant.ca

Paying homage to the old seaside town but updating dishes for a more modern sensibility, Chiado features what might best be described as "nouvelle Portuguese cuisine." The food is first-rate and fabulous, featuring an ocean's worth of fresh fish simply prepared with olive oil and herbs, as well as innovative takes on pheasant, game and poultry. To add to the authenticity of the experience, Chiado has the largest collection of fine Portuguese wines in North America and a superb selection of vintage ports. Spanish menu. Lunch, dinner. Reservations recommended. **$$$**

★★DYNASTY CHINESE

131 Bloor St. W., Toronto, 416-923-3323; www.dynasty.sites.toronto.com

Chinese menu. Lunch, dinner. Reservations recommended. **$$$**

★★★★THE FIFTH

225 Richmond St. W., Toronto, 416-979-3000; www.thefifthgrill.com

It takes work to make it to The Fifth. First, an alley entrance leads you to The Easy, an upscale nightclub and former speakeasy. Once inside The Easy, you are directed onto a Persian rug-lined vintage freight elevator. There, an attendant takes you to the fifth floor. Exit and you have finally arrived at The Fifth, a treasured contemporary French restaurant and supper club. The food is of the deliciously updated French variety, and the dishes are perfectly prepared, beautifully presented and easily devoured. Don't miss the sticky banana cake with rum butterscotch sauce for desert—it's heavenly. French menu. Dinner. Closed Sunday-Wednesday. Bar. Reservations recommended. Outdoor seating. **$$$$**

★GRANO

2035 Yonge St., Toronto, 416-440-1986; www.grano.ca

Italian menu. Outdoor seating. Lunch, dinner. **$$**

★★GRAZIE

2373 Yonge St., Toronto, 416-488-0822; www.grazie.ca

Italian menu. Pick up and delivery. Lunch, dinner. **$$**

★★★HEMISPHERES

108 Chestnut St., Toronto, 416-599-8000; www.metropolitan.com/hemis

Hemispheres elevates hotel dining to a whole new level with its stylish interior and international fusion cuisine. The menu includes European and Continental classics, many with an Asian bent. Wine lovers will appreciate the well-rounded and extensive cellar. International menu. Breakfast. Lunch, dinner. Reservations recommended. **$$**

★★★JOSO'S

202 Davenport Road, Toronto, 416-925-1903; www.josos.com

The walls are covered with the chef's racy art and celebrity pictures at this popular restaurant, which offers unique but excellent Mediterranean cuisine. Though it takes 20 minutes to prepare, the risotti is worth waiting for. Meditteranean menu. Dinner. Outdoor seating. **$$$**

★★★LA FENICE

319 King St. W., Toronto, 416-585-2377; www.lafenice.ca

The stark, modern dining room of this downtown restaurant recalls the chic design aesthetic of Milan. The pink and orange hues work to compliment the casual atmosphere and tasty Italian fare. The menu is large, so if you're undecided, just ask the helpful staff for house recommendations. Italian menu. Reservations recommended. Lunch, dinner. **$$$**

★★★LAI WAH HEEN

108 Chestnut St., Toronto, 416-977-9899; www.laiwahheen.com

Lai Wah Heen, meaning "luxurious meeting place," is truly luxurious with its two-level dining room featuring black granite, 12-foot ceilings and solarium-style glass wall. Exotic herbs and spices, skillful use of tropical fruits and seafood dishes make for a Cantonese menu rich with Pacific Rim flair. Cantonese, Chinese menu. Reservations recommended. Valet parking. **$$**

★MATIGNON

51 St. Nicholas St., Toronto, 416-921-9226, 866-211-6255; www.matignon.ca

French menu. Lunch, dinner. Bar. Reservations recommended. $$

★★MILLCROFT INN

55 John St., N. Alton, 519-941-8111, 800-383-3976; www.millcroft.com

French menu. Lunch, dinner, Sunday Brunch. Bar. $$$

★★★MISTURA

265 Davenport Road, Toronto, 416-515-0009; www.mistura.ca

Contemporary, seasonal Italian cuisine and a stylish, upscale environment are the hallmarks of this elegant Toronto restaurant. Past menu items like wild boar filled pasta with dried cherries have delighted guests along with fresh ingredients and artful presentation. Desserts are just as inventive. Italian menu. $$

★★★★NORTH 44

2537 Yonge St., Toronto, 416-487-4897; www.north44restaurant.com

Style, serenity and elegance infuse every aspect of North 44 Degrees. From the recently renovated loft-like dining room to the world-class New Continental cuisine, North 44 is a sublime and sexy dining experience. A sophisticated crowd fills the restaurant, named for the city's latitude, on most nights. Chef/owner Mark McEwan expertly blends the bright flavors of Asia with those of Italy, France and Canada. The service is smooth, refined and in perfect harmony with the cool space and stellar cuisine. International menu. Reservations recommended. Dinner. Bar. $$$$

★★★OLD MILL

21 Old Mill Road, Toronto, 416-236-2641, 866-653-6455; www.oldmilltoronto.com

The main dining room of the Old Mill Inn & Spa, a charming, English-style inn along the Humber River, features a warm and romantic atmosphere with beamed ceilings, a roaring fireplace, brick walls and soft lighting. Reinventing old classics like Beef Wellington Nouveau and Australian Lamb Souvlaki keeps diner guests guessing and the kitchen on their toes. International menu. Dinner. Jacket required (weekend dinner). Reservations recommended. Outdoor seating. Cover charge (Friday-Saturday from 8 p.m.) $$$

★★★★ONE RESTAURANT

116 Yorkville Ave., Toronto, 416-961-9600; www.onehazelton.com

One restaurant, housed in Toronto's grand Hazelton Hotel, means serious business. The main dining room caters to diners looking for quality food as well as sharp décor. Chocolate brown-leather booths line the walls of the main dining room, while the 16-seat Neil Young Room is reserved for those to discuss business, view presentations on the 52" plasma screen or just have an intimate meal with a small group. Red walls and mirrored doors make this room pop with sophistication. The menu is equally refined, thanks to chef Andrew Ellerby, whose roasted goose foie gras on warm toast will make you swoon, as will pastry chef Tony Accettola's apple charlotte with cinnamon ice cream. American menu. Breakfast, lunch, dinner, Saturday-Sunday brunch. $$$$

★★★OPUS RESTAURANT

37 Prince Arthur Ave., Toronto, 416-921-3105; www.opusrestaurant.com

This plush Yorkville restaurant is elegant, romantic and filled with the energy of Toronto's powerful and moneyed elite. International menu. Dinner. Reservations recommended. Outdoor seating. **$$$**

★★★ORO

45 Elm St., Toronto, 416-597-0155; www.ororestaurant.com

This restaurant has changed hands and names many times since it opened in 1922 and is famous for its patrons, who have included Ernest Hemingway and Prime Minister Jean Chrétien. The décor is contemporary and elegant, as is the food. International menu. Lunch, dinner. Bar. **$$$**

★★★PANGAEA

1221 Bay St., Toronto, 416-920-2323; www.pangaearestaurant.com

Vaulted ceiling and exotic floral arrangements set the stage for sophisticated continental cuisine using the wealth of each season's harvest. Tired Bloor Street shoppers will find this a great place to break for lunch or tea. International menu. Lunch, dinner. Reservations recommended. Business casual attire. Bar. **$$$**

★★PASTIS

1158 Yonge St., Toronto, 416-928-2212

French menu. **$$**

★★PIER 4 STOREHOUSE

245 Queen's Quay W., Toronto, 416-203-1440; www.pier4rest.com

Seafood menu. Reservations recommended. Outdoor seating. Lunch, dinner. **$$$**

★★IL POSTO NUOVO

148 Yorkville Ave., Toronto, 416-968-0469; www.ilposto.ca

Italian menu. Reservations recommended. Outdoor seating. Lunch, dinner. **$$$**

★★PROVENCE

12 Amelia St., Toronto, 416-924-9901; www.provencerestaurant.com

French menu. Outdoor seating. Lunch, dinner, Sunday Brunch. Reservations recommended. **$$$**

★★QUARTIER

2112 Yonge St., Toronto, 416-545-0505

Thai menu. Lunch, dinner. Reservations recommended. **$$**

★★RODNEY'S OYSTER HOUSE

469 King St. W., Toronto, 416-363-8105; www.rodneysoysterhouse.com

Seafood menu. Reservations recommended. Outdoor seating. **$$**

★★ROSEWATER SUPPER CLUB

19 Toronto St., Toronto, 416-214-5888; www.libertygroup.com

French menu. Reservations recommended. Outdoor seating. Lunch, dinner. **$$$**

ONTARIO

★
★
★
★
★

★★★★SCARAMOUCHE

1 Benvenuto Place, Toronto, 416-961-8011; www.scaramoucherestaurant.com

Up on a hillside overlooking the dazzling downtown lights, Scaramouche is the perfect hideaway for falling in love with food or your dining companion. This modern, bi-level space is known for its fantastic contemporary French fare and is often filled with dressed-up, savvy locals. The restaurant is divided between a formal dining room upstairs and a modestly priced pasta bar downstairs. French menu. Reservations recommended. $$$$

★★SENATOR

249 Victoria St., Toronto, 416-364-7517; www.thesenator.com

Seafood, steak menu. $$$

★★★★SPLENDIDO

88 Harbord St., Toronto, 416-929-7788; www.splendido.ca

Splendido has hit its stride tobecome one of Toronto's best restaurants, with interpretations of international cuisines and a focus on clean, flavorful sauces and local Canadian ingredients. Several charming details like the Champagne cart and the selection of petit fours make this a fun and enjoyable dining experience. The extensive selection of cheeses also makes for a nice late afternoon snack. International menu. Dinner. Closed Sunday-Monday, July-August. Reservations recommended. $$$

★★★SUSUR

601 King St. W., Toronto, 416-603-2205; www.susur.com

This internationally acclaimed restaurant blends flavors of the East and West to create innovative, eclectic dishes. Tasting menus, available in five or seven courses, change on a daily basis to reflect the fresh ingredients available at local markets, so you'll be treated to a new dining experience with each visit. International menu. Reservations recommended. $$$

★
★
★
★
★

★★TAKE SUSHI

22 Front St. W., Toronto, 416-862-1891; www.takesushi.ca.

Japanese, sushi menu. Reservations recommended. Lunch, dinner. $$

★★★★TRUFFLES

21 Avenue Road, Toronto, 416-964-0411; www.fourseasons.com

Filled with light and luxury, Truffles' dining room feels like the parlor room of a fabulous art collector with impeccable taste. Located in the Four Seasons Hotel Toronto, Truffles is known for its distinct, stylized brand of modern Provencal-style cuisine. Smooth service and an extensive wine list make Truffles a truly inspired dining event. If you're looking for a signature dish, order the spaghettini with Perigord black gold in a light truffle sauce. French menu. Dinner. Reservations recommended. $$$$

★UNITED BAKER'S DAIRY RESTAURANT

506 Lawrence Ave. West, Toronto, 416-789-0519

Jewish menu. $

★★ZACHARY'S RESTAURANT

950 Dixon Road, Etobicoke, 416-679-4394; www.zacharys.sites.toronto.com

Continental menu. Dinner. Reservations recommended. $$

SPAS

★★★★THE SPA AT THE HAZELTON HOTEL

The Hazelton Hotel, 118 Yorkville Ave., Toronto, 416-963-6307;
www.thehazeltonhotel.com

Toronto's prized hotel keeps up the second-to-none hospitality at its spa and health club. Linda McDonald-Ferris leads this excellent spa, whose experience as a skincare specialist for the past 20 years shows in the quality treatments that the spa offers. For complete relaxation, start with the lemon sea salt body scrub, followed by a shiatsu massage and an exfoliating session known as the Body Glow. Waxing, manicure and pedicure are also available. After you're done pampering and primping, end your spa day with a dip in the gorgeous indoor lap pool, which is outfitted in imported mosaic tile.

★★★★STILLWATER SPA AT PARK HYATT TORONTO

4 Avenue Road, Toronto, 416-925-1234; www.parktoronto.hyatt.com/hyatt/pure/spas

With its cool, crisp interiors—complete with a fireplace in the Tea Lounge and waterfalls and streams throughout the facility—and fabulous mind and body relaxation therapies, Park Hyatt Toronto's Stillwater Spa offers you an escape. The signature Stillwater massage customizes an aromatherapy blend to accompany a relaxing bodywork combination of Swedish massage, trigger-points pressure and stretching techniques. $$$

WINDSOR

Windsor is located at the tip of a peninsula and is linked to Detroit by the Ambassador Bridge and the Detroit-Windsor Tunnel. Aside from its status as the Ambassador City, thanks to its proximity to the United States, Windsor is also known as the City of Roses for its many beautiful parks. The Sunken Gardens and Rose Gardens in Jackson Park boast more than 500 varieties of roses, while Coventry Garden and Peace Fountain has the only fountain floating in international waters. A cosmopolitan and determinedly bilingual city with many French influences, Windsor enjoys a symphony orchestra, theaters, a light opera company, art galleries, nightlife and all the amenities of a large city.
Information: www.city.windsor.on.ca

WHAT TO SEE AND DO

ART GALLERY OF WINDSOR

401 Riverside Drive W., Windsor, 519-977-0013; www.artgalleryofwindsor.com

Collections consist of Canadian art, including Inuit prints and carvings, with an emphasis on Canadian artists from the past and the present. Children's gallery; gift shop.

COLASANTI FARMS, LTD

1550 Road 3 E., Kingsville, 519-326-3287; www.colasanti.com

More than 25 greenhouses with acres of exotic plants; large collection of cacti; farm animals, parrots and tropical birds. There is also arts and crafts and miniputt for the kids.

ONTARIO

COVENTRY GARDENS AND PEACE FOUNTAIN

Riverside Drive E. and Pillette Road, Windsor, 519-253-2300; www.citywindsor.ca

Riverfront park and floral gardens with a 75-foot-high floating fountain; myriad 3D water displays with spectacular night illumination. May-September, daily.

FORT MALDEN NATIONAL HISTORIC PARK

100 Laird Ave., Amherstburg, 18 miles (29 kilometers) south via City Road 20,
519-736-5416; www.parkscanada.gc.ca/malden

Ten-acre (4½-hectare) park with remains of fortification, original 1838 barracks and 1851 pensioner's cottage; visitor and interpretation centers with exhibits.

JACK MINER BIRD SANCTUARY

332 Road 3 W., Kingsville, 519-733-4034, 877-289-8328; www.jackminer.com

Canadian geese and other migratory waterfowl flock to this sanctuary. You can even catch the Canadian geese "air shows" during peak season.

JOHN FREEMAN WALLS HISTORIC SITE AND UNDERGROUND RAILROAD MUSEUM

859 Puce Road, 519-727-6555; www.undergroundrailroadmuseum.com

John Freeman Walls, a fugitive slave from North Carolina, built this log cabin in 1846. It subsequently served as a terminal of the Underground Railroad and the first meeting place of the Puce Baptist Church. It has remained in the possession of Walls's descendants. May-October, by appointment only.

NORTH AMERICAN BLACK HISTORICAL MUSEUM

277 King St., Amherstburg, 519-736-5433, 800-713-6336;
www.blackhistoricalmuseum.com

Chronicle achievements of Black North Americans, many of whom fled the United States for freedom in Canada. Permanent exhibits on the Underground Railroad including artifacts, archives and a genealogical library. April-November.

ODETTE SCULPTURE PARK

Between Church Street and Huron along the Detroit River,
519-253-2300, 888-519-3333

Walk or cycle the paths through this 2-mile park past large sculptures by Canadian and international artists. It's ideal for a picnic.

PARK HOUSE MUSEUM

214 Dalhousie St., Amherstburg, 519-736-2511

Solid log, clapboard-sided house circa 1795, considered to be oldest house in area. Built in Detroit, moved here in 1799. Restored and furnished to be as it was in the 1850s. There are demonstrations of tinsmithing, and samples for sale.

POINT PELEE NATIONAL PARK

407 Monarch Lane, 519-322-2365, 888-773-8888; www.parkscanada.gc.ca

The park is a 6-square-mile tip of the Point Pelee peninsula. Combination dry land and marshland, the park also has a deciduous forest and is situated on two major bird migration flyways. More than 350 species have been sighted in the park. A boardwalk winds through the 2,500 acres of marshland. Fishing, swimming, canoeing; picnicking, trails and interpretive center, biking.

UNIVERSITY OF WINDSOR-UNIVERSITY PLAYERS
401 Sunset Ave., Windsor, 519-253-3000; www.universityplayers.com
On campus is Essex Hall Theatre, featuring several productions per season. September-March.

WILLISTEAD MANOR
1899 Niagara St., Windsor, 519-253-2365; www.willisteadmanor.com
Restored English Tudor mansion built for Edward Chandler Walker, son of famous distiller Hiram Walker, on 15 acres of wooded parkland; elegant interiors with hand-carved woodwork; furnished in turn-of-the-century style. July-August, Sunday and Wednesday, September-June, first and third Sunday of each month.

WINDSOR'S COMMUNITY MUSEUM
254 Pitt St. W., Windsor, 519-253-1812; www.citywindsor.ca
Exhibits and collections interpret the history of Windsor and southwestern Ontario. Located in the historic Francois Baby House.

WRECK EXPLORATION TOURS
9 Robson Road, Leamington, 519-326-1566, 888-229-7325
Exploration of a 130-year-old wreck site. Shoreline cruise; artifact orientation. May-October, reservations required.

SPECIAL EVENTS
CARROUSEL OF THE NATIONS
519-255-1127; www.themcc.com
This family event features villages showcasing food, music traditions and dancing from all over the world. Three weekends in June.

FESTIVAL EPICURE: A CELEBRATION OF FOOD, WINE AND MUSIC
Riverside Festival Plaza, Windsor, 519-971-5005; www.festivalepicure.com
Sample food from local eateries and wine from regional wineries. Performances ranging from pop to bluegrass by Detroit and Windsor musicians. Mid-July.

INTERNATIONAL FREEDOM FESTIVAL
Riverside Drive and Ouelette Avenue, Windsor, 519-252-7264
Two-week joint celebration by Detroit and Windsor with many events, culminating in a fireworks display over the river. Late June-early July.

HOTELS
★★BEST WESTERN CONTINENTAL INN
3345 Huron Church Road, Windsor, 519-966-5541, 800-780-7234;
www.bestwestern.com
71 rooms. Complimentary continental breakfast. Restaurant, bar. Pool. High-speed Internet access. $

ONTARIO

★
★
★
★
★

★★★CAESARS WINDSOR HOTEL

377 Riverside Drive E., Windsor, 519-258-7878, 800-991-7777;
www.casinowindsor.com

An oasis from the frenetic casino activity, this hotel's guest rooms feature views of the Detroit skyline or the city of Windsor. A constant line-up of entertainers and a buzzing casino in the lobby will ensure that you'll never get bored. 758 rooms. Five restaurants, three bars. Casino. Pool. Fitness center. $$$

★COMFORT INN

1100 Richmond St., Chatham, 519-352-5500, 800-228-5150; www.comfortinn.com

80 rooms. Pets accepted, fee. Complimentary continental breakfast. High-speed Internet access. $

★★★HILTON WINDSOR

277 Riverside Drive W., Windsor, 519-973-5555, 800-774-1500; www.hilton.com

The waterfront location is key for both business and leisure travelers. The hotel is also conveniently interconnected to the Cleary International Convention Centre and close to other local attractions. The casual Park Terrace Restaurant serves breakfast, lunch and dinner. The River Runner Bar is a great place to catch the game. 305 rooms. Restaurant, bar. Pool. Business center. Children's menu. Pets accepted. $$

★★RADISSON RIVERFRONT HOTEL WINDSOR

333 Riverside Drive W., Windsor, 519-977-9777, 888-201-1718; www.radisson.com

207 rooms. Restaurant, bar. Pets accepted, fee. Pool. High-speed Internet access. Fitness center. $$

★★WHEELS INN

615 Richmond St., Chatham, 519-351-1100, 800-265-5257; www.wheelsinn.com

350 rooms. Four restaurants, bar. Pool. Business center. High-speed Internet access. $

RESTAURANTS

★★CHATHAM STREET GRILL

149 Chatham St. W., Windsor, 519-256-2555; www.chathamstreetgrill.com

Continental menu. Reservations recommended. Outdoor seating. Lunch, dinner. $$

★★COOK SHOP

683 Ouellette Ave., Windsor, 519-254-3377

Italian menu. Closed Monday; also two weeks in August. Reservations recommended. $$

★TUNNEL BAR-B-Q

58 Park St. E., Windsor, 519-258-3663, 877-285-3663; www.tunnelbarbq.com

American, steak menu. Breakfast, dinner. $$

ONTARIO

★
★
★
★
★

PRINCE EDWARD ISLAND

CANADA'S SMALLEST PROVINCE RESTS IN THE GULF OF ST. LAWRENCE ON THE EAST COAST, between Nova Scotia and New Brunswick. The island is just 40 miles (64 kilometers) wide at its broadest point, narrowing to only four miles (six kilometers) wide near Summerside and only 140 miles (224 kilometers) long. Charlottetown and Summerside are the only cities in the province. As charming as they are, it's no wonder this idyllic getaway, with its red soil, warm waters, fine white beaches and deep-cut coves, is more famed for its pastoral views and its promise of unspoiled, pristine relaxation.

Explore the Hillsborough River, one of the Canadian Heritage Rivers; scenic, red clay Heritage Roads; about 50 lighthouses (seven open to the public in the summer); three scenic routes—Lady Slipper Drive, Blue Heron Drive and Kings Byway—that travel around the islands coastline; 30 nine-hole and 18-hole golf courses; and a wealth of shops selling everything from traditional crafts to handmade soaps and Mi'kmaq figurines. Deep-sea fish, dig for clams, watch for more than 330 species of birds and sea kayak the coastline. Or simply unwind on one of many beaches.

Prince Edward Island is divided into six day-tour regions. "North by Northwest" encompasses the area from North Cape to Cedar Dunes Provincial Park, an area of unspoiled beauty with secluded beaches, picturesque fishing and farming communities and quaint churches. "Ship to Shore" covers the southwest, which proudly stewards a prosperous shipbuilding heritage, fox farming and world-famous Malpeque oysters. Also here is the city of Summerside, located on the Bedeque Bay. "Anne's Land," the white-sand beaches and central north shore of the province, brings literary fans to the real-life paradise of the beloved Anne of Green Gables, heroine of books written by Lucy Maud Montgomery. "Charlotte's Shore" encompasses the south central region, highlighted by Charlottetown, the provincial capital, as well as scenic red cliffs and warm waters. "Bays and Dunes," in the northeast corner, offers the island's best coastline views, with miles of white-sand beaches and spectacular dunes bordering the scenic countryside. "Hills & Harbors," through the southeast, is home to some of the most pleasing vistas and peaceful fishing villages in the province.

The 80-minute ferry ride to and from the island is a relaxing, scenic journey that is popular with visitors and locals alike. Northumberland ferries (888-249-7245; www.nfl-bay.com) operate between Caribou,

FUN FACTS

The Confederation Bridge is the longest bridge over ice-covered waters in the world and one of the most significant Canadian engineering feats of the 20th century. It took more than 6,000 people employed by the Strait Crossing organization four years to construct the bridge—from October 1993 through May 1997.

183

Nova Scotia and Wood Islands, Prince Edward Island about every 90 minutes from May-late December, weather permitting. A second ferry link, Corporation Transport Maritime Arien (CTMA), offers regular ferry service (about a five-hour trip) from Souris, P.E.I. to Cap-aux-Meules, les-de-la-Madeleine, Quebec except during February and March. For an equally interesting passage to Canada's beach-ridden gem, drive from New Brunswick to P.E.I. across the Confederation Bridge, the longest of its kind in the world.

CONFEDERATION BRIDGE

Not too long ago, the only way to get to Prince Edward Island was by air or water. That changed a decade ago when construction of the Confederation Bridge was completed. The bridge allows travel from New Brunswick to the town of Borden-Carleton on P.E.I. Built with more than 3.5 million tons of concrete and two million cubic yards of aggregate, the bridge has 44 main bridge spans, two traveling lanes and one emergency lane in either direction. There are 310 streetlights and 34 traffic lights (which remain green under normal conditions). The bridge is open only to motor vehicles; cyclists and pedestrians must use a shuttle to get across.

Information: www.confederationbridge.com

CONFEDERATION TRAIL

Those with enough pedal or foot power can travel the island from tip to tip on the Confederation Trail—a unique hiking, biking and snowmobile path that travels from Tignish on the west side of the island to Elmira on the east. The route totals more than 169 miles (270 kilometers), with branch trails extending into Charlottetown, Souris, Georgetown and Montague. There is also a link to the Confederation Bridge in Borden-Carleton. The easily traveled stone dust surface took the place of the Prince Edward Island railway, abandoned in 1989. Travelers pass woods, rivers and pastoral scenes along the route, in between small island communities. There are many places to stop for refreshments and a well-earned break. Prince Edward Island is the first province in Canada to complete its section (the Confederate Trail) of the Trans Canada Trail.

CAVENDISH

Located near the western end of Prince Edward Island National Park, Cavendish has more than 15 miles (24 kilometers) of world-famous beaches and is the heart and soul of Anne of Green Gables. Silky-white dunes, red sandstone cliffs and crystal blue water are all warmed by the Gulf Stream. Together with the allure of Canada's red-haired darling, Cavendish attracts thousands of visitors from around the world.

Information: www.cavendishbeachresort.com

WHAT TO SEE AND DO

AVONLEA-VILLAGE OF ANNE OF GREEN GABLES

Route 6, Cavendish, 902-963-3050; www.avonlea.ca

Families can spend a delightful day exploring Anne's world, meeting the novel's characters, visiting the barnyard, riding ponies and milking cows. Three music shows daily include children's shows; heritage buildings; museums; Avonlea Gardens. June-August: daily 10 a.m.-6 p.m.; September: daily 10 a.m.-4 p.m.

★
★
★
★
★

BIRTHPLACE OF LUCY MAUD MONTGOMERY

Junction of Highways 6 and 20, New London, 902-886-2099; www.gov.pe.ca

A replica of the "Blue Chest," the writer's personal scrapbooks containing copies of her many stories and poems, as well as her wedding dress and veil, are stored here. May-Thanksgiving: daily

GREEN GABLES

Prince Edward Island National Park, Routes 6 and 13, Cavendish, 902-672-6350; www.gov.pe.ca/greengables

Famous as the setting for Lucy Maud Montgomery's *Anne of Green Gables*. Surroundings portray the Victorian setting described in the novel. Tours available off-season. May-October: daily.

LUCY MAUD MONTGOMERY'S CAVENDISH HOME

Route 6, Cavendish, 902-963-2231; www.peisland.com/lmm

The site where Montgomery, author of *Anne of Green Gables* and 22 other novels, was raised by her grandparents from 1876 through 1911. The bookstore and museum houses the original desk, scales and crown stamp used in the post office. June-September: daily.

PRINCE EDWARD ISLAND NATIONAL PARK

Cavendish, 902-672-6350; www.canadianparks.com/prince_edward

Prince Edward Island National Park, 25 square miles (40 square kilometers), is one of Eastern Canada's most popular vacation destinations. Warm salt waters and sandy beaches abound. There are several supervised beach areas for swimmers and miles of secluded shoreline to explore. In addition to golf, tennis, bicycling and picnicking, the park offers campfires, beach walks, an interpretation program highlighting the natural and cultural features and stories of the area and more. Green Gables and its association with Lucy Maud Montgomery's *Anne of Green Gables* is a major attraction, with daily walks offered around the house and grounds. Many private cabins, hotels and campgrounds border the park.

RAINBOW VALLEY FAMILY FUN PARK

1 Ave. Wolfe, Montcalm, Cavendish, 902-963-2221; www.rainbowvalley.pe.ca

Approximately 40 acres of woodland, lakes and landscaped areas; children's farm with petting areas; playground, swan boats, flumes, water slides; entertainment; picnicking; café, Monorail ride. June-Labor Day.

HOTELS

★CAVENDISH CORNER

49 Pownal St., Charlottetown, 902-367-3205, 877-963-2251; www.resortatcavendishcorner.com

9-acre site, 46 cottages, 48 overnight rooms, 13 inn rooms. Closed mid-October-mid-May. Complimentary full breakfast (off-season only). Restaurant, children's activity center. $

★SILVERWOOD MOTEL

Green Gables Post Office, Cavendish Beach, 902-963-2439; www.silverwoodmotel.com

76 rooms. Restaurant. Pool. $

★★NEW GLASGOW LOBSTER SUPPERS

Route 258 New Glasgow, Cavendish, 902-964-2870; www.peilobstersuppers.com
Seafood menu. Closed November-May. $$

CHARLOTTETOWN

Having hosted the conference that led to the formation of Canada in 1864, Charlottetown today is a walkable, charm-filled heritage city with a scenic natural harbor, boating, yachting, swimming and plentiful seafood. Bistros, museums and artisan shopping, as well as a plethora of amenities, make this a traveler's headquarters. *Information: www.city.charlottetown.pe.ca*

WHAT TO SEE AND DO

ABEGWEIT SIGHTSEEING TOURS

157 Nassau, Charlottetown, 902-894-9966; www.abegweittours.ca
Charlottetown tours on authentic London double-decker buses; also north and south tours. Bilingual guide service available.

BEACONSFIELD

2 Kent St., Charlottetown, 902-368-6603
Mansard-style house built in 1877 for a shipbuilder is architecturally intact; guided tours. Headquarters of Prince Edward Island Museum and Heritage Foundation; bookstore. Regular and annual events.

186

CONFEDERATION CENTRE OF THE ARTS

145 Richmond St., Charlottetown, 902-628-1864, 800-565-0278;
www.confederationcentre.com
Canada's National Memorial to the Fathers of Confederation; opened by Queen Elizabeth II to honor the centennial of the 1864 Confederation Conference. Contains provincial library, Confederation Centre Museum and Art Gallery, theaters and the Robert Harris Collection of portraiture. Courtyard restaurant, gift shop. Home of the Charlottetown Festival. Gallery and museum.

FORT AMHERST/PORT LA JOYE NATIONAL HISTORIC PARK

2 Palmers Lane, Near Rocky Point Highway 19 across the harbor mouth,
Charlottetown, 902-566-7626; www.pc.gc.ca
The only earthworks of the former French fort Port la Joye (built in 1720) are still visible at this site. Captured by the British in 1758, it was abandoned in 1768. Cafe, boutique. Interpretive center. Mid-June-Labor Day: daily.

FOUNDER'S HALL-CANADA'S BIRTHPLACE PAVILION

6 Prince St., Charlottetown, 902-368-1864; www.foundershall.ca
Learn about the nation's history beginning in 1864 in this 21,000-square-foot (1,951-square-meter) waterfront attraction, with state-of-the-art displays and multimedia presentations. Restaurant; shop.

PRINCE EDWARD ISLAND

GOVERNMENT HOUSE

Charlottetown, 902-368-5480; www.gov.pe.ca

Tour the lieutenant governor's official residence. The Victorian Fanningbank Historic House was built in 1832. Tours explain the history of the house and the room furnishings. Visitors are free to explore the lovely flower gardens around the property after the tour. July-August: Monday-Friday 10 a.m.-4 p.m.

GREEN PARK SHIPBUILDING MUSEUM

Port Hill, 902-831-7947; www.gov.pe.ca/peimhf

Former estate of James Yeo, Jr., whose family members were leading shipbuilders of the 19th century. House restored to reflect life during the prosperous shipbuilding era. Photos of famous ships and artifacts in interpretive center; audiovisual presentation in Museum Theater. Lecture series and concerts. Annual events. Swimming; camping at Malpeque Bay. Mid-June-Labor Day: daily.

ORWELL CORNER HISTORIC VILLAGE

Charlottetown, 902-651-8515; www.orwellcorner.isn.net

Reconstructed rural crossroads community of late 19th century. Combined store, post office and farmhouse; school, church, cemetery and barns. Farming activities as they were practiced 100 years ago. Annual events. Ceilidhs (Wednesday evenings).

PROVINCE HOUSE

165 Richmond St., Charlottetown, 902-566-7626

Birthplace of the Canadian nation and a national historic site. Confederation room where delegates met in 1864 to discuss confederation. National memorial, seat of Provincial Legislature. Tours.

ST. DUNSTAN'S BASILICA

45 Great George St., Charlottetown, 902-894-3486; www.stdunstans.pe.ca

Largest church on the island. Gothic cathedral with distinctive triple towers contains beautiful stained-glass windows and an impressive altar: It is 37 feet (11 meters) high, made of many types of marble and crowned with a beautiful rose window.

SPECIAL EVENTS

CHARLOTTETOWN FESTIVAL

Confederation Centre of the Arts, 145 Richmond St., Charlottetown, 902-566-1267;
www.conferderationcentre.com

During this festival, you'll find original Canadian musicals, including *Anne of Green Gables* and other productions, as well as special gallery presentations and theater. Late May-mid-October.

FESTIVAL OF LIGHTS

Charlottetown Waterfront, Confederation Landing Park. Water and Great George Streets, Charlottetown, 902-629-1864

Buskers, children's concerts, Waterfront Magic, children's midway. Fireworks display over Charlottetown Harbor on July 1 (Canada Day). Late June-early July.

PRINCE EDWARD ISLAND

PRINCE EDWARD ISLAND STUDIO TOUR

94, Euston St., Prince Edward Island, 902-368-6300;
www.peibusinessdevelopment.com

Shoppers delight at this annual weekend-long event. Purchase island-made crafts and giftware at more than 140 participating craft studios, galleries, shops and museums across the island, without paying the provincial sales tax. Pick up the official directory and map at any P.E.I. visitor information center. Late September.

HOTELS

★★BEST WESTERN CHARLOTTETOWN

238 Grafton St., Charlottetown, 902-892-2461, 800-528-1234; www.bestwestern.com
146 rooms. Restaurant, bar. Pets accepted. Fitness room. Pool. $

★★THE CHARLOTTETOWN

75 Kent St., Charlottetown, 902-894-7371, 800-565-7633; www.rodd-hotels.ca
115 rooms. Restaurant, bar. Pets accepted, fee. Pool. $$$

★★★DELTA PRINCE EDWARD

18 Queen St., Charlottetown, 902-566-2222, 800-268-1133; www.deltahotels.com
Overlooking Charlottetown Harbor in an area of shops and restaurants, this large red-brick hotel is located at the foot of Queen Street at Peake's Wharf. Renovated guest rooms have a modern flair and are comfortable and well appointed. The hotel features its own marina, and guests can walk along the waterfront or take a harbor cruise from the hotel. 211 rooms. Two restaurants, bar. Pets accepted, fee. Pool. Spa. Business center. $$$

★★RODD ROYALTY INN

Highways 1 and 2, Charlottetown, 902-894-8566, 800-565-7633; www.rodd-hotels.ca
121 rooms. High-speed Internet access. Pets accepted. Pool. Restaurant, bar. $$

188

PRINCE EDWARD ISLAND

★
★★
★★
★★
★

QUÉBEC

AN ENCLAVE OF EUROPE IN THE HEART OF NORTH AMERICA, QUÉBEC IS A DIVERSE AND colorful province that is fiercely proud of its French heritage. Delightfully blending Old and New World, and passionate politics with a unique joie de vivre, this nation within a nation hums with incredible cuisine and nightlife alongside glorious mountains, charming villages, First Nations culture and an untamed wilderness. French is the language used by the majority of Québecers, though English is spoken or understood almost everywhere in the province.

By reason of its history and culture, Québec has forged a unique personality. Québecers enjoy fine dining and entertainment as evidenced by the busy calendar of festivals and other events—but they also maintain a classic Canadian hardiness and sense of adventure. As a place where both European and North American cultural influences play out, Québec has always produced a fertile creative energy and cultural vitality. The result is a thriving literature, theatrical, art, sculpture and crafts scene.

Historic yet resolutely modern, vibrant and festive, the cities of Montréal, Québec and Gatineau embody urban Québec with their rich architectural heritage, dynamic cultural melting pot and splendid surroundings. The wider river region, centered around the historic St. Lawrence river (one of the largest in the world), is home to old coastal villages, islands, bird sanctuaries, marine mammals and lighthouses, all bound by rural and rugged coastline.

189

Further afield, Québecers have mastered the art of resort living and eco-tourism. Québec's vast natural heritage comprises 27 national parks, numerous wildlife reserves and three biosphere reserves recognized by UNESCO. Ecotourism and adventure tour guides can support your discovery of the most beautiful sites in Québec on foot, by canoe or by kayak. During the summer enjoy golf, biking, tennis, hiking, swimming and water sports, and in winter get outside to snowmobile, ski, skate and even dog-sled. Whatever the day holds, fine cuisine will await you on the patio or by the hearth. For the more independent wanderer, Québec has pushed the boundaries of adventure since the days of the fur traders. In this vast territory, bears, deer and caribou are often the only inhabitants. Explore the province's length and breadth by canoe, snowmobile or seaplane, with nature as your travel companion.

QUÉBEC

★ **FUN FACTS** The old quarter of Québec City is the only fortified city in North America, with ramparts that look down into the maze of cobblestoned streets below. There's a funicular a few blocks away that descends to Lower Town, not far from the docks, a very steep (but short) ride that delights children.

Information: www.bonjourquebec.com

MONT TREMBLANT

In 1894, the provincial government of Québec established this 482-square-mile (1,248-square kilometer) wilderness reserve as a park in order to protect its abundant wildlife, 300 lakes, three rivers, three major hydrographical basins, innumerable streams, waterfalls and mountains that reach as high as 3,120 feet (960 meters). Today it is a center of fishing, hiking, canoeing, biking, swimming, sailing, snowmobiling, snowshoeing and cross-country and downhill skiing—and in the fall, people come here in droves for the foliage.

Information: www.tremblant.ca

SPECIAL EVENTS

MUSIC IN THE MOUNTAINS

Mont Tremblant Provincial Park, 888-736-2526; www.tremblant.com

Special music performances, workshops and activities. Late August-early September.

TREMBLANT INTERNATIONAL BLUES FESTIVAL

Mont Tremblant Provincial Park, 888-736-2526; www.tremblant.com

Ten days of the biggest blues festival in Canada, featuring more than 400 artists in almost 200 performances on indoor and outdoor stages. Mid-July.

HOTELS

★★CLUB TREMBLANT

121 rue Cuttle, Ville de Mont-Tremblant, 819-425-2731, 800-567-8341; www.clubtremblant.com

100 rooms. Restaurant, bar. Children's activity center. Pool. Tennis. $$

★★★FAIRMONT TREMBLANT

3045 Chemin de la Chapelle, Mont Tremblant, 819-681-7000; www.fairmont.com

The Fairmont's location at the base of the Laurentian Mountains makes it a skier's paradise, with ski-in, ski-out access to the slopes. Its plentiful menu of activities ensures that non-skiers are also cosseted. The guest rooms and suites offer a sophisticated twist on traditional ski lodge décor while incorporating creature comforts. 314 rooms. Restaurant, bar. Pool. Business center. $$

★★GRAY ROCKS RESORT AND CONVENTION CENTRE

2322 rue Labelle, Mont Tremblant, 819-425-2771, 800-567-6762; www.grayrocks.com

156 rooms. Restaurant, bar. Children's activity center. Beach. Seaplane base. Pool. Golf. Tennis. $

★★★LE WESTIN RESORT, TREMBLANT

100 Chemin Kandahar, Mont Tremblant, 819-681-8000, 888-736-2526; www.westin.com

A resort for all seasons, this hotel has luxurious guest rooms, many with balconies and fireplaces, a separate entrance for skiers and an outdoor heated saltwater pool Twenty outdoor tennis courts and two 18-hole golf courses challenge guests. After an activity-filled day, try Soto's Japanese cuisine or the American fare at Panache. 126 rooms. Complimentary continental breakfast. Restaurant, bar. Children's activity center. Spa. Beach. Pool. Golf. Tennis. Business center. $$

QUÉBEC

★
★
★
★
★

RESTAURANTS
★AUBERGE SAUVIGNON
2723 Chemin Principal, Mont Tremblant, 819-425-5466, 866-665-5466;
www.aubergesauvignon.com
French menu. Dinner. **$$$**

★LE SHACK
3035 De La Chapelle, Mont Tremblant, 819-681-4700; www.leshack.com
American menu. Lunch, dinner. **$$**

★PIZZATERIA
118 Chemin Kandahar Village Center, Mont Tremblant, 819-681-4522;
www.pizzateria.com
Lunch, dinner. **$**

MONTREAL

Blessed by its location on an island at the junction of the St. Lawrence and Ottawa rivers, Montreal has served for more than three centuries as a gigantic trading post. However, despite its status as a commercial, financial and industrial center, Montreal has an unconventional, eclectic heart. An internationally recognized patron of the fine arts, the city hosts several acclaimed festivals attended by the international elite, and its cosmopolitan flavor is enhanced by its two-thirds French-speaking population, as well as more than 80 ethnic communities that welcome visitors to colorful neighborhoods, attractions and markets.

Montreal is made up of two parts: the Old City, which is a maze of narrow streets, restored buildings and old houses best seen on foot; and the modern Montreal, with its many skyscrapers, museums, theaters, restaurants and nightlife. The boutiques and department stores of Sainte-Catherine Street are a shopper's paradise, while the café terraces of Crescent Street encourage peoplewatching. In the brisk winter, locals and visitors alike take refuge in Montreal's underground city, an impressive pedestrian network more than 19 miles (30 kilometers) long with hundreds of shops, restaurants, attractions and one of the most unique subway systems anywhere—in which each station has been decorated by a different architect for what's been called the largest underground art gallery in the world.

Information: www.tourisme-montreal.org

WHAT TO SEE AND DO
BIODOME DE MONTREAL
4777 Pierre-De Coubertin Ave., Montreal, 514-868-3000; www.biodome.qc.ca
The former Olympic Velodrome has been transformed into an environmental museum that combines elements of a botanical garden, aquarium, zoo and nature center. Four ecosystems—Laurentian Forest, Tropical Forest, Polar World and St. Laurent Marine—sustain thousands of plants and small animals. The Biodome also features a 1,640-foot (500-meter) nature path with text panels and maps.

QUÉBEC

★
★
★
★
★

CASINO MONTREAL

1 Ave. du Casino, Montreal, Expo 67's famous French Pavilion,
514-392-2746, 800-665-2274; www.casinos-quebec.com

The Casino de Montreal offers a variety of games, with more than 120 gaming tables as well as 3,060 slot machines. Open 24 hours.

CHÂTEAU RAMEZAY

280 rue Notre-Dame E., Montreal, 514-861-3708; www.chateauramezay.qc.ca

This historic building was constructed in the 18th century and was once the home of the governors of Montreal, the West Indies Company of France and the Governors-General of British North America. It opened as a museum in 1895 and today is the oldest private museum in Québec. Collections include furniture, paintings, costumes, porcelain, manuscripts and art objects of the 17th through 19th centuries.

DAVID M. STEWART MUSEUM

20 Chemin Tour L'Ile, St. Helen Island, 514-861-6701; www.stewart-museum.org

The Stewart Museum houses artifacts such as maps, firearms, kitchen utensils, engravings and navigational and scientific instruments that trace Canadian history from the 16th through the 19th centuries.

DORCHESTER SQUARE

1555 Peel St., Montreal

In the center of Montreal, this park is a popular meeting place. Also here is Mary Queen of the World Cathedral, a one third-scale replica of St. Peter's in Rome, as well as the information center of Montreal and Tourisme Québec.

★
★
★
★
★

FLORAL PARK

Le Notre-Dame, Montreal

Site of Les Floralies Internationales 1980; now permanent, it displays a collection of worldwide flowers and plants. Walking trails; pedal boats, canoeing; picnic area, restaurant. Third week in June-mid-September, daily.

FORT LENNOX

Saint-Paul-de-l'ile-aux-Noix, 1 61st Ave., Montreal,
450-291-5700; www.parcscanada.gc.ca

Located on le-aux-Noix, Fort Lennox was designed to protect against an American invasion. Costumed guides provide visitors with insight into the history of these fortifications.

INSECTARIUM DE MONTREAL

4581 Sherbrooke E., Montreal, 514-872-1400: www.ville.montreal.qc.ca

The Insectarium features a collection of more than 350,000 insects in a building designed to resemble a stylized insect. Interactive and participatory exhibits take visitors through aviaries and living displays in six geographically themed areas. Includes a butterfly aviary summer and a children's amusement center.

THE LAURENTIANS

www.laurentides.com

The Laurentian region, just 45 miles (72 kilometers) from Montreal, is a rich tourist destination. Surrounded by forests, lakes, rivers and the Laurentian Mountains, this area provides ample open-air activities year-round. Water sports abound in summer, including canoeing, kayaking, swimming, rafting, scuba diving and excellent fishing. Hunting, golfing, horseback riding and mountain climbing are also popular in warmer months, as is bicycling along the 125-mile (201-kilometer) P'tit train du Nord trail. Brilliant fall colors lead into a winter ideal for snow lovers. The Laurentian region boasts a huge number of downhill ski centers, 600 miles (966 kilometers) of cross-country trails and thousands of miles of snowmobiling trails. The territory of the Laurentian tourist zone is formed on the south by the Outaouais River, des Deux-Montagnes Lake and the Milles-iles River. On the east, its limits stretch from the limit of Terrebonne to Entrelacs. It is bounded on the north by Ste. Anne du Lac and Baskatong Reservoir and on the west by the towns of Des Ruisseaux, Notre-Dame de Pontmain and Notre Dame du Laus.

LA FONTAINE PARK

Sherbrooke and Avenue du Parc Lafontaine, Montreal, 514-872-2644

Outdoor enthusiasts delight in this park for its many recreational opportunities. Along with paddle boating on two manmade lakes, visitors may enjoy footpaths and bicycle trails and, in winter, cross-country skiing, ice-skating and snowshoeing.

LA RONDE

Le Sainte-Helene, 22 Chemin Macdonald, Montreal, 514-397-2000; www.laronde.com

A 135-acre amusement park with 35 rides, including a 132-foot (40-meter-high) wooden roller coaster; arcades, entertainment on a floating stage; waterskiing; live cartoon characters, children's village; circus, boutiques and restaurants. Mid-May-late October.

MAISON ST. GABRIEL

Pointe-Saint-Charles, 2146 place de Dublin, Montreal, 514-935-8136;
www.maisonsaint-gabriel.qc.ca

Built in the late 17th century as a farm; also served as school for Marguerite Bourgeoys, founder of the Sisters of the Congregation de Notre-Dame, who looked after young French girls who were to marry the early colonists. The site includes vegetable, herb and flower gardens. The house itself has period furnishings and tools and items of French-Canadian heritage, including woodcuts from ancient churches and chapels. Mid-April-late June, September-mid-December, Tuesday-Sunday 1-5 p.m.; late June-early September, Tuesday-Sunday 11 a.m.-6 p.m.

MCCORD MUSEUM OF CANADIAN HISTORY

690 rue Sherbrooke Ouest, Montreal, 514-398-7100; www.mccord-museum.qc.ca

Extensive and diverse collections, including the most important First Nations collection in Québec, Canadian costumes and textiles and the Notman photographic archives.

QUÉBEC

MONTREAL BOTANICAL GARDEN

4101 rue Sherbrooke E., Montreal, 514-872-1400; www.ville.montreal.qc.ca/jardin

Within 180 acres (73 hectares) grow more than 26,000 species and varieties of plants; 30 specialized sections include roses, perennial plants, heath gardens, flowery brooks, bonsai, carnivorous plants and an arboretum; one of the world's largest orchid collections; seasonal flower shows. The bonsai and penjing collections are two of the most diversified in North America. Chinese and Japanese gardens; restaurant, tearoom.

MONTREAL CANADIENS (NHL)

1260 de La Gauchetière S.W., Montreal, 514-790-1245; www.canadiens.com

Professional hockey team.

MONTREAL MUSEUM OF FINE ARTS

1379-80 rue Sherbrooke Ouest, Montreal, 514-285-2000, 800-899-6873;
www.mmfa.qc.ca

Canada's oldest art museum, founded in 1860, has a wide variety of displays ranging from Egyptian statues to 20th-century abstracts. Canadian section features old Québec furniture, silver and paintings.

MONTREAL PLANETARIUM

1000 rue Saint-Jacques Ouest, Montreal, 514-872-4530;
www.planetarium.montreal.qc.ca

See the stars at the Montreal Planetarium, where a 385-seat theater holds multimedia astronomy shows with projectors creating features of the night sky. Just outside the theater are temporary and permanent exhibits on the solar system, meteorites, fossils and other astronomy-related topics.

THE MONTREAL SCIENCE CENTRE

King-Edward Pier, 333 rue de la Commune Ouest, Montreal, 514-496-4724, 877-496-4724;
www.centredessciencesdemontreal.com/en

Uncover the mysteries of science and technology through multimedia and hands-on exhibits, an IMAX theater and more.

MUSEÉ D'ART CONTEMPORAIN DE MONTREAL

185 rue Sainte-Catherine Ouest, Montreal, 514-847-6226; www.macm.org

The only museum in Canada that is devoted exclusively to modern art. Gift shop, bookstore, garden, restaurant.

MUSEUM OF DECORATIVE ARTS

2200 rue Crescent, Montreal

Historic mansion Chateau Dufresne, built in 1918 And partially restored and refurnished, now houses international exhibitions of glass, textiles and ceramic art; changing exhibits.

★
★
★
★
★

NOTRE-DAME BASILICA

110 rue Notre-Dame Ouest, Montreal, 514-842-2925, 866-842-2925;
www.basiliquenddm.org

Completed in 1829, this church features Le Gros Bourdon, a bell cast in 1847 and weighing 24,780 pounds (11,240 kilograms). Built of Montreal limestone, the basilica is neo-Gothic in design with a beautiful main altar, pulpit and numerous statues, paintings and stained-glass windows.

NOTRE-DAME-DE-BON-SECOURS CHURCH

400 rue St. Paul E., Montreal, 514-282-8670

Founded in 1657 by teacher Marguerite Bourgeoys and rebuilt 115 years later, this is one of the oldest churches still standing in the city. With its location near the Port of Montreal, parishioners often prayed here for the safety of the community's sailors. In recognition of this, many fishermen and other mariners presented the church with miniature wooden ships, which hang from the vaulted ceiling today. The tower offers views of the river and city. Housed here is the Marguerite Bourgeois museum, which features objects pertaining to early settlers.

THE OLD FORT

Oldest remaining fortification of Montreal, built between 1820 and 1824; only the arsenal, powder magazine and barracks building still stand. Two military companies dating to the 18th century, La Compagnie Franche de la Marine and the 78th Fraser Highlanders, perform colorful military drills and parades. Late June-August, Wednesday-Sunday.

OLD (VIEUX) MONTREAL

Bounded by McGill, Berri, Notre-Dame streets and the St. Lawrence River

The city of Montreal evolved from the small settlement of Ville-Marie founded by de Maisonneuve in 1642. The largest concentration of 19th-century buildings in North America is found here; several original dwellings remain while many other locations are marked by bronze plaques. The expansion of this settlement led to what is now known as Old Montreal. The area roughly forms a 100-acre (40-hectare) quadrangle which corresponds approximately to the area enclosed within the original fortifications.

QUÉBEC

★
★
★
★

OLD PORT OF MONTREAL

333 Rue de la Commune St., Montreal, 514-496-7678, 800-971-7678;
www.oldportofmontreal.com

A departure point for boat cruises, and a recreation and tourist park hosting exhibitions, special events and entertainment.

OLYMPIC PARK

4141 Pierre de Coubertin Ave., Montreal, 514-252-4141, 877-997-0919;
www.rio.gouv.qc.ca

The stadium was the site of the 1976 Summer Olympic Games and is now home to les Alouettes de Montreal football team. The world's tallest inclined tower (626 feet or 191 meters, leaning at a 45-degree angle) is here. Tours of the stadium are given daily.

PARC DU MONT-ROYAL

Cote des Neiges and Remembrance roads, Montreal, 514-843-8240;
www.lemontroyal.qc.ca

Designed by Frederick Law Olmsted, the creator of Central Park in New York City, Parc du Mont-Royal is also a park located in the heart of a city. Popular with visitors to Montreal, if affers something for everyone: cycling, hiking, picnicking, paddle boating, cross-country skiing and snowshoeing. Bikes, paddleboats, skis and snowshoes may be rented at the park. Daily 6 a.m.-midnight.

PARC JEAN-DRAPEAU

1 Circuit Gilles-Villeneuve, Montreal, 514-872-6120; www.parcjeandrapeau.com

Two islands in the middle of the St. Lawrence River; access via Jacques-Cartier Bridge or Metro subway. Ile Ste. Helene St. St. Helen's Island was the main anchor site for Expo '67; now a 342-acre (138-hectare) multipurpose park with three swimming pools; picnicking; cross-country skiing, snowshoeing. Le Notre-Dame Notre Dame Island, to the south, was partly built up from the riverbed and was an important activity site for Expo '67. Here is Gilles-Villeneuve Formula 1 racetrack; also beach, paddleboats, windsurfing and sailing.

PLACE D'ARMES

Rue St. Jacques, Montreal

A square of great historical importance and center of Old Montreal. The founders of Ville-Marie encountered the Iroquois here in 1644 and rebuffed them. In the square's center is a statue of de Maisonneuve, first governor of Montreal and at one end is the St. Sulpice seminary 1685, with an old wooden clock. At 119 St. Jacques Street is the Bank of Montreal. This magnificent building contains a museum (open Monday-Friday) with a collection of currency, mechanical savings banks, photographs and a reproduction of an old-fashioned teller's cage. Some of the most important financial houses of the city are grouped around the square.

PLACE DES ARTS

260 Blvd. de Maisonneuve Oeste, 514-842-2112; www.pdarts.com

This four-theater complex is the heart of Montreal's artistic life. L'Opera de Montreal, the Montreal Symphony Orchestra, les Grands Ballets Canadiens and La Compagnie Jean-Duceppe theatrical troupe have their permanent homes here. Other entertainment includes chamber music, recitals, jazz, folk singers, variety shows, music hall, theater, musicals and modern and classical dance.

PLACE JACQUES-CARTIER

Between rue Notre-Dame and rue de la Commune, Montreal

Named for the discoverer of Canada, this was once a busy marketplace. Today, restaurants, cafés, bars, cyclists, in-line skaters and street performers are found around the plaza, which is closed to traffic. The oldest monument in the city, the Nelson Column, is in the square's upper section.

★
★
★
★
☆

POINTE-À-CALLIÈRE, THE MONTREAL MUSEUM OF ARCHAEOLOGY AND HISTORY

350 Place Royale, Montreal, 514-872-9150; www.pacmuseum.qc.ca

Built in 1992 over the site of the founding of Montreal, the main museum building, the Eperon, actually rests on pillars built around ruins dating from the town's first cemetery and its earliest fortifications, which are now in its basement. Two balconies overlook this archaeological site and a 16-minute multimedia show is presented using the actual remnants as a backdrop. From here, visitors continue underground, amid still more remnants, to the Archaeological Crypt, a structure that allows access to many more artifacts and remains; architectural models beneath a transparent floor illustrate five different periods in the history of Place Royale. The Old Customs House Ancienne-Douane houses thematic exhibits on Montreal in the 19th and 20th centuries. Permanent and changing exhibits.

RUE SAINT-PAUL

The oldest street in Montreal. The mansions of Ville-Marie once stood here, but they have been replaced by commercial houses and office buildings.

ST. JOSEPH'S ORATORY OF MONT ROYAL

3800 Chemin Queen Mary, Montreal, 514-733-8211; www.saint-joseph.org

The chapel was built as a tribute to St. Joseph in 1904. A larger crypt church was completed in 1917. Today, the main church is a famous shrine attracting more than two million pilgrims yearly. A basilica with a seating capacity of 2,200 was founded in 1924; the dome towers over the city and a 56-bell carillon made in France is outstanding. The Oratory's museum features 200 nativity scenes from 100 different countries.

SPECIAL EVENTS

CANADIAN GRAND PRIX

Parc Jean-Drapeau, Montreal, 514-350-0000

Held annually since 1967, this Formula 1 race took place on the Mont-Tremblant Circuit until 1977. At that time, the track was considered too dangerous and the then-named le-Notre-Dame Track was built. The first race at the new track was held in 1978 and was won by Gilles Villeneuve, Canada's first F1 driver. In 1982, when Villeneuve was killed during practice laps at the Belgian Grand Prix, the track was re-named in his honor. If you wish to attend this event, make sure to purchase tickets well in advance; they can be extremely hard to come by. Mid-June.

FETE NATIONALE

82 rue Sherbrooke Ouest, Montreal, 514-849-2560; www.fetenationale.qc.ca

St. Jean-Baptiste, patron saint of the French Canadians, is honored with three days of festivities surrounding the provincial holiday. The celebration includes street festivals, a bonfire, fireworks, musical events and parades. Mid-June.

INTERNATIONAL FIREWORKS COMPETITION

Le Sainte-Helene, 22 Chemin Macdonald, Montreal, 514-397-2000;
www.montrealfireworks.com

Held in Montmorency Falls Park, this musical fireworks competition attracts master fireworks handlers from around the world. Fireworks start at 10 p.m., rain or shine. Late June-late July.

QUÉBEC

JUST FOR LAUGHS FESTIVAL

2095 Blvd. St. Laurent, Montreal, 514-845-2322, 888-244-3155; www.hahaha.com

This comedy festival features comic talent from all over the world. Shows are performed in more than 25 venues along St. Denis Street and are broadcast to millions of viewers worldwide. Artists who have performed at past festivals include Jerry Seinfeld, Jay Leno, Rowan Atkinson, Jon Stewart, Lily Tomlin and the cast of *The Simpsons*. Mid-July.

MONTREAL BIKE FEST

1251 rue Rachel E., Montreal, 514-521-8356, 800-567-8356; www.velo.qc.ca

An entire week of events celebrating the bicycle, ending when 40,000 cyclists ride through the streets of Montreal. Includes a 16-mile (26-kilometer) outing for up to 10,000 children. Late May-early June.

MONTREAL HIGH LIGHTS FESTIVAL

822 rue Sherbrooke E., Montreal, 514-288-9955, 888-477-9955;
www.montrealhighlights.com

Spotlights the city's cultural and artistic diversity. Mid-February-early March.

MONTREAL INTERNATIONAL JAZZ FESTIVAL

822 rue Sherbrooke E., Montreal, 514-871-1881, 888-515-0515;
www.montrealjazzfest.com

More than 1,200 musicians and 1 million music lovers from around the world gather to celebrate jazz and other types of music. The 10-day fest includes more than 350 indoor and outdoor concerts. Late June-early July.

WORLD FILM FESTIVAL

1432 de Bleury St., Montreal, 514-848-3883; www.ffm-montreal.org

Montreal's World Film Festival was organized to celebrate all types of cinema, from documentaries and drama to comedy and science fiction. Amateur and well-known filmmakers alike participate in the event, which screens films from nearly 70 countries. Late August-early September.

HOTELS

★★★AUBERGE DU VIEUX-PORT

97 rue de la Commune E., Montreal, 514-876-0081, 888-660-7678;
www.aubergeduvieuxport.com

This historic landmark building served several functions before becoming a full-service inn. Rooms have contemporary furnishing and loft-like exposed beams and brick walls. Les Ramparts restaurant serves up fine, French cuisine and a rooftop terrace offers a panoramic view of the St. Lawrence River. Guests are pampered with a full breakfast, afternoon wine and cheese and more. 27 rooms. Complimentary full breakfast. Restaurant, bar. $$

★★★AUBERGE HANDFIELD

555 Blvd. Richelieu, St. Marc-Sur-Richelieu, 450-584-2226;
www.aubergehandfield.com

This country inn, located 45 minutes from central Montreal, offers comfortable rooms with views of the garden or nearby river. The onsite restaurant serves full, traditional dinners drawing on local ingredients as well as an extensive Sunday brunch. 56 rooms. Restaurant, bar. Exercise room. Pool. Spa. **$**

★★★CHATEAU VERSAILLES HOTEL

1659 rue Sherbrooke Ouest, Montreal, 888-933-8111, 514-933-8111;
www.versailleshotels.com

Located at the start of Montréal's famous Miracle Mile shopping district and the foot of Mont Royal, this 1800s hotel features unique rooms in four renovated Victorian townhouses. The property is also just minutes by metro to the Molson Centre and the Place des Arts. 65 rooms. Complimentary continental breakfast. Restaurant, bar. Pets accepted, fees. Exercise room. Business center. **$$**

★★COURTYARD MONTREAL DOWNTOWN

410 rue Sherbrooke Ouest, Montreal, 514-844-8855, 800-449-6654; www.marriott.com
157 rooms. Complimentary continental breakfast. Restaurant, bar. Pool. **$**

★★★DELTA MONTREAL

475 President Kennedy Ave., Montreal, 514-286-1986, 877-286-1986;
www.deltamontreal.com

This modern, inviting hotel is located in the heart of downtown, near the Convention Centre and the Place des Arts. Have a game on the squash courts at Delta's elaborate spa and sports center, then enjoy French cuisine at Le Bouquet or relax at Le Cordial, the hotel's full-service bar. 456 rooms. Restaurant, bar. Children's activity center. Pets accepted, fees. Exercise room. Pool. Business center. **$**

★★★FAIRMONT THE QUEEN ELIZABETH

900 Blvd. Rene Levesque Ouest, Montreal, 514-861-3511, 800-441-1414;
www.fairmont.com

This contemporary hotel is located in the city center, above the train station and linked to the underground system of shops and restaurants. The hotel's Beaver Club is a favorite for its gourmet meals and the convivial, Mediterranean-inspired Le Montrealais Bistrot-Bar-Restaurant is a more casual spot for dinner or drinks. 1,039 rooms. Two restaurants, bar. Pets accepted, fees. Exercise room. Pool. Business center. **$$**

★★★HILTON MONTREAL, BONAVENTURE

900 de la Gauchetiere Ouest, Montreal, 514-878-2332, 800-267-2575;
www.hiltonmontreal.com

This hotel is perched on top of the Place Bonaventure Exhibition Hall. There are rooftop gardens to explore and a year-round outdoor pool. The central city location is perfect for sightseeing in Old Montreal, gambling at the casino or shopping the underground boutiques. 395 rooms. Restaurant, bar. Pets accepted, fees. Exercise room. Pool. Business center. **$$**

★★★HILTON MONTREAL DORVAL AIRPORT

12505 Cote de Liesse, Dorval, 514-631-2411; www.dorval.hilton.com

Perfect for business or leisure travelers, this hotel has a location that is only a two-minute drive to the airport. Guests can relax in either the pool or jacuzzi and then retreat to their renovated, contemporary rooms. Dine at Au Coin du Feu and enjoy the seafood and steak menu, then have a cocktail at Eclipse. 486 rooms. Restaurant, bar. Pets accepted, fees. Exercise room. Pool. Business center. $

★★HOLIDAY INN SELECT MONTREAL

99 Viger Ave. Ouest, Montreal, 514-878-9888, 888-878-9888;
www.yul-downtown.hiselect.com

235 rooms. Restaurant, bar. Exercise room. Pool. Business center. $$

★★★HOSTELLERIE LES TROIS TILLEULS

290 rue Richelieu, St. Marc-Sur-Richelieu, 514-856-7787; www.lestroistilleuls.com

This 1880s farmhouse is located 30 minutes south of Montreal on the Richelieu River. The inn has comfortable rooms decorated in soothing neutrals with down duvet-topped beds. The onsite Spa Givency offers a full menu of treatments including hot stone massages, facials and body wraps. 41 rooms. Restaurant, bar. Pool. Tennis. Business center. $

★★★HOTEL DU FORT

1390 rue du Fort, Montreal, 514-938-8333, 800-565-6333; www.hoteldufort.com

Located steps from rue Ste. Catherine, this property is close to the city's top attractions, shops and restaurants. Understated guest rooms offer city views and traditional furnishings in neutral tones. Room service options include menus from area restaurants. 124 rooms. Complimentary continental breakfast. Restaurant, bar. Business center. $

★★★HOTEL GAULT

449 rue Ste. Héléne, Montreal, 514-904-1616, 866-904-1616; www.hotelgault.com

You might not expect to find an ultramodern hotel in a historic neighborhood, but Hotel Gault is exactly that. Inside, you'll find interiors of glass, concrete and steel, balanced with warm woods. Sound proofed guest rooms feature flatscreen TVs, CD and DVD players and comfortable workstations, and some have private terraces. A variety of living spaces are available-30 rooms. Restaurant, bar. Exercise room. Business center. $$

★★★HOTEL INTERCONTINENTAL MONTREAL

360 rue Ste Antoine Ouest, Montreal, 514-987-9900;
www.montreal.intercontinental.com

This sophisticated, elegant hotel is located across from the Convention Center in downtown Montreal. It's a short walk from the popular Old Town. Rooms are comfortable and traditional with plush bedding and ample workspaces. The hotel's building houses shops and businesses, with the guest rooms starting on the 10th floor. 357 rooms. Pets accepted, some restrictions; fee. Two restaurants, bar. Fitness room. Indoor pool. Business center. $

★★HOTEL LE CANTLIE SUITES

1110 rue Sherbrooke Ouest, Montreal, 514-842-2000, 800-567-1110;
www.hotelcantlie.com
251 rooms, all suites. Restaurant, bar. Pool. Business center. **$$**

★★★HOTEL LE GERMAIN

2050 rue Mansfield, Montreal, 514-849-2050, 877-333-2050; www.hotelgermain.com
This distinctive boutique hotel offers hospitality, comfort and relaxation in an elegant
setting. The convenient downtown location makes it close to shopping, museums,
concert halls and movie theaters. Guest rooms feature original photos by Louis Duc-
harm and elegant comfortable décor. 101 rooms. Complimentary full breakfast. Res-
taurant, bar. Pets accepted, fees. Exercise room. **$$**

★★★★HOTEL LE ST. JAMES

355 Saint Jacques St., Montreal, 514-841-3111, 866-841-3111;
www.hotellestjames.com
At the majestic Hotel Le St. James, each room and suite is individually decorated with
antiques and art. Housed in a former bank, the building's imposing façade features
ornate moldings and details fully restored to their 1870s grandeur. The convention
center, downtown business area, Old Port area and the St. Lawrence River are a short
stroll away from the hotel. Lunch, dinner and afternoon tea in the hotel's restaurant
feature regional, market-driven fare. 61 rooms. Restaurant, bar. Spa. Pets accepted.
Fitness center. Business center. **$$$$**

★★★HOTEL L'EAU A LA BOUCHE

3003 Blvd. Ste. Adele, Sainte Adèle, 450-229-2991; www.leaualabouche.com
Located just 45 minutes from Montreal, Hotel L'Eau A La Bouche is amid the greenery of the Laurentian Mountains. Rooms offer mountain views. The property includes
a heated outdoor pool and a full-service spa. Having a meal at the hotel's restaurant, where the award-winning cuisine of chef Anne Desjardins is served, is a must.
25 rooms. Restaurant, bar. Spa. Exercise room. **$$**

★★★HOTEL NELLIGAN

106 rue St. Paul Ouest, Montreal, 514-788-2040, 877-788-2040;
www.hotelnelligan.com
This boutique hotel consists of two connected buildings. The exposed-brick and
stone walls hint at its lengthy history, but the hotel provides all the modern touches
that guests expect in an urban hotel. A wine and cheese reception is offered daily.
Verses, the hotel's restaurant, serves French fare in a hip and trendy setting. 44 rooms,
53 suites. Complimentary continental breakfast. Restaurant, bar. Exercise room.
Business center. **$$**

★★★HOTEL OMNI MONT-ROYAL

1050 rue Sherbrooke Ouest, Montreal, 514-284-1110, 800-843-6664;
www.omnihotels.com
This elegant property is centrally located in the historic Golden Square Mile in the
heart of downtown and at the foot of Mont Royal. Shops, museums, nightlife and
fine dining are within walking distance. Pets are not only welcome at the hotel, they

receive specially designed treats. 299 rooms. Two restaurants, bar. Spa. Pets accepted. Exercise room. Pool. Business center. $$

★★★HOTEL PLACE D'ARMES

55 Saint-Jacques Ouest, Montreal, 514-842-1887, 888-450-1887; www.hotelplacedarmes.com

Step from Old Montreal's centuries-old charm into new millennium mod at Le Place d'Armes Hotel and Suites. The boutique hotel's ultramodern décor makes for a refreshing departure of the more traditional hotels in the area. Service is polished and professional, the onsite restaurant serves a full breakfast daily. 135 rooms. Complimentary continental breakfast. Restaurant, bar, spa. $$$

★★★HOTEL ST. PAUL

355 rue McGill, Montreal, 493-062-9011, 866-380-2202; www.hotelstpaul.com

Set in a restored Beaux Arts building, the Hotel St. Paul is all about contemporary cool. Lighting above guest room doors revolve around two themes: earth (lit in red) and sky (lit in blue). The spare accommodations feature large windows, modern furnishings and animal-print accents. The onsite restaurant, Cube, serves fresh seasonal cuisine. 120 rooms. Complimentary continental breakfast. Restaurant, bar. Pets accepted, fees. Exercise room. Business center. $$

★★★HYATT REGENCY MONTREAL

1255 Jeanne-Mance, Montreal, 514-982-1234, 866-816-3871; www.montreal.hyatt.com

Enjoy a lively urban retreat at the Hyatt Regency Montréal. Located in the Cultural District, the Hyatt is part of the elaborate shopping, dining and entertainment center Complexe des Jardins and is located adjacent to Place des Arts. The hotel also has underground access to the Montréal Convention Center. 605 rooms. Restaurant, bar. Exercise room. Pool. Business center. $$

★★★LE SAINT SULPICE HOTEL MONTREAL

414 rue Saint Sulpice, Montreal, 514-288-1000, 877-785-7423; www.lesaintsulpice.com

Step back in time at this luxury hotel, located in the historic section of Montreal, just steps from the Notre-Dame Basilica and the Old Port. Sample steaks and seafood as well as regional specialties in S Le Restaurant. The Essence Health Center features beautifying treatments in addition to modern exercise equipment. 108 rooms, all suites. Complimentary continental breakfast. Restaurant, bar. Spa. Exercise room. $$$

★★★LOEWS HOTEL VOGUE

1425 rue de la Montagne, Montreal, 514-285-5555, 800-465-6654; www.loewshotels.com

The fresh spirit and chic modernity of the Loews Hotel Vogue breathes new life into old-world Montreal. The accommodations provide sleek shelter with silk upholstered furnishings while creature comforts like oversized bathrooms appeal to every guest. Stop in at L'Opéra Bar, a lively after-dark gathering spot. 142 rooms. Restaurant, bar. Pets accepted, fees. Business center. $$

★★★MARRIOTT MONTREAL CHATEAU CHAMPLAIN

1050 de la Gauchetiere Ouest, Montreal, 514-878-9000, 800-200-5909;
www.marriott.com

Charming Art Nouveau décor adorns the guest rooms which ahve views of the Cathedral, Parc Mont Royal and Old Montréal. Hospitality rules at the Mediterranean-flavored Le Samuel de Champlain restaurant, while Le Senateur Bar satisfies discriminating tastes. 611 rooms. Restaurant, bar. Exercise room. Pool. $$

★★NOVOTEL

1180 rue de la Montagne, Montreal, 514-861-6000, 800-668-6835;
www.novotelmontreal.com

228 rooms. Restaurant, bar. Pets accepted, fee. Exercise room. Business center. $

★★★PETITE AUBERGE LES BONS MATINS

1401 Argyle Ave., Montreal, 514-931-9167, 800-588-5280; www.bonsmatins.com

Guests stay in rooms in adjoining restored century-old townhomes in the heart of Montréal. This inn is located close to main thoroughfares Sainte-Catherine Street and Crescent Street and just steps away from the Lucien L'Allier metro stop. Antiques and paintings by a family artist decorate rooms, each of which have private baths with bathrobes and natural bath products. A full gourmet breakfast is served daily in the dining room. 21 rooms. Pets accepted, some restrictions. Complimentary full breakfast. $$

★★QUALITY INN

6680 Taschereau Blvd., Brossard, 450-671-7213, 800-267-3837; www.qualityinn.com

100 rooms. Complimentary continental breakfast. Check-out noon. Restaurant, bar. Outdoor pool. $

★★★THE RITZ-CARLTON, MONTREAL

1228 Sherbrooke St. West, Montreal, 514-842-4212,
800-363-0366; www.ritzmontreal.com

This classic hotel is a leisure traveler's dream, with the quaint Old Town, Olympic Center and renowned museums located just a short distance away. The hotel is currently undergoing renovations, and it is scheduled to reopen in November 2009. 231 rooms. Restaurant, bar. Pets accepted, fees. Exercise room. Business center. High-speed Internet access. $$

★★★SOFITEL MONTREAL

1155 Rue Sherbrooke Ouest, Montreal, 514-285-9000; www.sofitel.com

Modern and elegant, this hotel is set at the foot of Parc Mont Royal on Sherbrooke Street and close to galleries, boutiques and the historic center of the city. Enjoy morning croissants and evening cocktails in Le Bar or dine on Provencal-inspired cuisine in Renoir. 258 rooms. Restaurant, bar. Pets accepted, fee. Exercise room. Business center. Wireless Internet access. Fitness centre. $$$

SPECIALITY LODGINGS

ANGELICA BLUE BED & BREAKFAST

1213 Ste. Elizabeth, Montreal, 514-844-5048, 800-878-5048; www.angelicablue.com

Six rooms Complimentary full breakfast, Free wireless Internet access. not accepted Pets. $

AUBERGE DE LA FONTAINE
1301 rue Rachel E., Montreal, 514-597-0166, 800-597-0597;
www.aubergedelafontaine.com
21 rooms. Complimentary full breakfast. Wireless Internet access. Bar. **$$**

LE PETIT PRINCE BED & BREAKFAST
1384 Overdale Ave., Montreal, 514-938-2277, 877-938-9750;
www.montrealbandb.com
Four rooms. Complimentary full breakfast, Wireless Internet access. **$$**

RESTAURANTS
★★★AU PIED DE COCHON
536 Ave. Duluth E., Montreal, 514-281-1114; www.restaurantaupieddecochon.ca
The "Pig's Foot" serves hearty regional cuisine with an emphasis on beef, lamb, venison, duck and yes, pork. There are several varieties of foie gras and fish, along with local favorite sides like poutine (fries doused in gravy). The cozy atmosphere and historic Montreal location make for an authentic dining experience. French menu. Dinner. Closed Monday. Reservations recommended. **$$$**

★AU TOURNANT DE LA RIVIERE
5070 Salaberry, Carignan, 450-658-7372; www.restaurantautournantdelariviere.com
French menu. Dinner, Sunday Brunch. **$$$**

★★AUBERGE HANDFIELD
555 Blvd. Richelieu, St. Marc-Sur-Richelieu, 450-584-2226, 800-361-6162;
www.aubergehandfield.com
French menu. Dinner. Closed Monday; also mid-January-early May. Reservations recommended. Outdoor seating. **$$$**

★★BIDDLE'S JAZZ AND RIBS
2060 rue Aylmer, Montreal, 514-842-8656
American menu. Dinner. Reservations recommended. Outdoor seating. **$$**

★★★BISTRO À CHAMPLAIN
75 Chemin Masson, Ste. Marguerite, 450-228-4988; www.bistroachamplain.com
Located on the edge of Lake Masson in the Laurentian Mountains, this elegant, rustic restaurant serves a varied menu with everything from braised caribou to grilled steak making an appearance on the menu. A lengthy wine list and views of a nearby lake add to the ambience. French menu. Dinner. Closed Monday-Tuesday. Reservations recommended. **$$$**

★★★CAFE FERREIRA
1446 rue Peel, Montreal, 514-848-0988; www.ferreiracafe.com
This restaurant is one of the most stylish dining rooms in Montreal. The friendly staff serve up wonderful Portuguese cuisine, with an emphasis on fresh fish and a comprehensive selection of Portuguese wines and ports. Portuguese menu. Dinner. Closed Sunday. Bar. Reservations recommended. Outdoor seating. **$$$**

204

QUÉBEC

★
★
★
★
★

★CAFE STE. ALEXANDRE

518 rue Duluth E., Montreal, 514-849-4251

Italian, Greek, seafood menu. Reservations recommended. Outdoor seating. **$$**

★★★CHEZ L'EPICIER

311 rue Saint-Paul E., Montreal, 514-878-2232; www.chezlepicier.com

This cozy and informal French restaurant is located in a building in Old Montreal that dates to the late 1800s. The restaurant uses fresh, local produce for its daily-changing menu, and its food products are available for sale in a neighborhood market setting. French menu. Lunch, dinner. Closed for two weeks in January. Reservations recommended. **$$$**

★★★CHEZ LA MERE MICHEL

1209 rue Guy, Montreal, 514-934-0473; www.chezlameremichel.com

In a city with volumes of competition, this fine French restaurant has succeeded in its downtown historic-home location since 1965. The menu is classic and well prepared and includes a fantastic strawberry Napoleon for dessert. French menu. Dinner. Closed Sunday. **$$$**

★★GLOBE

3455 St. Laurent, Montreal, 514-284-3823; www.restaurantglobe.com

French menu. Reservations recommended. **$$$**

★★JARDIN NELSON

407 Place Jacques-Cartier, Montreal, 514-861-5731; www.jardinnelson.com

Italian menu. Lunch, Saturday-Sunday brunch. Closed November-March. Reservations recommended. Outdoor seating. **$$**

★★THE KEG

25 rue St. Paul E., Montreal, 514-871-9093; www.kegsteakhouse.com

Steak menu. Dinner. Bar. Reservation recommended. **$$$**

★★★★L'EAU A LA BOUCHE

3003 Blvd. Sainte-Adèle, Ste. Adele, 450- 229-2991; www.leaualabouche.com

Tucked into forests surrounding the Laurentian Mountains, near the village of Sainte-Adèle, you will find L'eau a la Bouche, a charming little restaurant located on the property of the Hotel L'eau a la Bouche. The gourmet menu is built around local produce, fish, meat and homegrown herbs and vegetables, woven together and dressed up with a perfect dose of French technique and modern flair. Attentive, thoughtful service and a vast wine list make this luxurious dining experience unforgettable. French menu. Breakfast, dinner. Bar. **$$$**

★★L'EXPRESS

3927 St. Denis, Montreal, 514-845-5333

French menu. Reservations recommended. **$$**

★★LA GAUDRIOLE

825 rue Laurier E., Montreal, 514-276-1580; www.lagaudriole.com

French menu. Closed first week in January, mid-July-early August. Reservations recommended. **$$$**

★LA LOUISIANE
5850 Sherbrooke St. W., Montreal, 514-369-3073; www.lalouisiane.ca
Cajun menu. Dinner. Closed Monday. **$$**

★★★LA MAREE
404 Place Jacques Cartier, Montreal, 514-861-9794; www.restaurant.ca
Situated in Old Montreal, this romantic dining room offers classic French cuisine in an ornate, Louis XIII atmosphere. The historic 1808 building is just the place to enjoy old-fashioned, formal service and a great bottle of wine from the cellar. French menu. Reservations recommended. Outdoor seating. **$$$**

★★★LA RAPIERE
1155 rue Metcalfe, Montreal, 514-871-8920
Southwestern French cooking with a personal touch is the draw at this sophisticated restaurant in downtown Montreal. Cassoulet, foie gras and other specialties from southwest France are served in a typical country-French setting. French menu. Dinner. Jacket required. Closed Sunday; also mid-July-mid-August, 15 days in December. Reservations recommended. **$$$**

★LA SAUVAGINE
1592 Route 329 Nord, Ste. Agathe, 819-326-7673; www.lasauvagine.com
French menu. Closed Monday-Tuesday off-season. **$**

★★★LALOUX
250 Pine Ave. E., Montreal, 514-287-9127; www.laloux.com
One of Montreal's most appealing Parisian-style bistros, this cozy spot delivers traditional bistro fare in a crisp, white-tableclothed environment. In addition to an excellent steak frites, you can sample hearty dishes like mushroom and herb casserole or seafood risotto with leeks and spinach. Polish it all off with a classic French dessert such as chocolate pot de crème. French menu. Reservations recommended. Outdoor seating. **$$$**

★
★
★
★
★

★★LE CAFE FLEURI
1255 rue Jeanne Mance, Montreal, 514-841-2010; www.montreal.hyatt.com
French menu. Breakfast, lunch. Outdoor seating. **$$**

★★★LE LUTETIA
1430 rue de la Montagne, Montreal, 514-288-5656; 800-361-6262;
www.hoteldelamontagne.com
Located in the popular l'Hotel de la Montagne, this restaurant serves breakfast only in a formal rococo setting. The service is gracious and accommodating, and the creative dishes make a special occasion out of the simplest meal of the day. French menu. Breakfast. Reservations recommended. **$$$**

★★★LE MAS DES OLIVIERS
1216 rue Bishop, Montreal, 514-861-6733; www.lemasdesoliviers.ca
This small, traditional French restaurant has been offering rich cuisine in a Provencal setting for more than 30 years. Settle in to the rustic room, with its white tablecloth-topped

tables and exposed brick walls, and dig into classic dishes such as frog legs with garlic or rack of lamb with herbs de Provence and mustard sauce. French menu. Dinner. Reservations recommended. $$$

★★LE PARCHEMIN

1333, rue University, Montreal, 514-844-1619; www.leparchemin.com

French menu. Lunch, dinner. Closed Sunday. Reservations recommended. $$$

★★★LE PIÉMONTAIS

1145 Ave. de Bullion, Montreal, 514-861-8122; www.lepiemontais.com

Experience authentic, Italian cuisine at this comfortable, elegant restaurant. Fresh pastas appear on the menu nightly, from linguine to gnocchi. The wine list features bottle from the Piedmont region of Italy and service is prompt and professional. Italian menu. Lunch, dinner. Closed Sunday; mid-July-mid-August. Reservations recommended. $$$

★★★LE PIMENT ROUGE

1170 Peel St., Montreal, 514-866-7816; www.lepimentrouge.com

The spicy cuisine of China's Szechwan province is served in an airy, contemporary restaurant located in the former Windsor Hotel. Signature dishes include spicy peanut butter dumplings, a recipe the restaurant is credited with inventing in Montreal. Le Piment Rouge also stocks more than 3,000 wines. Chinese menu. Dinner. $$

★★★LES CAPRICES DE NICOLAS

2072 rue Drummond, Montreal, 514-282-9790; www.lescaprices.com

The intimate candlelight and a romantic indoor/outdoor garden combine to make this restaurant a special occasion destination. Given the classic, formal service, it is a pleasant surprise to find the French dishes on the menu refreshingly updated with light, vibrant flavors and seasonal market produce. A wine list of 500 labels adds to the excitement. French menu. Dinner. Jacket required. Reservations recommended. $$$

★★★LES CONTINENTS

360, rue St. Antoine Ouest, Montreal, 514-847-8729, 800-361-3600;
www.intercontinental.com

Located on the second floor of the Hotel InterContinental Montreal, Les Continents has beautiful views of Jean-Paul Riopelle Park and the colorful Convention Centre. The menu features contemporary French cuisine with Canadian influences. French-Canadian menu. Breakfast, lunch, dinner. $$$

★★★LES REMPARTS

93, rue de la Commune E., Montreal, 514-392-1649; www.restaurantlesremparts.com

Located in the basement of the Auberge du Vieux-Port, on the site of Montreal's original fortress, this French restaurant offers a comfortable, cozy atmosphere with professional, attentive service. The restaurant is decorated with candles on each table, stone floors and exposed brick walls with parts of the old fort's stonework on display. French menu. Reservations recommended. Outdoor seating. $$$

★
★
★
★
★

★★★MED BAR AND GRILL

3500 Blvd. St. Laurent, Montreal, 514-844-0027; www.medgrill.com

If you're seeking a spot to see-and-be-seen, or a chic place to linger over cocktails while perched amidst Montreal's most stylish set, Med Bar and Grill is an excellent option. The food is upscale but remains fun and inviting. Classic dishes of the Mediterranean are given a modern spin here, reflecting the seasons and incorporating the regions bountiful produce. Mediterranean menu. Dinner. Closed Sunday-Monday. Reservations recommended. **$$$**

★★MIKADO

399 Laurier West, Montreal, 514-279-4809; www.mikadomontreal.com

Japanese menu. Lunch, dinner. Bar. Reservations recommended. **$$**

★★MOISHE'S

3961 Blvd. St. Laurent, Montreal, 514-845-3509; www.moishes.ca

Steak menu. Dinner. Reservations recommended. **$$$**

★★★NUANCES

1 Ave. de Casino, Montreal, 514-392-2708, 800-665-2274;
www.casinosduquebec.com/montreal/fr/restaurants-bars/nuances

This stylish, modern bistro, located within the Montreal Casino, is swathed in soothing earth tones and decorated with original works that were custom-designed for the space by local artists. The upscale menu stars exquisitely updated French cuisine assembled from a cast of nature's best seasonal products. French menu. Lunch, dinner. Jacket required. Reservations recommended. **$$$**

★★PRIMADONNA

3479 Blvd. St. Laurent, Montreal, 514-282-6644; www.primadonnaonline.com

Italian menu, sushi. Reservations recommended. **$$$$**

★★★QUEUE DE CHEVAL

1221 Blvd. Rene-Levesque Ouest, Montreal, 514-390-0090; www.queuedecheval.com

Prime, dry-aged meats are the showstoppers at Queue de Cheval, a rustic, chateau-styled steakhouse accented with rich maple wood and tall, vaulted ceilings in the heart of Montreal. The menu also has a generous raw bar, a terrific selection of salads and vegetarian appetizers and a shimmering fresh fish market. Steak menu. Lunch, dinner. Reservations recommended. Outdoor seating. **$$$**

★★RESTAURANT CHEZ LÉVÈQUE

1030, rue Laurier Ouest, Montreal, 514-279-7355; www.chezleveque.ca

French menu. Reservations recommended. **$$**

★★RESTAURANT SHO-DAN

2020, rue Metcalfe, Montreal, 514-987-9987; www.sho-dan.com

Japanese menu. Lunch (weekdays only), dinner. **$$**

★★★RISTORANTE DA VINCI

1180, rue Bishop, Montreal, 514-874-2001; www.davinci.ca

This charming restaurant offers an authentic atmosphere, warm, attentive service and well-prepared traditional dishes made with fresh ingredients. The menu includes everything from freshly prepared pasta to grilled steaks. Italian menu. Dinner. Closed Sunday. Reservations recommended. Outdoor seating. **$$$**

★★ROSALIE RESTAURANT

1232, rue de la Montagne, Montreal, 514-392-1970; www.rosalierestaurant.com

French bistro menu. Lunch (weekdays only) dinner. Reservations recommended. Outdoor seating. **$$**

★★★★TOQUE!

900 place Jean-Paul Riopelle, Montreal, 514-499-2084; www.restaurant-toque.com

Toque! is a graceful, luxurious, contemporary French restaurant located across from the Convention Centre and Jean-Paul Riopelle Park. Plates are garnished with such impeccable attention to detail that you may spend several minutes debating whether or not to ruin the presentation. The talented and hospitable chef, Norman Laprise wields magic with a whisk and uses locally farmed ingredients to create a miraculous menu of sophisticated, avant-garde French fare. French menu. Closed Sunday-Monday; also two weeks in late December-early January. Reservations recommended. **$$$**

★★ZEN

1050, rue Sherbrooke Ouest, Montreal, 514-284-1110; www.omnihotels.com

Chinese menu. Lunch, dinner, Sunday brunch. Reservations recommended. **$$$**

QUÉBEC CITY

Nestled on a historic rampart, Québec, the provincial capital, is historic, medieval and lofty, a place of mellowed stone buildings and weathered cannons, horse-drawn calches, ancient trees and narrow, steeply angled streets. Once the "Gibraltar of the North," Québec's Upper Town is built high on a cliff and surrounded by fortress-like walls. One of the split-level city's best-known landmarks, Le Chateau Frontenac, is a hotel towering so high that it's visible 10 miles (16 kilometers) away. The Lower Town surrounds Cape Diamond and spreads up the valley of the St. Charles River, a tributary of the St. Lawrence. The two sections are divided by a funicular, which affords magnificent views of the harbor, river and hills beyond. The most ardently French of all Canadian cities, Québec City is a place where it's not uncommon to encounter folks who don't (or won't) speak English, and who proudly stick to their Gallic Traditions. The historic streets of Québec City provide an easy clue as to what this city looked like in Colonial days, and the cafés and shops tucked within them deliver hours of distractions.

Information: www.quebecregion.com

WHAT TO SEE AND DO

ARTILLERY PARK NATIONAL HISTORIC SITE

2 d'Auteuil St., Québec City, 418-648-4205; www.pc.qc.ca/ihn-nhs/qc/artiller

A 4-acre (2-hectare) site built by the French to defend the opening of the St. Charles River. By the end of the 17th century, it was known as a strategic site and military engineers began to build fortifications here. Until 1871, the park housed French and British soldiers, eventually becoming a large industrial complex.

BASILICA OF STE. ANNE-DE-BEAUPRE

10018 Royale Ave., Québec City, 418-827-3781; www.ssadb.qc.ca

This basilica is noted as the oldest pilgrimage in North America. The first chapel was built on this site in 1658; the present basilica, built in 1923, is made of white Canadian granite and is regarded as a Romanesque masterpiece. Capitals tell the story of Jesus' life in 88 scenes; vaults are decorated with mosaics; unusual techniques were used for 240 stained-glass windows outlined in concrete.

GASPÉ PENINSULA

357, route de la Mer Sainte-Flavie, Québec City, 418-775-2223, 800-463-0323; www.tourisme-gaspesie.com

Jutting out into the Gulf of St. Laurent, the Gaspé Peninsula is a region of varying landforms including mountains, plateaus, beaches and cliffs. It is blessed with abundant and rare wildlife and some unique flora, including 12-foot-tall (4-meter-tall), centuries-old fir trees. The rivers, teeming with trout, flow to meet the salmon coming from the sea. Called "Gespeg" meaning ? "land's end" by the aborigines, the area was settled primarily by Basque, Breton and Norman fishermen, whose charming villages may be seen clinging to the shore beneath the gigantic cliffs. The French influence is strong, although English is spoken in a few villages.

GRAND THEATRE

269 Blvd. Rene-Levesque, Québec, 418-643-8131; www.grandtheatre.qc.ca

Ultramodern theater has giant mural by sculptor Jordi Bonet in lobby; home of the Québec Symphony Orchestra and Opera; theatrical performances, concerts.

HARBOR CRUISES

124 St. Pierre St., Québec City, 418-692-1159, 800-563-4643

M/V *Louis Jolliet* offers daytime, evening dance and dinner cruises on the St. Lawrence River. Bar service, entertainment. May-October.

ILE D'ORLÉANS

490, côte du Pont, Saint-Pierre-de-l'Île-d'Orléans, Québec City, 418-828-9411; www.iledorleans.com

This 23-mile-long (37-kilometer-long) island was visited by Champlain in 1608 and colonized in 1648. Old stone farmhouses and churches of the 18th century remain. Farms grow an abundance of fruits and vegetables, especially strawberries, for which the island is famous.

JACQUES-CARTIER PARK

Route 175, Stoneham, (40 km from downtown Québec City), 418-844-2358, 877-844-5358; www.jacques-cartier.com

This park features beautiful views in a boreal forest valley. Fishing, rafting, canoeing, mountain climbing, wilderness camping, cross-country skiing, hiking, mountain biking, snowshoeing, dogsledding and picnicking are among the many activities available here. Visitors may also enjoy the serenity of its wilderness by walking the magnificent nature trail, as well as through nature interpretation activities. Late May-mid-October, mid-December-mid-April.

JEANNE D'ARC GARDEN

835 Wilfrid Laurier, Québec City, 418-649-6159

This floral jewel was created in 1938 by landscape architect Louis Perron. It combines the French Classical style with British-style flower beds and features more than 150 species of annuals, bulbs and perennials.

LA CITADELLE

1 Cote de la Citadelle, Québec City, 418-694-2815; www.lacitadelle.qc.ca

Forming the eastern flank of the fortifications of Québec, La Citadelle was begun in 1820. Work on it continued until 1850. Vestiges of the French regime, such as the Cap Diamant Redoubt and a powder magazine can still be seen. Panoramic views; 50-minute guided tours. Changing of the guard (late June-Labor Day, daily 10 a.m.). Beating the Retreat, a recreation of a 16th-century ceremony late June-Labor Day, Tuesday, Thursday, Saturday-Sunday.

LAURENTIDES WILDLIFE RESERVE

Québec City, 418-686-1717; www.sepaq.com

A variety of animals including moose, wolves, bears and numerous birds can be found here. Nature fans will find many recreational opportunities such as canoeing, fishing, hunting and camping, as well as boat, ski and snowshoe rental. Located here are 140 cabins and 134 campsites. Late May-Labor Day, mid-December-mid-April.

MONT-STE-ANNE PARK

2000 Blvd. Beau Pre, Beaupre, 418-827-4561; www.mont-sainte-anne.com

Gondola travels to summit of mountain 2,625 feet or 800 meters, affording beautiful view of St. Lawrence River late June-early September, daily. Skiing November-May: 12 lifts, 50 trails; snowmaking; cross-country, full service. Two 18-hole golf courses; bicycle trail. 166 campsites. The migration of 250,000 snow geese occurs in spring and fall at nearby wildlife reserve Cap Tourmente. Park daily; closed May.

MUSÉE DE LA CIVILISATION

85, rue Dalhousie, Québec, 418-643-2158; www.mcq.org

At the entrance is La Debacle, a massive sculpture representing ice breaking up in spring. Separate exhibition halls present four permanent and several changing exhibitions dealing with the history of Québec and the French Canadian culture, as well as cultures of other civilizations from around the world.

MUSÉE DES ANCIENS CANADIENS

332 Ave. de Gaspé W., Saint-Jean-Port-Joli, 418-598-3392; www.quebecweb.com

This museum features an impressive collection of wood carvings by St. Jean artisans, as well as original carvings by the Bourgault brothers. Visitors may watch a wood-carver at work and ask questions about his craft and purchase wood-carved pieces. Mid-May-October, daily.

QUÉBEC

★
★
★
★
★

MUSÉE DU FORT

10 Sainte-Anne St., Québec City, 418-692-2175; www.museedufort.com

Narrated historical recreation of the six sieges of Québec between 1629 and 1775, with a sound and light show.

MUSÉE NATIONAL DES BEAUX-ARTS DU QUÉBEC

Parc des Champs-de-Bataille, Québec city, 418-643-2150; www.mnba.qc.ca

Features collections of ancient, modern and contemporary Québec paintings, sculpture, photography, drawings and decorative arts.

MUSEUM OF THE ROYAL 22E REGIMENT

Succursale Haute-Ville, Québec City, 418-694-2815; www.lacitadelle.qc.ca

Powder magazine circa 1750, flanked on both sides by massive buttresses, contains replicas of old uniforms of French regiments, war trophies, 17th-20th-century weapons; diorama of historic battles under the French; old military prison contains insignias, rifle and bayonet collections, last cell left intact. Mid-March-October: daily. Changing of the guard mid-June-Labor Day: daily 10 a.m.

NATIONAL ASSEMBLY OF QUÉBEC

Grande-Allee and Honore-Mercier Ave., Québec City, 418-643-7239;
www.assnat.qc.ca

Take a 30-minute guided tour of Québec's Parliament Building, constructed between 1877 and 1886. Guides provide an inside look into the proceedings of the Québec National Assembly, while explaining the building's architectural features.

★
★
★
★

NATIONAL BATTLEFIELDS PARK

835 Wilfrid Laurier, Québec City, 418-648-4071

Two hundred fifty acres (101 hectares) along edge of bluff overlooking St. Lawrence River from Citadel to Gilmour Hill. Also called the Plains of Abraham, the park was site of 1759 battle between the armies of Wolfe and Montcalm and the 1760 battle of Ste. Foy between the armies of Murray and Levis. Visitor reception and interpretation center present history of the Plains of Abraham from the New France period to the present. In the park are two Martello towers, part of the fortifications, a sunken garden, many statues and the Jeanne d'Arc Garden.

NOTRE-DAME DE QUÉBEC BASILICA-CATHEDRAL

20 De Buade St., Québec City, 418-694-0665; www.patrimoine-religieux.com

View the richly decorated Cathedral, over 350 years old and the crypt, where most of the governors and bishops of Québec are buried. Guided tours offered daily from early May-early November.

OLD PORT OF QUÉBEC INTERPRETATION CENTRE

25 Eddy St., Gatineau, Québec city, 418-648-3300; www.pc.gc.ca

Located in an ancient cement works and integrated into harbor installations of Louise Basin. Permanent exhibit shows importance of city as a gateway to America in the mid-19th century; timber trade and shipbuilding displays; films, exhibits; guides.

PARC DE LA CHUTE-MONTMORENCY

2490 Ave. Royale, Beauport, 418-663-2877; www.sepaq.com

Visitors to this park can enjoy walking and hiking in the summer and skiing, ice climbing and downhill sliding on Sugarloaf Ice Hill and slide in the winter. Sights to see include Manoir Montgomery, a restored villa built in 1780 that houses a restaurant, café, bar and shops; the Panoramic Stairway, offering views atop its 487 steps; Montmorency Falls, which are 100 feet (30 meters) higher than Niagara Falls and the subject of many 18th- and 19th-century paintings; and the Wolfe House and Redoubt, which served as the headquarters for English general James Wolfe before the battle of the Plains of Abraham.

PLACE-ROYALE

27 Notre Dame St., Québec City, 418-646-9072; www.mcq.org

This site encompasses the earliest vestiges of French civilization in North America. Once a marketplace and the city's social center, it has been restored to its historic appearance. Today, visitors come to enjoy the many restaurants and retail stores, as well as theater performances that take place during summer.

QUÉBEC AQUARIUM

1675 Ave. des Hotels, Sainte-Foy, 418-659-5264; www.sepaq.com/paq/en

Extensive collection of tropical, fresh and saltwater fish, marine mammals and reptiles; overlooks St. Lawrence River.

QUÉBEC CITY WALLS AND GATES

Encompassing Old Québec. Eighteenth-century fortifications encircle the only fortified city in North America; includes Governor's Promenade and provides scenic view of The Citadel, St. Lawrence River and Levis. Daily except Governor's Promenade.

QUÉBEC ZOO

9300 Faune St., Charlesbourg, 418-622-0312; www.spsnq.qc.ca

More than 270 species of native and exotic animals and birds in a setting of forests, fields and streams; children's zoo, sea lion shows.

SOUND AND LIGHT SHOW "HEAVENLY LIGHTS"

20 De Buade St., Québec City, 418-694-0665; www.patrimoine-religieux.com

This 30-minute multimedia show in both French and English takes place on three giant screens within the cathedral. Early May-mid-October, first show at 3:30 p.m., then every 60 minutes. Last show is at 8:30 p.m.

ST. ANDREW'S PRESBYTERIAN CHURCH

5 Cook St., Québec City, 418-694-1347; www.standrewsquebec.ca

Serving the oldest English-speaking congregation of Scottish origin in Canada, which traces back to 1759. The church itself was built in 1810. Its interior is distinguished by a long front wall with a high center pulpit, as well as stained-glass windows and historic plaques. The original petition to King George III asking for a "small plot of waste ground" on which to build a Scotch church is on display in the Church Vestry. A spiral stairway leads to the century-old organ. July-August.

SPECIAL EVENTS

CARNAVAL DE QUÉBEC

290, rue Joly, Québec City, 418-626-3716; www.carnaval.qc.ca

This internationally acclaimed French Canadian festival, billed as the world's biggest winter carnival, is celebrated throughout Old Town. Activities include parades, a canoe race on the St. Lawrence River, a dogsled race, a snow and ice sculpture show, a soapbox derby and the "snow bath," where participants brave the snow in their bathing suits. Late January-mid-February.

DU MAURIER QUÉBEC SUMMER FESTIVAL

226, rue St-Joseph Est., Québec City, 418-529-5200, 888-992-5200;
www.infofestival.com

This 11-day event is one of the largest music festivals in North America. Performances are held at various locations throughout Old Québec. Major local and international artists are showcased, but the festival also serves as a springboard for up-and-coming artists. Early-mid-July.

EXPO QUÉBEC

250 Blvd. Wilfrid-Hamel, Québec City, 418-691-7110; www.expocite.com

This commercial, agricultural and industrial fair attracts more than 400,000 people each year. Staged at Exhibition Park, the event features arts and science pavilions, rides, a sand sculpture competition and a food exhibit. Late August.

NEW FRANCE CELEBRATION

5, rue du Cul-de-Sac, Québec City, 418-694-3311, 866-391-3383;
www.nouvellefrance.qc.ca

This family-oriented historical event in Old Québec recreates the life of the colonists in New France in the 16th and 17th centuries. During this festival, the streets are filled with theatrical events, storytellers, song and dance performances and children's entertainment. Both children and adults who attend often dress in period costumes. Early August.

HOTELS

★★★AUBERGE SAINT-ANTOINE

8, rue Saint-Antoine, Québec City, 418-692-2211, 888-692-2211;
www.saint-antoine.com

Explore historic Québec City from this sleek hotel housed in a building that has been occupied since the beginning of the French colony. A cannon battery runs through the lobby. Stone walls and wooden beams enhance the décor in this small hotel, located in the middle of Old Québec's Port District on the St. Lawrence River. 95 rooms. Restaurant, bar. Business center. $$$

★★CHATEAU LAURIER HOTEL

1220 Georges 5th Ouest, Québec City, 418-522-8108, 800-463-4453;
www.old-quebec.com/laurier

57 rooms. Restaurant, bar. Free wireless Internet access. $

★★CLARENDON HOTEL

57, rue Ste. Anne, Québec City, 418-692-0222, 800-463-5250;
www.hotelclarendon.com

151 rooms. Restaurant, bar. Free wireless Internet access. $

★★COURTYARD QUÉBEC CITY DOWNTOWN

850 Place d'Youville, Québec City, 418-694-4004; www.marriott.com

102 rooms. Restaurant, bar. Business center. High-speed Internet access. Pets not accepted. $

★★★FAIRMONT LE CHATEAU FRONTENAC

1, Rue Des Carrieres, Québec City, 418-692-3861, 800-441-1414; www.fairmont.com

Reigning over this historic walled city from its perch atop the roaring St. Lawrence River is the majestic Fairmont Le Chateau Frontenac. Built as a classic, sprawling railway hotel at the end of the 19th century, the hotel features rooms decorated in a classic European style. The cavernous, wood-clad lobby is watched over by the hotel's resident canine Santol and serviced by a friendly staff. 618 rooms. Five restaurants, bar. Pool. Business center. High-speed Internet access. $$$

★★★FAIRMONT LE MANOIR RICHELIEU

181, rue Richelieu, Charlevoix, 418-665-3703, 800-441-1414; www.fairmont.com

This majestic hotel, located east of Québec City in the heart of Québec's scenic Charlevoix countryside, welcomes visitors with historic charm and world-class sophistication. Rooms and suites have a classic country appeal and are stocked with modern amenities. Guests can opt for nearby skiing and golf or enjoy the hotel's fitness and spa facilities. 405 rooms. Restaurant, bar. Pool. Business center. High-speed Internet access. $$$

★★★HOTEL DOMINION 1912

126, rue Saint-Pierre, Québec City, 418-692-2224, 888-833-5253;
www.hoteldominion.com

Old Québec is considered the cradle of French culture in North America, and Hotel Dominion 1912 is a wonderful base from which to explore it. This small, sleek hotel takes full advantage of the early 20th-century building's historic architectural features while providing updated, contemporary rooms with down-duvet topped beds. 60 rooms. Restaurant, bar. Free wireless Internet access. $$

★★★LOEWS LE CONCORDE

1225 Cours du General De Montcalm, Québec City, 418-647-2222, 800-463-5256;
www.loewshotels.com

See a vision of Paris out your window from this hotel on Québec City's version of the Champs-Elysees. Just 15 minutes from the airport, the tower has views of the St. Lawrence River, the city lights and the historic Plains of Abraham. A visit is not complete without a peek, and hopefully a meal, at L'Astral, the revolving rooftop restaurant. 404 rooms. Restaurant, bar. Pets accepted, fees. Pool. Business center. High-speed Internet access. $

QUÉBEC

★
★
★
★
★

★★★QUÉBEC HILTON

1100 Blvd. Rene Levesque E., Québec City, 418-647-2411; www.hilton.com

Located next to the Congress Centre and a 10 minute walk to Old Town, and other local attractions, the hotel is convenient for business travelers or families. After a busy day of sightseeing, enjoy the cuisine and modern art at the hotel's Allegro Restaurant. 571 rooms. Restaurant, bar. Pets accepted, fees. Pool. Business center. High-speed Internet access. **$$**

RESTAURANTS

★★AUX ANCIENS CANADIENS

34, rue Ste. Louis, Québec City, 418-692-1627; www.auxancienscanadiens.qc.ca

French menu. Dinner. **$$$**

★★★LA PINSONNIERE

124 Saint-Raphaël, La Malbaie, 418-665-4431, 800-387-4431; www.lapinsonniere.com

Situated on a hill above the St. Lawrence, La Pinsonnière provides personalized service and attention to diners. Once the home of Senator Marc Drouin, the building now houses an inn and restaurant. Each room is unique in size and shape, yet filled with modern amenities. The restaurant menu changes daily, based on season and local ingredients. 18 rooms. Restaurant, bar. Pool. **$$**

★★★L'ASTRAL

1225 cours du General de Montcalm, Québec City, 418-647-2222; www.loewshotels.com

Each rotation of this rooftop restaurant atop the Loews Le Concorde takes 90 minutes, which is plenty of time to enjoy its fine cuisine and the spectacular panoramic views of Québec City. Contemporary recipes such as roasted Cornish hen with kalamata olives and grapes, or grilled salmon with sweet corn foam make up the seasonally-driven menu. French menu. Breakfast, lunch, dinner. Reservations recommended. **$$$**

★★★LAURIE RAPHAËL

117 Dalhousie St., Québec City, 418 692 4555; www.laurieraphael.com

Owners Daniel Vezina and Suzanne Gagnon head this popular restaurant, which they named after their children, with well-known friendliness. Focusing on simple, gourmet fusion cuisine allows the flavor and taste of some of their best dishes, like jerusalem artichoke blinis with abitibi sturgeon egg cream, to come shining through. The impressive wine cellar includes a broad range of countries. French menu. Dinner. Reservations recommended. **$$$**

★★★LE CONTINENTAL

26, rue Ste. Louis, Québec City, 418-694-9995; www.restaurantlecontinental.com

Deep colors and oak dominate the rich décor and European atmosphere at this fine dining restaurant in Upper Québec. Order one of the flambé specialties for a unique tableside show. The remainder of the menu is filled with grilled steak and seafood options, and a solid list of French bottles makes up the wine list. French menu. Dinner. **$$$**

★LE MANOIR DU SPAGHETTI

3077 Chemin Ste. Louis, Ste. Foy, 418-659-5628

French and Italian menu. Dinner. **$$**

★★★LE SAINT-AMOUR

48, rue Ste. Ursule, Québec City, 418-694-0667; www.saint-amour.com

Family-owned and operated since opening in Old Québec in 1978, this charming restaurant is away from the bustle of the tourist beat. Fresh, local products are highlighted and the vast wine room houses more than 12,000 bottles. French menu. Outdoor seating. $$$

★★LE VENDOME

36 Cote de la Montagne, Québec City, 418-692-0557; www.restaurantvendome.com

French menu. Outdoor seating. $$

★L'OMELETTE

66, Rue Ste. Louis, Québec City, 418-694-9626; www.quebecweb/mgs

French menu. Breakfast, lunch, dinner. Closed November-March. $

★★★MONTE CRISTO L'ORIGINAL

3400 Chemin Ste. Foy, Québec City, 418-653-5221; www.chateaubonneentente.com

Monte Cristo is a relaxed yet modern restaurant where guests are treated to traditional and original Québec cooking that emphasizes the use of local products. Both the décor and the menu are contemporary, with dishes such as polenta with pea purée or duck tartare with wasabi on the menu. French menu. Breakfast, lunch, dinner. $$$

★★★★RESTAURANT INITIALE

54, rue Saint-Pierre, Québec City, 418-694-1818; www.restaurantinitiale.com

This modern French-cuisine restaurant is located in a former bank about one block from the St. Lawrence River in the Old Port district. Country products from local producers result in fresh, pure flavors. Service is crips and professional, and the staff can aptly recommend an appropriate wine from the lengthy list. French menu. Closed Sunday-Monday; also first two weeks in January. Reservations recommended. $$$

★
★
★
★
★

SHERBROOKE

Nestled in a land of natural beauty at the juncture of the Magog and Saint-Francois rivers, Sherbrooke is a bilingual and bicultural community. The principal city of Québec's Eastern Townships, Sherbrooke is the center of one of Canada's fastest developing winter sports areas. In summer, its historic river system forms a vast linear park right through the center of the city, allowing visitors and residents to benefit from nearly 20 kilometers of walking and cycling paths along the banks of the lovely Magog River. The region also bustles with entertainment: outdoor concerts, shows and performances, bistros, cafés and plentiful pubs. Sherbrooke's downtown offers nature, culture and architecture, with lively people, wide green spaces and an undeniable charm.

Information: www.tourismesherbrooke.com

WHAT TO SEE AND DO

BASILIQUE-CATHEDRALE DE SAINT-MICHEL

130, rue de la Catheral, Sherbrooke, 819-563-9934

This Gothic-style cathedral is decorated with sculptures, mosaics and other works of art.

BEAUVOIR SANCTUARY

675, Cote de Beauvoir, Sherbrooke, 819-569-2535; www.sanctuairedebeauvoir.qc.ca

Built in 1920, this church is located in a setting of natural splendor on a hill. A statue of the Sacred Heart has been here since 1916, making it a regional pilgrimage site. May-October, daily; November-April, Sunday. Picnic tables, restaurant, gift shop open in summer.

LOUIS S. ST. LAURENT NATIONAL HISTORIC SITE

6790 Route Louis-St-Laurent, Compton, 819-835-5448, 800-463-6769; www.parcscanada.qc.ca/stlaurent

Birthplace of Louis S. St. Laurent (1882-1973), Prime Minister of Canada from 1948 to 1957; landscaped grounds; general store and adjacent warehouse with sound and light show. May-September, daily.

ORFORD ARTS CENTRE

3165 Chemin Du Parc, Orford, 819-843-9871, 800-567-6155; www.arts-orford.org

Located here are a pavilion with teaching and practice studios and a 500-seat concert hall, where performances are given by noted artists during Orford Summer Festival. The center also features a visual arts program. May-September.

PARC DU MONT-ORFORD

3321 Chemin du Parc Canton, Orford, 819-843-9855, 800-665-6527; www.sepaq.com/montorford

Parc du Mont-Orford offers a wide array of both summer and winter activities, like golfing, cycling, swimming, backpacking, hiking, snowboarding, downhill and cross-country skiing and snowshoeing. For visitors wanting a more relaxed experience, there are walking trails, campsites and opportunities for viewing wildlife. Some may also choose to sit back and relax and take in the spectacular views of the park's many mountains and peaks.

SKI MONT ORFORD

4380 Chemin du Parc, Orford, 819-843-6548, 866-673-6731; www.orford.com

Mount Orford features some of the best facilities in Québec. It includes 54 runs, the longest 2½ miles, or 4 kilometers, and eight lifts, as well as 20 acres (8 hectares) of glade and 25 miles (40 hectares) of cross-country skiing. November-April, daily.

HOTEL

★★HOTEL GOUVERNEUR SHERBROOKE

3131 King St. Ouest, Sherbrooke, 819-565-0464, 888-910-1111; www.gouverneur.com

124 rooms. Restaurant, bar. Pool. High-speed Internet access. $

TROIS-RIVIÈRES

Considered the second-oldest French city in North America, Trois-Rivières was founded in 1634 and many 17th- and 18th-century buildings remain today. The St. Maurice River splits into three channels here as it joins the St. Lawrence, giving the name to this major commercial and industrial center and important inland seaport.

WHAT TO SEE AND DO

CATHEDRALE DE L'ASSUMPTION

363 rue Bonaventure, Trois-Rivières, 819-374-2409

Built in 1858 in the Gothic Westminster style, this cathedral contains huge stained-glass windows, brilliantly designed by Nincheri. The cathedral was renovated in 1967.

LE MANOIR DE TONNANCOUR

864, rue des Ursulines, Trois-Rivières, 819-374-2355; www.galeriedartduparc.qc.ca

This historic structure is the oldest house in the city. It was built between 1723 and 1725 and rebuilt in 1795. When the government acquired the house in 1812, it was used as a barracks for soldiers. In 1852, it became the bishop's home. Today, the house contains the Art Gallery in the Park and features displays of paintings, pottery, sculpture, engravings, serigraphy and jewelry.

LES FORGES DU ST. MAURICE NATIONAL HISTORIC SITE

10000 Blvd. des Forges, Trois-Rivières, 819-378-5116, 800-463-6769;
www.pc.qc.ca/ihn-nhs/qc/saintmaurice

This site commemorates the founding of Canada's first industrial community. Visitors may see the remains of the first ironworks industry in Canada, the blast furnace and Ironmaster's House interpretation centers and a sound-and-light show at the Grande Maison. Mid-May-mid-October, daily 9:30 a.m.-5 p.m.; after Labor Day, daily 9:30 a.m.-4:30 p.m.

NOTRE DAME-DU-CAP SHRINE

626, rue Notre Dame Est., Trois-Rivières, 819-374-2441; www.sanctuaire-ndc.ca

The site includes a small church that was built in 1714, making it the oldest preserved stone church in Canada. It was turned into a shrine in 1888. Also here is a large octagonal basilica featuring stained-glass windows made by Dutch glassmaker Jan Tillemans, as well as a neoclassic Casavant organ with 5,425 pipes. Summer organ recitals are held here from June to September. May-October, daily.

OLD PORT

800 Parc Portuaire, Trois-Rivières, 819-372-4633

Magnificent view of the St. Lawrence River. Built over part of the old fortifications. Pulp and paper interpretation center; riverside park; monument to La Vrendrye, discoverer of the Rockies in 1743.

SIGHTSEEING TOUR: M/S JACQUES-CARTIER

1515, rue de Fleuve, Trois-Rivières, 819-375-3000; www.jacquescartier.croisieres.qc.ca

A 400-passenger ship offering cruises around Trois-Rivières Harbor and on the St. Lawrence River. Options include dinner cruises, country cruises, fireworks cruises and a Captain's Christmas cruise. Late May-mid-September.

ST. JAMES ANGLICAN CHURCH

811, Rue Des Ursulines, Trois-Rivieres, 819-374-6010

Constructed in 1699 and rebuilt in 1754, at various times the building was used as a storehouse and a court; the rectory was used as a prison, hospital and sheriff's office. In 1823, it became an Anglican church and is now shared with the United Church.

QUÉBEC

Carved woodwork was added in 1917; the cemetery dates from 1808. The church is still used for services.

URSULINE MUSEUM

734, rue des Ursulines, Trois-Rivières, 819-375-7922; www.ursulines-uc.com
Constructed in 1700, this Norman-style building has been enlarged and restored many times. A historic chapel, museum and art collection are located here. May-August, Tuesday-Sunday; October-April, Wednesday-Sunday.

SPECIAL EVENT

TROIS-RIVIÈRES INTERNATIONAL VOCAL ARTS FESTIVAL

Bonaventure and Royale, Trois-Rivières, 819-372-4635; www.artvocal.com
A celebration of song. Religious, lyrical, popular, ethnic, traditional singing. Late June-early July.

HOTELS

★★DELTA TROIS-RIVIÈRES

1620, rue Notre-Dame, Trois-Rivières, 819-376-1991, 888-890-3222;
www.deltahotels.com
159 rooms. Restaurant, bar. Pets accepted, fees. Exercise room. Pool. Wireless Internet access. **$**

★★HOTEL GOUVERNEUR TROIS-RIVIÈRES

975, rue Hart, Trois-Rivières, 888-910-1111; www.gouverneur.com
127 rooms. Complimentary continental breakfast. Restaurant. Pool. **$**

220

QUÉBEC

SASKATCHEWAN

SASKATCHEWAN, THE MIDDLE OF CANADA'S THREE PRAIRIE PROVINCES, IS GEOGRAPHICALLY located in the center of North America. Within its borders is more road surface than in any other province, totaling 150,000 miles (241,400 kilometers). Half of the province is covered by forest, one-third is farmland and one-eighth is fresh water, with nearly 100,000 lakes. The province is a paradise of unspoiled hunting and fishing, with extraordinary sunshine to boot—the city of Estevan in the southeastern region is Canada's sunshine capital, averaging 106 sun-filled days each year. These sunny days make it easy to enjoy close to 5 million acres (more than 2 million hectares) of parkland, including two national and 26 provincial parks.

The province is popularly explored from behind the wheel of a car or recreational vehicle—roads are easy going, amenities along the way are plentiful, and the experiences are authentic prairie. Follow the route taken in 1874 by the North West Mounted Police, forerunners of today's Mounties, when they came west to quell the whiskey trade. Take in historic sites, panoramic views, cultural icons and friendly people, along with a slew of museums celebrating everything from the province's love of the sport of curling, its wild west beginnings and its discovery of vast deposits of dinosaur fossils. Wander through what locals call "parkland," a rolling and evocative combination of "not quite prairie and not quite forest." This was fur-trade country, where rivers run clear, lakes are inviting and well-tended campgrounds are plentiful.

Information: www.sasktourism.com

MOOSE JAW

Despite its humble beginnings as a village of sod huts and shanties, the city of Moose Jaw offers everything from high-energy adrenaline to laid-back relaxation. The city's "Tunnels of Little Chicago," an underground network of passages built to smuggle liquor during the Prohibition era, are a wink to the city's raucous history, which is well represented across several museums and sites. Take in sporting events, cultural extravaganzas, mineral spas and walking trails along with a small-town friendliness that makes Moose Jaw a must-see prairie destination.

Information: www.citymoosejaw.com

WHAT TO SEE AND DO

BUFFALO POUND PROVINCIAL PARK/ WHITE TRACK SKI AREA

110 Ominica St., Moose Jaw, 306-694-3659; www.envoirmental.gov.sk.ca

This 4,770-acre (1,930-hectare) park was established in 1963 and is known for its free-ranging buffalo that traverse the Qu'Appelle River Valley. The name of the park refers

FUN FACTS

Near Regina is North America's oldest bird sanctuary, established in 1887 at Last Mountain Lake.

Curling was named Saskatchewan's official sport in 2001, although many have considered it so for years. Once called the "roaring game" because of the thunderous noise made by corn brooms used to sweep rocks down the ice, curling has a rich history and enthusiastic following in the province.

to the aboriginal people's method of corralling bison by using the topography as a means to hold the animals in place. The park has a large outdoor pool, beaches, fishing, boating, mini-golf and hiking trails. It is also home to the White Track Ski Resort, with downhill skiing, as well as a number of snowshoeing and cross-country skiing trails.

CASINO MOOSE JAW

21 Fairford St. E., Moose Jaw, 306-694-3888, 800-555-3189; www.casinomoosejaw.com

This casino has a 1920s theme and embraces Moose Jaw's unique history. It also has 20 indoor and outdoor wall murals that portray specific periods of the city's history. There are more than 150 slot machines to test your luck, as well as all table game favorites including blackjack, roulette and "Let It Ride" Bonus.

CRANBERRY ROSE GALLERY AND GIFTS

316, Main St., Moose Jaw, 306-693-7779, 800-970-7328; www.cranberryrose.com

The Cranberry Rose Gallery and Gifts shop is located in a historic house. While here, shop, enjoy a cup of tea or indulge your sweet tooth with one of the scrumptious homemade desserts.

MOOSE JAW MUSEUM AND ART GALLERY

461 Langdon Crescent, Moose Jaw, 306-692-4471; www.mjmag.ca

The permanent collections of the Moose Jaw Museum and Art Gallery feature a wide variety of works from a vast collection of local, provincial, national and international artists. The pieces from this collection are on exhibit at various times throughout the year. Don't miss the Norma Lang Gallery and the discovery center.

ST. VICTOR PETROGLYPH PARK

206-110 Ominica St. W., Moose Jaw; www.saskparks.net

At this mysterious place, there are more than 300 carvings in the sandstone of a huge exposed rock that depict stories of ancient times.

TUNNELS OF MOOSE JAW

18 Main St. N., Moose Jaw, 306-693-5261; www.tunnelsofmoosejaw.com

These tunnels between many of the buildings in Moose Jaw's downtown are said to have been dug by Chinese immigrants in the late 1800s. Rumors surround all aspects of the tunnels; they were allegedly used during the Prohibition years by bootleggers and smugglers trying to avoid the law. Two 50-minute tours can help visitors draw their own conclusions.

WESTERN DEVELOPMENT MUSEUM

50 Diefenbaker Drive, Moose Jaw, 306-693-5989; www.wdm.ca

There are four Western Development Museums across Saskatchewan, each focusing on a different form of history of the province. The Moose Jaw location traces the development of transportation in the west through displays and artifacts.

WOOD MOUNTAIN POST PROVINCIAL HISTORICAL PARK

206-110 Ominica St. West, Moose Jaw, 306-266-4322, 800-205-7070; www.saskparks.net

At this historic site, learn how the Northwest Mounted Police arrived in the area and designated it as a post. The stories told during a visit through the historic buildings and sites paint a vivid picture of the important history that unfolded while people here policed the Northwest. June-mid-August: daily 10 a.m.-5 p.m.

HOTELS
★★HERITAGE INN

1590 Main St. N., Moose Jaw, 306-693-7550, 888-888-4374; www.heritageinn.net

104 rooms. Restaurant, bar. Pool. $

★★TEMPLE GARDENS MINERAL SPA

24 Fairford St. E., Moose Jaw, 306-694-5055; www.templegardens.sk.ca

181 rooms. Restaurant, bar, spa. Pool. $

RESTAURANT
★HOUSTON PIZZA & STEAK HOUSE

117 Main St. N., Moose Jaw, 306-693-3934

Pizza, steak menu. Dinner. $$

NORTH BATTLEFORD

The city of North Battleford and its neighbor, the town of Battleford, are located in the historic heart of Saskatchewan. Despite a relatively small population (less than 14,000), attractions abound—the city's northern lakes offer fishing, boating, swimming and camping, and nearby Table Mountain is one of the best ski hills in Saskatchewan. Fort Battleford National Historic Site, an old North West Mounted Police post, dates to the late 1800s and offers fresh air, big skies and living heritage.

Information: www.city.north-battleford.sk.ca

WHAT TO SEE AND DO
ALLEN SAPP GALLERY

1 Railway Ave. E., North Battleford, 306-445-1760; www.allensapp.com

This gallery displays the works of Cree artist Allen Sapp. The collection also includes First Nation and Inuit artists.

BATTLEFORDS PROVINCIAL PARK

Cochin, 30 minutes from North Battleford, 306-386-2212;
www.tpcs.gov.sk.ca/TheBattlefords

The park offers something for everyone, from family picnics to parasailing and golf. It is also great for cross-country skiing—nestled within its large rolling hills and forests are 25 miles (40 kilometers) of trails for all skill levels.

BLUE MOUNTAIN OUTDOOR ADVENTURE CENTRE

RR1, North Battleford, 306-445-4941; www.bluemountaincanada.com

These 2,400 wooded acres (971 hectares) have some of the best trails and facilities in the world for cross-country skiing. If you're feeling adventurous, you can take a shot at skate skiing, a form of skiing resembling skating on ice.

FINLAYSON ISLAND

North Battleford on the North Saskatchewan River, 306-445-6044;
www.tourismbattlefords.com

This island was named in honor of Donald (Dan) Matheson Finlayson, who served as a Member of Parliament from 1908 to 1934. It is a popular hiking and cross-country skiing destination with many miles of groomed ski trails.

FORT BATTLEFORD NATIONAL HISTORICAL PARK

Battleford

Located at the confluence of the North Saskatchewan and Battle Rivers, Fort Battleford is an excellent site to achieve a better understanding of the historic role of the area's North West Mounted Police. The fort came into being in 1876 and was maintained until 1924. Learn its story through its five original buildings, reconstructed stockades and bastions, and other period pieces. Open Victoria Day weekend-Labor Day weekend.

GOLD EAGLE CASINO

11902 Railway Ave., North Battleford, 306-446-3833, 877-446-3833;
www.battlefords.com

The 15,000-square-foot (1,394 square meter) casino features traditional casino games as well as "Let It Ride," Caribbean Stud Poker, progressive jackpots and Sega horse racing. Enjoy its lounge, restaurant and a nightclub that features weekend entertainment.

MAKWA LAKE PROVINCIAL PARK

Loon Lake, Saskatchewan, 306-837-2410; www.tpcs.gov.sk.ca

Makwa Lake Provincial Park offers boating and fishing on five connected lakes. Try the nine-hole golf course in the summer and the 12 miles (19 kilometers) of intermediate cross-country ski trails in the winter. These trails double as hiking paths in the summertime; there are many camping opportunities as well.

STEELE NARROWS

Loon Lake, Saskatchewan, 306-837-2410

This site owes its existence to a battle between the North West Mounted Police and the Cree tribe. Named after Inspector Sam Steele, it is the site where he and his troops fought a three-hour battle with the Cree. This battle left several dead and was the last of the Northwest Rebellion.

WESTERN DEVELOPMENT MUSEUM HERITAGE FARM AND VILLAGE

North Battleford at Highways 16 and 40, 306-445-8033; www.wdm.ca

Visitors will find a large barn filled with livestock and see how a typical farmer of the 1920s spent his workday in the fields. Walk along the boardwalk and enter the town, where you can experience more aspects of this lifestyle, such as a co-op store, a church or a typical home or business of the period.

PRINCE ALBERT

Prince Albert is located in the broad valley of the North Saskatchewan River near the geographical center of the province, where the agricultural prairie of the south and the rich forest belt of the north meet. The province's third-largest city, Prince Albert is a gateway to the recreational opportunities in the far northern region. Its center bustles with attractions, festivals, golf courses, casinos and museums. At the Fort Carlton Provincial Historic Site in the city's southwest, see how life was lived in the days of the fur trade from the vantage point of a booming trading post circa mid-1800s, when swarthy trappers ruled along the North Saskatchewan River.

Information: www.citypa.ca

WHAT TO SEE AND DO

ATHABASCA SAND DUNES

La Ronge, 150 miles (241 kilometers) north of Prince Albert, accessible only by air or by boat from the Lake Athabasca communities, 306-425-4234

The Athabasca Sand Dunes, the northernmost dunes in the world, are located along the south shore of Lake Athabasca in northwest Saskatchewan. This untarnished area has several dune fields that extend for approximately 60 miles (96½ kilometers). Two major rivers in the park, the William and the MacFarlane, he create the unforgettable scenery here. Visitors must be self-sufficient for wilderness travel, taking along all food and supplies. All garbage must be packed out and visitors must be aware of special park regulations designed to protect the fragile environment.

CANDLE LAKE PROVINCIAL PARK

Candle Lake, 306-929-8400; www.tpcs.gov.sk.ca/CandleLake

Candle Lake has more than 19,457 acres (7,874 hectares) of recreational park and is known for its beaches and sand dunes. Visitors can enjoy a number of activities in this nature park, including swimming, fishing, waterskiing, golfing, camping, hiking, biking and horseback riding. Many facilities and services are located in the nearby community of the Resort Village of Candle Lake.

LAC LA RONGE PROVINCIAL PARK

La Ronge, 145 miles/233 kilometers north of Prince Albert, 306-425-4234; www.tpcs.gov.sk.ca/LacLaRonge

Lac La Ronge Provincial Park is Saskatchewan's largest provincial park, covering 851,204 acres (344,470 hectares) and containing more than 100 lakes. There are beautiful waterfalls on the Churchill River, and the park is famous for its whitewater rapids. It also has excellent canoeing, fishing and hiking. If you enjoy skiing, you can bask in the beautifully diverse scenery along the 35 miles (56 kilometers) of cross-country trails, including three miles (five kilometers) of lighted trails for night skiing.

NORTHERN LIGHTS CASINO

44 Marquis Road W., Prince Albert, 306-764-4777, 888-604-7711; www.siga.sk.ca

Northern Lights appends its casino games with monthly blackjack and slot tournaments. The casino also promotes and showcases Aboriginal artists on its stage. The Northstar Restaurant and Prince Albert Inn are part of the complex.

SPECIAL EVENT

PRINCE ALBERT CANADA DAY CELEBRATION

1410C Central Ave., Prince Albert, 306-922-0405

Canada Day celebrations take place at Kinsmen Park during the day and at D.G. Steuart Park at night. Festivities include sports, picnics, flag raising, a color ceremony, contests and children's games. Early July.

225

SASKATCHEWAN

REGINA

The capital acts as the commercial, industrial and financial center of the province while still maintaining a small-town feel. Since the first pioneers homesteaded in the early 1880s, local residents have worked by hand to transform the flat, treeless prairie into a city of shaded parks and streets. Regina sparkles with rich artistic and multi-cultural traditions, with Canada's longest continuously operating symphony orchestra and the Globe Theatre, a company that stages innovative productions in the round. The Wascana Centre, in the heart of Regina, is one of North America's largest urban parks, measuring 2,300 acres (931 hectares). Regina is also the home of the Royal Canadian Mounted Police.

Information: www.tourismregina.com

WHAT TO SEE AND DO

CASINO REGINA

1880 Saskatchewan Drive, Regina, 306-565-3000, 800-555-3189; www.casinoregina.com

Casino Regina boasts more than 800 slot machines, and 35 table games and features a spectacular showroom.

ECHO VALLEY PROVINCIAL PARK

Fort Qu'Appelle, 45 miles (72 kilometers) east of Regina, 306-332-3215;
www.tpcs.gov.sk.ca/EchoValley

In this 1,606-acre (650-hectare) park, enjoy the picturesque Qu'Appelle Valley in addition to Echo and Pasqua lakes. Other activities such as swimming, waterskiing, sailing and bird-watching await visitors to the park. In addition, 6 miles (9.6 kilometers) of groomed cross-country trails are popular in winter and may be used in the summer for walking or biking.

GLOBE THEATRE

1801 Scarth St., Regina, 306-525-6400; www.globetheatrelive.com

View plays performed by the province's oldest professional theater company. Season runs September to May.

GOVERNMENT HOUSE MUSEUM AND HERITAGE PROPERTY

4607 Dewdney Ave., Regina, 306-787-5773; www.graa.gov.sk.ca/govhouse

Opened in 1891 as the residence of the Queen's representative, the house became the official residence of Saskatchewan's Lieutenant Governor from 1905 to 1945. Fourteen rooms are decorated with period furnishings and almost 100,000 artifacts.

LAST MOUNTAIN HOUSE

146-3211 Albert St., Regina, 5 miles (8 kilometers) northwest of Craven on Highway 20,
approximately 45 minutes from Regina, 306-787-7031; www.se.gov.sk.ca/saskparks

Last Mountain House is a reconstructed Hudson's Bay Company post from 1869. While touring the area, visitors will see the Master's House and Last Mountain House, as well as artifacts that give the history of the area and show how the fur trade in this part of Saskatchewan ended. July 1-Labor Day.

SASKATCHEWAN

★
★
★
★
☆

MACKENZIE ART GALLERY

3745 Albert St., Regina, Wascana Centre, T.C. Douglas Building, 306-584-4250;
www.mackenzieartgallery.sk.ca

The focus of this 100,000-square-foot (8,290-square-meter), tri-level gallery is Canadian and Saskatchewan artists. The collection of 1,600 works also features contemporary American artists and 15th- to 19th-century European prints, drawings and paintings.

REGINA SYMPHONY ORCHESTRA

Saskatchewan Centre of the Arts, 200 Lakeshore Drive, Regina, 306-586-9555;
www.reginasymphony.com

Canada's longest continuously operating symphony.

ROYAL CANADIAN MOUNTED POLICE TRAINING ACADEMY AND MUSEUM

5607 Dewdney Ave., Regina, 306-522-7333; www.rcmpmuseum.com

The Royal Canadian Mounted Police has been located in Regina since 1885. The museum explains the police's role in Canadian history. The tour shows visitors the oldest building in Regina, the chapel and provides a chance to view cadets in training.

ROYAL SASKATCHEWAN MUSEUM

2445 Albert St., Regina, Wascana Centre at Albert Street and College Avenue,
306-787-2815, 306-787-2816; www.royalsaskmuseum.ca

Visitors to this museum learn about the anthropological and natural history of the province. The museum houses earth and life science galleries and a fossil station.

SASKATCHEWAN LEGISLATIVE BUILDING

123 Legislative Building, 2405 Legislative Drive, Regina, Wascana Centre,
306-787-2376; www.legassembly.sk.ca

The building was completed in 1912 and houses many provincial governmental activities. The building itself is worth a look, but if you take the tour, you will get a better feel for how Canadian government functions.

SASKATCHEWAN SCIENCE CENTRE

2903 Powerhouse Drive, Regina, Wascana Centre at Winnipeg Street and Wascana Drive,
306-522-4629, 800-667-6300; www.sasksciencecentre.com

Hands-on exhibits explore physics, genetics, biology, ecology, geology and space and a Discovery Lab houses an array of reptiles and amphibians. Live demonstrations of static electricity, cryogenics, lasers, sound, ecology and anatomy are given daily. The SaskTel 3D Laser Theatre (one of only 10 in the world) provides a unique experience. Visitors can also climb the 60-foot (18-meter) climbing wall or take in one of the many entertaining and informative stage shows. The Kramer IMAX Theatre has a five-story screen and powerful surround sound.

WASCANA CENTRE

2900 Wascana Drive, Regina, 306-522-3661; www.wascana.sk.ca

At Wascana Lake (manmade), take a ferry to Willow Island for a picnic. Swimming in the lake is prohibited, but once it freezes, ice skating is encouraged. Ski trails are groomed on the north shore from the Royal Saskatchewan Museum to Douglas Park. Phone ahead for trail conditions.

SPECIAL EVENTS

BUFFALO DAYS
IPSCO Place, Lewvan Drive, Regina, 306-781-9200; www.ipscoplace.com
At this city festival, enjoy activities ranging from midway rides to livestock shows to a parade. Late July.

MOSAIC
2144 Cornwall St., Regina, 306-757-5990; www.reginamosaic.com
Mosaic is an annual three-day festival of cultures that celebrates the rich ethnic history of the prairie settlers of this area. Experience 17 different countries and their cultures through food and dance. Early June.

RCMP SUNSET RETREAT CEREMONIES
RCMP Training Academy, Dewdney Avenue W., Regina, 306-780-5777
Traditional lowering of the flag, drill display by cadet band and march performed by the troops. Held on Parade Square, weather permitting. July-mid-August: Tuesday 6:45-7:30 p.m.

HOTELS

★COUNTRY INN & SUITES BY CARLSON
3321 Eastgate Drive, Regina, 306-789-9117; www.countryinns.com
76 rooms. Wireless Internet access. Complimentary continental breakfast. Pets accepted. Fitness center, fee. $

★★★DELTA REGINA
1919 Saskatchewan Drive, Regina, 306-525-5255, 888-890-3222; www.deltahotels.com
Contemporary and comfortable, the Delta Regina offers a range of accommodations. Have some aquatic fun at the onsite Waterworks Recreation Complex, complete with a waterslide, pool, children's pool and whirlpool. Families are particularly welcomed here with children's menus, individual check-in cards for kids and age-specific kids' essentials kits. 274 rooms. Restaurant, bar. Children's activity center. Pets accepted, fee. Exercise room. Pool. $$

★★★RADISSON PLAZA HOTEL SASKATCHEWAN
2125 Victoria Ave., Regina, 306-522-7691, 800-667-5828; www.hotelsask.com
Overlooking Regina Park, this historic landmark is elegant and welcoming to both business and leisure guests. The Cortlandt Dining Room offers fine dining and Sunday brunch and Sunday buffet. Enjoy high tea in the Victoria Tea Room or something a bit stronger in Monarch's Lounge. 224 rooms. High-speed Internet access. Restaurant, bar. Pets accepted, fee. $$

★TRAVELODGE
4177 Albert St. S., Regina, 306-586-3443; www.travelodgeregina.com
200 rooms. Restaurant, bar. Pool. $

SASKATCHEWAN

★
★
★
★
★

★★WEST HARVEST INN

4025 Albert St., Regina, 306-586-6755, 800-858-8471; www.regina.westharvest.ca
105 rooms. Restaurant, bar. **$**

RESTAURANTS
★★★CORTLANDT HALL DINING ROOM

2125 Victoria Ave., Regina, 306-337-4316, 800-667-5828; www.hotelsask.com
Situated in the Radisson Plaza Hotel Saskatchewan, the Cortlandt Hall Dining Room offers fine dining in an elegant and relaxing atmosphere. Memorable entrée options include grilled swordfish, prosciutto-wrapped pork tenderloin and smoked duck breast. Traditional favorites are offered at the Sunday brunch and Sunday evening buffet. International menu. Breakfast, lunch, dinner, Sunday brunch. **$**

★★★DANBRY'S CONTEMPORARY CUISINE

1925 Victoria Ave., Regina, 306-525-8777
Creative menu selections with locally produced products are offered at this casual, elegant restaurant housed in the historic Assiniboia Club building. An extensive cocktail menu is offered, as well as a cigar menu. International menu. Closed Sunday. Outdoor seating. **$$$**

★MEDITERRANEAN BISTRO

2589 Quance St. East, Regina, 306-757-1666; www.mbistro.sasktelwebhosting.com
Mediterranean menu. Outdoor seating. **$$**

SASKATOON

Saskatoon is Saskatchewan's largest city, named from "mis-sask-quah-toomina," the Cree name for an indigenous berry. The jams and pies made from those berries are still local specialties. The South Saskatchewan River is the main waterway; bike, jog or take a stroll along its banks. Along the river and in the downtown are many craft shops and galleries, a fine symphony orchestra, a plethora of summer festivals, four professional theater companies and an active amateur theater community.
Information: www.tourismsaskatoon.com

WHAT TO SEE AND DO
BLACKSTRAP PROVINCIAL PARK

102-112 Research Drive, Saskatoon, 306-492-5675
This park is located on Blackstrap Lake near Mount Blackstrap. Many activities can be enjoyed on the lake such as windsurfing, waterskiing and swimming; fishing is popular as well. If you're adventurous, climb Mount Blackstrap and take in the scenery of the lake and more than 1,310 acres (530 hectares) of park below. The hill at Blackstrap was built to accommodate events of the 1971 Canada Winter Games. There are a couple of sections for skiing along the 3 miles (5 kilometers) available, though the trails are not long.

FORT CARLTON PROVINCIAL HISTORICAL PARK

102-112 Research Drive, Saskatoon, 306-467-5205; www.tpcs.gov.sk.ca/FortCarlton
This is the original site of a Hudson's Bay Company fur-trading post that operated between 1810 and 1885 on the North Saskatchewan River. Today, visitors can check

SASKATCHEWAN

★
★
★
★
★

out a reconstructed stockade, fur and provisions store and clerks' quarters. Each of the buildings appears much like they would have in the 1860s. See, touch and smell items such as buffalo hides, beaver pelts, war clubs, blankets, guns, twist tobacco and birch bark baskets. Mid-May-early September.

MENDEL ART GALLERY & CIVIC CONSERVATORY

950 Spadina Crescent E., Saskatoon, 306-975-7610; www.mendel.ca

Both permanent and temporary exhibits showcase historical and contemporary art by international, national and regional artists. The gallery holds a number of special programs, including "ART for LIFE," "Something on Sundays" and the annual "School Art" exhibit, which presents the works of Saskatoon's students.

PIKE LAKE PROVINCIAL PARK

102-112 Research Drive, Saskatoon, 306-933-6966; www.se.gov.sk.ca

Just 20 minutes south of Saskatoon, Pike Lake is an escape that has something for everyone: swimming, fishing, boating, nature trails, tennis courts, golfing, picnicking and year-round camping. The Leisure Pool and Waterslide Complex are designed for all, from first-time water sliders to the more experienced.

WANUSKEWIN HERITAGE PARK

RR 4 Penner Road, Saskatoon, 306-931-6767; www.wanuskewin.com

Wanuskewin Heritage Park is set on 760 acres (308 hectares) along the South Saskatchewan River, 10 miles (16 kilometers) from Saskatoon in the Opamihaw Valley. The park focuses on the rich native heritage of the aboriginal people who lived here 6,000 years ago through cultural, archaeological, historical and geographical interpretation. There are self-guided trails, an interpretation center and a 500-seat amphitheater where native dances and songs are performed and stories are told.

WESTERN DEVELOPMENT MUSEUM

2610 Lorne Ave. S., Saskatoon, 306-931-1910; www.wdm.ca

This tour shows many of the aspects of life in a typical prairie town. Through the many displays you will be transported to this time in history and learn what life was like.

SPECIAL EVENTS

CANADA REMEMBERS INTERNATIONAL AIR SHOW

101-3515 Thatcher Ave., Saskatoon, 306-975-3155;
www.canadaremembersairshow.com

This popular air show is held as a tribute to Canadian veterans. Opening ceremonies feature a parade of veterans and are followed by performances from the Canadian Armed Forces, the U.S. Air Force, the U.S. Air National Guard and the Royal Canadian Air Force. Mid-August.

CLARICA MID-SUMMER MASTERS

Ebon Stables, Highway 16 E., Saskatoon, 306-477-0199; www.ebonstables.com

This five-day event attracts the best equestrian athletes in Western Canada, who compete for $20,000 in prizes. Mid-August.

★
★
★
★

SASKTEL SASKATCHEWAN JAZZ FESTIVAL

701-601 Spadina Crescent E., Saskatoon, 306-652-1421; www.saskjazz.com

At the end of June, thousands of visitors and local residents come together to enjoy the sounds of more than 800 of the best provincial, national and international jazz, blues, gospel and world-beat musicians. Events are held in venues like the Broadway Theatre and the Adam Ballroom and require tickets, but there are also many free-staged events throughout downtown and in parks. Late June.

SHAKESPEARE ON THE SASKATCHEWAN

602-245 Third Ave. S., Saskatoon, 306-653-2300;
www.shakespeareonthesaskatchewan.com

This annual festival features outdoor performances of different plays written by the bard. July-mid-August.

HOTELS

★COUNTRY INN & SUITES BY CARLSON

617 Cynthia St., Saskatoon, 306-934-3900, 888-201-1746; www.countryinns.com

77 rooms. High-speed Internet access. Pets accepted, fee. $

★★★DELTA BESSBOROUGH

601 Spadina Crescent E., Saskatoon, 306-244-5521, 888-890-3222;
www.deltahotels.com

This full-service chateau-style hotel overlooks the Saskatchewan River. Guests can relax by the indoor pool or whirlpool. Children have fun here as well with activities and a playground. Enjoy a dinner at the Japanese steakhouse. 225 rooms. High-speed Internet access. Restaurant, bar, spa. Exercise room. Pool. $$

★★RADISSON HOTEL SASKATOON

405 20th St. East, Saskatoon, 306-665-3322; www.radisson.com

291 rooms. High-speed Internet access. Restaurant, bar. Pets accepted, fee. Pool. $

★★★SHERATON CAVALIER HOTEL

612 Spadina Crescent E., Saskatoon, 306-652-6770;
www.sheratonsaskatoon.com

Located in a business and shopping district, 6 miles from downtown and 5 miles from Calgary International Airport, this renovated hotel offers a variety of amenities. The Carvers Steakhouse provides a wonderful steak and seafood menu. Complimentary shuttle service is offered. 249 rooms. High-speed Internet access. Restaurant, bar. Exercise room. Pool. $

RESTAURANTS

★★2ND AVE GRILL

123 Second Ave. S., Saskatoon, 306-244-9899; www.2ndavegrill.com

International menu. Outdoor seating. $$

★CHIANTI

102 Idylwyld Drive N., Saskatoon, 306-665-8466

Italian menu. Outdoor seating. $$

YORKTON

In Yorkton, immigrants primarily from the Ukraine who were well experienced in plains farming, settled the fertile region. These pioneers brought with them a philosophy of community cooperation and cultural pride—and their legacy is that the city of Yorkton still boasts a rich ethnic diversity evident in the architecture of its churches, museums and handcrafts.

Information: www.tourismyorkton.com

WHAT TO SEE AND DO

CANNINGTON MANOR PROVINCIAL HISTORICAL PARK

Kenosee Lake, Yorkton, 306-787-2700

Cannington Manor, built in the early 1880s by a British captain who lost his fortune in England, is located in southeast Saskatchewan. The captain wanted to create an aristocratic society of British people living in western Canada. Inside the house, learn the history of Captain Edward Pierce, the founder, as well of the house itself. Mid-May-Labor Day: Wednesday-Monday; closed Tuesday.

DUCK MOUNTAIN PROVINCIAL PARK

Kamsack, 306-542-5500; www.tpcs.gov.sk.ca

Enjoy the highlands of east-central Saskatchewan in beautiful contrast to its prairies. The park also offers a vista of aspen forests and gorgeous valleys that cradle the sparkling Madge Lake. There are beaches, convenient campgrounds and lake fishing, along with golf, boating and hiking to enjoy. At the southern end of the park, find downhill skiing and 45 miles (72 kilometers) of cross-country ski trails.

MOOSE MOUNTAIN PROVINCIAL PARK

Yorkton, 306-577-2600; www.tpcs.gov.sk.ca

This park features many lakes and offers such recreational opportunities as horseback riding, bird-watching, hiking, camping and cross-country skiing. Also here are two 18-hole golf courses, a 36-hole miniature golf course and a casino.

PAINTED HAND CASINO

30 Third Ave. N., Yorkton, 306-786-6777, 888-604-7711; www.siga.sk.ca

This 25,000-square-foot (2,323-square-meter), Native American owned-and-operated casino features 134 slot machines and 12 table games, including blackjack, progressive jackpots, slot machines, red dog, poker and roulette. The casino also hosts major events, such as curling tournaments.

ST. MARY'S UKRAINIAN CATHOLIC CHURCH

155 Catherine St., Yorkton, 306-783-4594

St. Mary's was built in 1914 and is Yorkton's most unique feature. On the inside of the dome of the church is the "Coronation of the Virgin," painted by Steven Meush from 1939 to 1941. This beautiful painting is as similar to the Baroque painted domes in German and Italian churches as you will find in this part of Canada.

★
★
★
☆
☆

WESTERN DEVELOPMENT MUSEUM

Highway 16 W., Yorkton, 306-783-8361; www.wdm.ca

The Yorkton Western Development Museum has re-created the times and styles of some of the many immigrants who settled in Western Canada. Scenes illustrate the cultural roots of these new peoples: Ukrainians, English, Swedes, Germans, Doukhobors and Icelanders. Outdoors, the challenge of turning sod is demonstrated in the lineup of agricultural equipment, which includes the gigantic 1916 Twin City gas tractor, one of only two in North America.

SPECIAL EVENT

YORK COLONY QUILTERS GUILD QUILT FAIR AND TEA

Yorkton, 306-783-8361; www.wdm.ca

This two-day fair has been going strong for more than a decade. Its quilt show celebrating the York Colony Quilters Guild is a major attraction of the event. Early May.

HOTELS

★COMFORT INN

22 Dracup Ave., North Yorkton, 306-783-0333, 800-228-5150; www.comfortinn.com

80 rooms. Complimentary continental breakfast. Pets accepted, fee. Exercise room. Pool. $

★DAYS INN

2 Kelsey Bay, Yorkton, 306-783-3297, 800-544-8313; www.daysinn.com

74 rooms. Complimentary continental breakfast. High-speed Internet access. Pool. $ **233**

SASKATCHEWAN

INDEX

237

INDEX

★
★
★
★
★

239

INDEX

241

INDEX

★
★
★
★
★

★
★
★
★
☆

244

INDEX

★
★
★
★

★
★
★
✩

Museum of the Royal 22e
Regiment (Québec
City), *212*
Music in the Mountains
(Mont Tremblant
Provincial Park), *190*
Muttart Conservatory
(Edmonton), *24*
Myrtleville House
Museum (Brantford),
121

★
★
★
★

249

INDEX

★
★
★
★
★

251

INDEX

★
★
★
★
★

253

INDEX

★
★
★
★
★